ALASTAIR SAWDAY'S

SPECIAL

BED AND BREAKFAST FOR
GARDEN
LOVERS

An irresistible collection of very special
houses in Britain - and some in France - with
gardens to match. Sleep and stroll in peace.

EDITED BY NICOLA CROSSE

Design:	Caroline King
Maps & Mapping:	Bartholomew Mapping, a division of HarperCollins, Glasgow
Printing:	Canale, Italy
UK Distribution:	Portfolio, Greenford, Middlesex

Published in January 2003

Alastair Sawday Publishing Co. Ltd
The Home Farm Stables, Barrow Gurney, Bristol BS48 3RW
Tel: +44 (0)1275 464891 Fax: +44 (0)1275 464887
E-mail: info@specialplacestostay.com Web: www.specialplacestostay.com

Second edition

Copyright © January 2003 Alastair Sawday Publishing Co. Ltd

ISBN 1-901970-50-7 in the UK

Printed in Italy

The publishers have made every effort to ensure the accuracy of the information
in this book at the time of going to press. However, they cannot accept any
responsibility for any loss, injury or inconvenience resulting from the use of
information contained therein.

ALASTAIR SAWDAY'S
SPECIAL PLACES TO STAY

BED AND BREAKFAST FOR
GARDEN
LOVERS

ALASTAIR
SAWDAY
PUBLISHING

Alastair Sawday Publishing
Bristol, UK

CONTENTS

Acknowledgements • A word from Alastair Sawday • A word from Sue Colquhoun • Introduction • General map • Maps

england

CONTENTS

wales

CONTENTS

scotland

CONTENTS

france

Map & French Garden History

Entries

See the back of the book for:

- Garden organisations • Good gardens to visit •
- What is Alastair Sawday Publishing? •
- www.specialplacestostay.com •
- Alastair Sawday Special Places to Stay series •
- Little Earth Book • Report form • Quick reference indices •
- Index by surname • Index by place name •
- Exchange rates • Explanation of symbols •

ACKNOWLEDGEMENTS

Nicola Crosse has managed this project with flair and tenderness – and beautiful manners. Half-way through it all she had a major operation on her neck, yet I suspect that her editorial brain hardly stopped functioning. She was back at work within weeks of the operation, utterly undaunted. The book is shot through with her commitment and her passion for gardens and people. She is perfect for the job.

Elsewhere we have talked about our new union with Sue Colquhoun but this is the place to acknowledge her achievements. She set up *Bed & Breakfast for Garden Lovers* in 1994 and has run it, virtually single-handed, ever since. She has been entrepreneur, administrator, saleswoman and PR expert. We are delighted that she will continue to promote the new book and to represent its ideals wherever she goes.

Inspecting gardens as well as houses is a challenge – though fun for the right person. Sue has done lots of it and Kim Lawrence has been brilliant, earning special praise from the owners she visited.

Julia Richardson has co-ordinated a complex production project with her usual panache, Paula Brown has marketed magnificently and we are indebted, too, to Jo Boissevain's creativity and passion for gardens.

Alastair Sawday

Series Editor:	Alastair Sawday
Editor:	Nicola Crosse
Editorial Director:	Annie Shillito
Production Manager:	Julia Richardson
Web Producer:	Russell Wilkinson
Production Assistants:	Rachel Coe, Tom Dalton, Paul Groom
Accounts:	Bridget Bishop
Additional writing	Jo Boissevain, Sue Colquhoun
Photo of Alastair Sawday:	Fiona Duby
Country photos:	Mark Bolton, Hidehara Imai
Inspections:	Sue Colquhoun, Kim Lawrence

A special thank you, too, to other inspectors who saw just one or two houses for us.

Photos of Thorpe Lodge courtesy of Rosalind Simon.

A WORD FROM ALASTAIR SAWDAY

Only recently have I become aware of the passions involved in gardening. Wow! One woman's Virginia creeper is another's poison ivy. Even the humble vegetable can make people see red. Someone wrote an article in the *Atlantic Monthly* entitled 'Against Broccoli'. It contained the memorable headline: 'The local grocers are all out of broccoli – lockily!'. But it all comes, really, from a deep love of gardening, a very real joy in watching things that you have planted grow. My wife has become an allotment gardener and I hardly see her any more. Bill tells her how to plant; Fred lavishes radishes and beans upon her. Monty Don's words of wisdom are excitedly heeded. I am a mere, and very humble, spud-peeler and consumer.

So, others can wax lyrical about gardening. I will confine myself to the particular joys of this book: the combination of fine gardens and fine bedrooms, in which latter 'strangers' may sleep. For I do believe that it is a rare pleasure to be able to ring up a complete stranger and invite yourself not only to sleep in one of his or her bedrooms but to wander around the garden too – a rare privilege.

We have joined forces with the inimitable *Bed and Breakfast for Garden Lovers* organisation to produce this second edition of our own popular book. BBGL has been a force in the gardens world for many years and we all owe Sue Colquhoun a great debt. I think we now have an especially ravishing selection of houses and gardens for you to choose from. They are gardens where you may wander at will, snooze upon the lawn, peer at plants, perhaps take cuttings with the owner's permission, chat about gardening until the cows come home or the owner wants to sleep. I doubt you will escape without a stimulating exchange of ideas and some powerful hints for your own gardening – in strict defiance of the gardening maxim that 'you get the most of what you need the least'.

Have a wonderful time using this book – I'll be astonished if you don't.

Alastair Sawday

A WORD FROM
SUE COLQUHOUN

When *Bed and Breakfast for Garden Lovers* was founded in 1994 with 25 keen gardening hosts, nobody quite realised that it would catch the mood of the age in quite the way that it did. The concept of guests and hosts sharing a common interest just happened to coincide with a burgeoning interest in gardening.

BBGL gained a loyal following through the concerted efforts of everyone involved with the scheme. Particular thanks go to:

* Sue Ferguson and all at Livesey Ltd of Shrewsbury, who printed seven editions of the BBGL brochure.

* Derek St Romaine for the lovely brochure cover photographs, and Jane Harman for the drawing that was the BBGL logo for many years.

* Tony and Andy Merry of Milford Associates for the brilliant web site.

* Angela Reid and Caroline Long for their administrative help and support.

* Gardens, nurseries and other outlets that made BBGL brochures available to their visitors.

* Journalists and editors for mentioning BBGL in articles.

* Regular guests for encouraging us and keeping us up to the mark.

* My family for their patient support.

* Above all, the members who worked so hard to make BBGL what it is: those who featured in the 2002 brochure are listed in an index at the back of the book.

All of us who knew and loved the little BBGL brochure will miss it, but interest in the organisation ultimately became so great that Alastair Sawday's offer to produce the title in book form seemed the logical step forward. I am confident that the excellent reputation of the *Special Places to Stay* guides means that *Bed and Breakfast for Garden Lovers* is in safe hands. I do hope that regular visitors will continue to support BBGL in this format, and I wish the book and the hosts who feature in it every success.

Sue Colquhoun

INTRODUCTION

With, we hope, an open mind. One of the things that makes our guide books different and special is that we don't judge people and places by the same yardstick as other publishers. A little cobweb here and there, or a cat snoozing on the table can be forgiven, particularly if the house and owners are charming and the food is fresh and local. This is a book about people and their homes, not a list of commercially minded business people with laminated rules. And the homes in this book are described honestly so that you can take what you like and leave the rest; in other words, unlike hotel brochures, tourist board guides and glossy magazines, you'll be able to read between the lines.

There are some magnificent architectural gems in this book, but not one of them would have been given page space if their owners were glum, cold or even over-professional in their outlook. The dull, the corporate-minded and the plain snooty – even those with five-star 'facilities' are not for us. Our owners form part of a growing band of folk who do B&B – not only because it contributes to their living, but also because they care about people; we like those who are generous with their time (a lift to a station or bus stop, an early supper for your children or the gift of a cutting from a plant you've admired). Our owners are willing to go out of their way for their guests – that's why they're special – and we know that an encounter with genuine kindness will be remembered for a lot longer than any amount of luxury.

In this book there are simple farmhouses, Palladian mansions, cottages, modern timber A-frames, 60s brick-built and many manor houses; stunning modern art collections, antiques to die for, snazzy designer sofas and William Morris wallpapers, so you've masses of choice. And that's just the houses. A special garden is part of the package – but not just a garden that is perfect and cared for by a team of gardeners: the owners must be garden lovers. There are huge estates, parklands, policies, tiny courtyards and town gardens in the book; there are alpine gardens, clematis gardens, bog gardens and no end of herbaceousness – many of which are good enough to open for the *National Gardens Scheme*, and some of which appear in the *Good Gardens Guide*. Our criteria for choosing them have been that the owners love them, are knowledgeable about them and want to share that joy with guests. Some of the gardens are

INTRODUCTION

'finished' and being maintained perfectly. Some of them are starting out and one hasn't even been built yet – nearly all of the owners have future plans that excite them and that they love to talk about. That doesn't mean that you have to be an expert, you may just want to look, but if you do have questions they will be answered.

Our owners are experts on their own gardens, of course, but they can often organise visits to private gardens nearby, direct you to excellent nurseries and give you the low down on which public gardens are worth going to see. For lovers of the *Yellow Book* and *The Good Gardens Guide*, our book gives you the choice of many wonderful places to stay whether you are focused on a single trip or embarking on a gentle roam around the country, and we've 15 places in France, too!

How we go about it

Again, our criteria are our own. All of our places have been visited. If other books or organisations visit their owners – and many don't – there is often no evaluation of the people, their taste, character or style. Through our succinct and vibrant writing we aim to give an honest opinion that is fun to read. Writing each entry is quite challenging – lawns can only really 'sweep', although they have on occasion 'romped' and even 'rolled' – but what we try to avoid completely is that dreadful 'estate agent' language and cliché that litters many guide books. Some of our owners have gone into battle with us over a write-up that they don't like! If there are inaccuracies or small changes then we are happy to be flexible – but the essence must remain – a certain Sawdayness. I met an old friend, a devout user of our *British Bed and Breakfast* book, who told me that Alastair was one of her "best friends" – even though she'd never met him! That sort of loyalty can only be generated by accurate research, perceptive writing – and trust.

Subscriptions

Owners pay to go into this guide. Their fee goes some way towards covering the inspection and production costs of an all-colour book. It is not possible however, for people to buy their way into the book – whatever our rivals may suggest!

What to expect

The last time I went to stay in a Sawday B&B I was upset about the hollow fibre pillow on my bed. Normally, being very British, I would maintain a stiff upper lip (but a wobbling lower one) and not complain. But I had a very bad neck problem so I did

INTRODUCTION

say something. Hey presto! Within minutes two lovely feather pillows appeared, along with the perfectly reasonable explanation that some guests cannot tolerate feathers because of asthma and other allergies. If you feel your needs are not being met – within reason – then do say something; your hosts want you to be happy.

Owners tell me that they love having Sawday guests; among other things they understand that they are not staying in a hotel. So, don't expect room service, your bags to be carried or shoes to be cleaned. Do, however, expect to be treated like a human being rather than the occupant of Room 307.

If you know that you're fussy about other guests, traffic noise, arrival times or food, or if you want to be there in the afternoon to watch an important match on TV, check the entry carefully; then phone the owner and ask about it. Most owners are willing to be extremely flexible but it wouldn't be fair to spring a 6am breakfast, a difficult elderly relative or a wet shaggy dog on them. Ask first. Good manners and humour go a long way and not just in the house – garden etiquette dictates that we don't take our secateurs and help ourselves to anything we fancy, as I gather coachloads of wicked old ladies are apt to do in public gardens. Just ask – some owners will be happy to give you a cutting, others charge. One of our owners encourages her guests to weed for her; others would not be happy for guests to do anything but look. Many hosts will be deeply keen to give you a guided tour of their garden, others might be particularly busy at the time you ask. Be flexible and pick your moment.

Finding the right place for you

Quick reference indices. At the back of the book we list those owners:

- who were in the 2002 BBGL brochure
- willing to let you bring your pet
- that accept children of any age
- that are licensed
- that have wheelchair access or rooms suitable for limited mobility
- who let you stay all day
- who offer evening meals
- who offer mostly organic or home-grown food

INTRODUCTION

How to use this book

Map

Look at the map in the front of the book, find the area you want to visit and look for the nearest houses by number. In cities, check individual entries for their position.

Rooms

Double, twin, family or single. Sometimes these can be juggled or extra beds added (for three or more people), so do ask.

Bathrooms

If a room has an en suite bathroom, we now say 'with' bathroom or shower. If the bathroom is not actually in the room then we state whether it is shared – nearly always by guests in the same party – or private.

Prices

We state the room price rather than the per person price. A single occupancy rate will show what is charged if you choose to loll in a double bed on your own. This book will last for two years and prices may change.

Breakfasts

Unless it says otherwise, a full breakfast is included in the room price. In most cases this will be a fabulous cooked blow-out but check first – especially if you are the sort of person who might be disappointed by something healthier.

Symbols

At the back of the book we explain our, much discussed, loved or hated symbols. They are just a guide and occasionally owners may want to bend their own rules.

Practical matters

Apart from breakfast, don't expect to be provided with any other meal unless you arrange it; even owners who do dinner or packed lunch need notice. If you book dinner – and you will not find better, fresher and more seasonal food in any hotel – then try to be on time. If you are delayed then telephone – just good manners again! Prices for dinner are quoted per person. Very few of our houses are licensed but some owners offer a drink before, and wine, with dinner; if you want to bring your own then just ask.

INTRODUCTION

Price variations

Some of our houses offer a discount for a stay of more than two or three nights, and some charge extra for a stay of one night. Others may charge supplements at certain times. Do book early for popular holidays or if you know you want a particular room.

Booking

Bookings are usually made by phone. This gives you the chance to ask any questions you may have and to get the feel of the people and place. It's a good idea to get written confirmation of the room booked, the price for B&B and for meals, and state roughly what time you will arrive. You may be asked for a deposit which may be non-refundable. Be sure you know what their policy is – the contract is between you and the owner.

Cancellations

If you have to cancel your booking, telephone the owner as soon as possible. You may lose your deposit or have to pay part of the cost of your booking, depending on the amount of notice.

Payment

All our owners take cash and cheques with a cheque card. If they also take credit cards, we have given them the appropriate symbol. Do check that yours is acceptable.

Children

The teddy bear symbol is given to houses that accept children of any age – angels or horrors. Don't assume though that the owners have all the toys, sterilising equipment and high chairs that you may need.

Dogs

The dog collar symbol means that pets are welcome. They may have to sleep in another part of the house or in the car – do check, and do be honest about the size and nature of your pet.

Smoking

A 'No Smoking' symbol means that you can't smoke anywhere in the house – and that includes hanging out of the window.

INTRODUCTION

Owners do not expect tips. If you are overwhelmed with gratitude then write a lovely letter or leave a little present.

Environment

We try to be as 'green' as possible. We lend bicycles to staff and provide a pool car. We celebrate the use of organic, home-grown and locally produced food. We are working to establish an organic standard for B&B's and run an Environmental Business Trust to stimulate business interest in the environment.

We also publish *The Little Earth Book*, a collection of essays on environmental issues. A new title, *The Little Food Book*, is another hard-hitting analysis – this time of the food industry. To try to reduce our impact on the environment we plant trees: the emissions directly related to our office, paper production, printing and distribution have been 'neutralised' through the planting of indigenous woodlands with Future Forests. We are, officially, Carbon Neutral.

Internet

Our web site www.specialplacestostay.com has online pages for all the places featured here and in our other books. For more details see the back of the book.

Disclaimer

We do not claim to be purely objective in choosing our *Special Places*. They are here because we like them. Our opinions and tastes are ours alone and this book is a statement of them; we hope that you share them.

We have tried hard to get our facts right but I would like to apologise if you find any mistakes lurking between the pages. If you are burning to tell us of any inaccuracies or flaws then write to us – we always act on feedback and welcome it.

And finally

We hope that you will be inspired by the people, houses and gardens in this book and enjoy using it. It's all about bringing people together. We can lead you to parts of this country – and France, too – that you haven't seen before, and the owners can lead you to the best bits of their patch. Happy travels.

Nicola Crosse

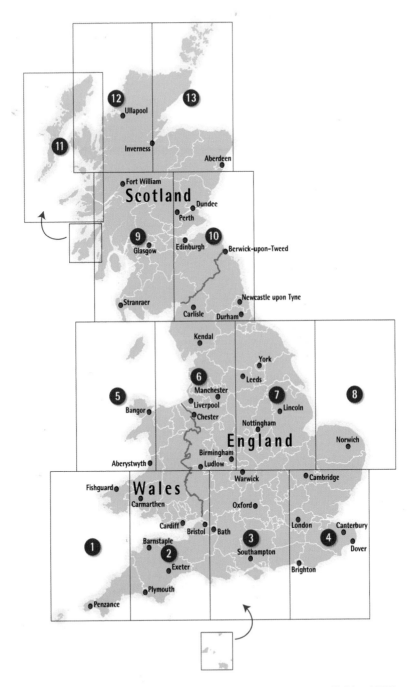

Ullapool

12

13

Inverness

11

Aberdeen

Fort William

Scotland

Dundee

Perth

9

Glasgow

Edinburgh

10

Berwick-upon-Tweed

Stranraer

Newcastle upon Tyne

Carlisle

Durham

Kendal

York

Leeds

6

Manchester

5

Liverpool

7

Lincoln

Bangor

Chester

Nottingham

England

Aberystwyth

Birmingham

8

Ludlow

Norwich

Fishguard

Wales

Warwick

Cambridge

Carmarthen

Oxford

Cardiff

Bristol

Bath

London

Canterbury

Barnstaple

2

3

4

Dover

1

Southampton

Exeter

Brighton

Plymouth

Penzance

©Bartholomew Ltd, 2002

A guide to our map numbers

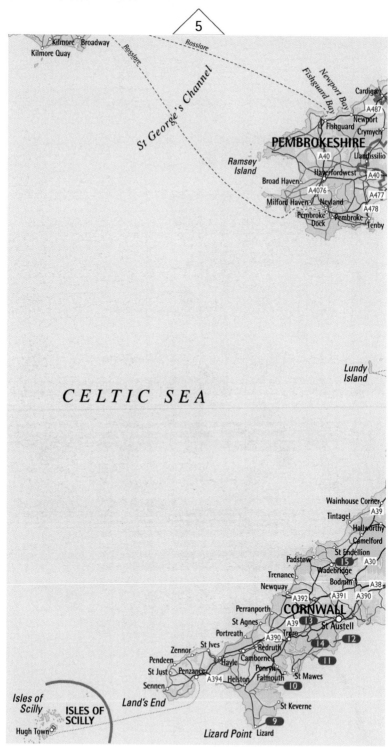

Map 1

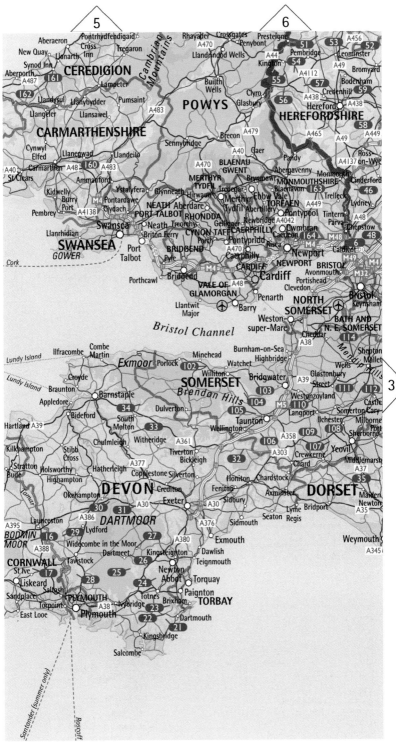

Map 2

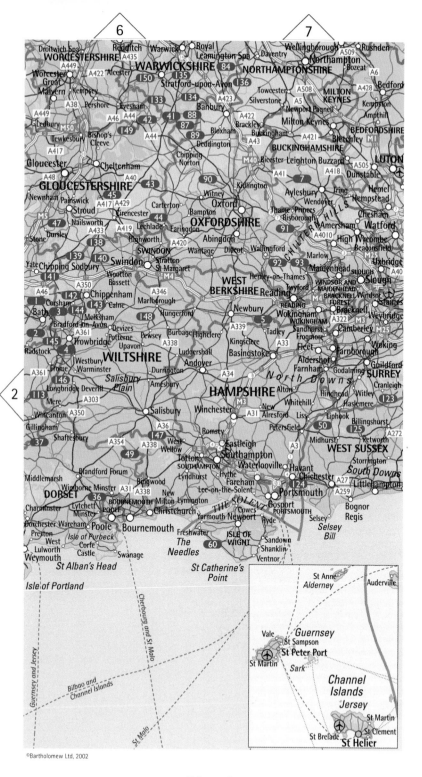

Map 3

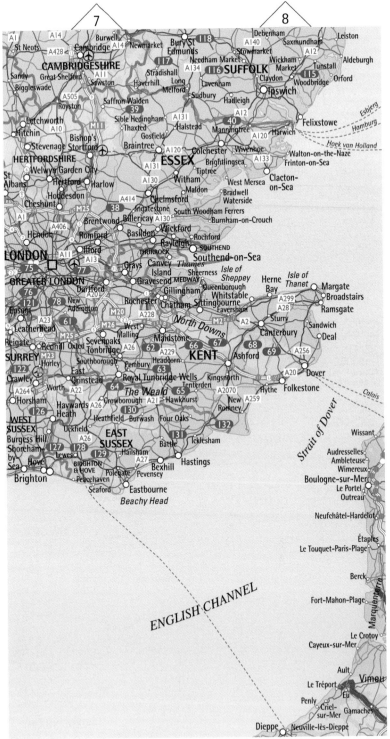

Map 4

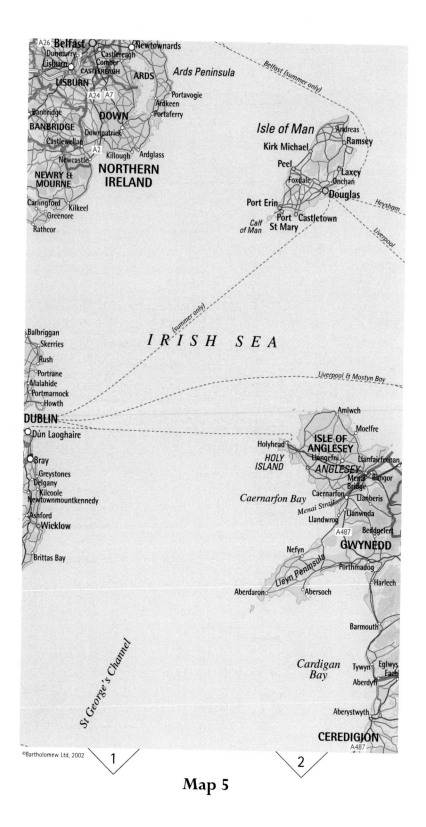

Map 5

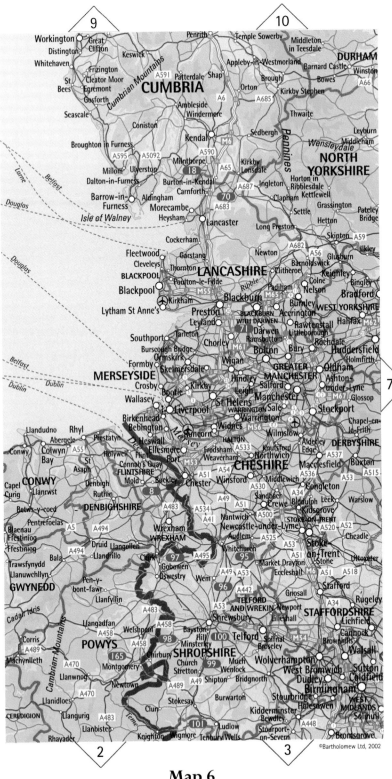

Map 6

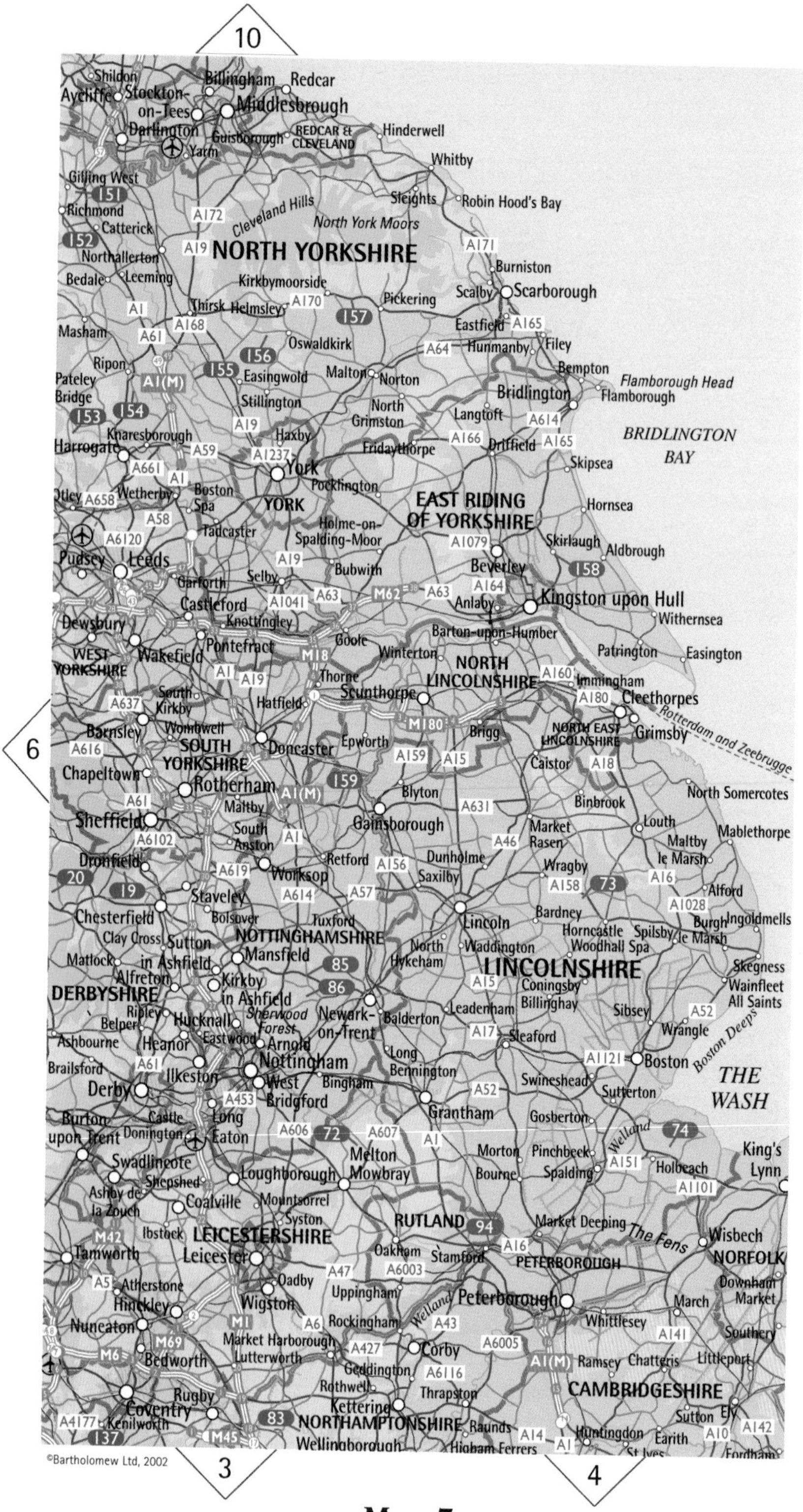

Shildon
Aycliffe Stockton-
on-Tees Redcar
Darlington Billingham
Middlesbrough
Yarm REDCAR et Hinderwell
Gilling West CLEVELAND
Guisborough Whitby
Richmond A172 Sleights Robin Hood's Bay
Catterick Cleveland Hills North York Moors
Northallerton A19 NORTH YORKSHIRE A171
Bedale Leeming Burniston
Kirkbymoorside Scalby Scarborough
Masham Thirsk Helmsley A170 Pickering
Ripon A61 A168 Oswaldkirk Eastfield A165
Pateley A1(M) Easingwold Malton Norton Hunmanby Filey
Bridge Stillington North A64 Bempton Flamborough Head
Knaresborough Grimston Bridlington Flamborough
Harrogate A59 Haxby Langtoft A614 BRIDLINGTON
Otley Wetherby A1237 York Friadythorpe A166 Driffield A165 BAY
Boston Pocklington Skipsea
Pudsey Spa Taddaster YORK EAST RIDING
Leeds Holme-on- OF YORKSHIRE Hornsea
Garforth Selby Spalding-Moor A1079
Dewsbury Castleford Bubwith Beverley Skirlaugh Aldbrough
WEST Wakefield A1041 A63 M62 A63 Anlaby A164 Kingston upon Hull
YORKSHIRE Knottingley Goole Barton-upon-Humber Withernsea
Pontefract Winterton Patrington Easington
South A1 A19 Thorne NORTH A160 Immingham
Barnsley Kirkby Hatfield Scunthorpe LINCOLNSHIRE A180 Cleethorpes
A637 Wombwell M180 NORTH EAST Grimsby
SOUTH Doncaster Epworth LINCOLNSHIRE Rotterdam and Zeebrugge
Chapeltown YORKSHIRE 159 A159 A15 Caistor A18
A61 Rotherham A1(M) Blyton North Somercotes
Sheffield Maltby Binbrook Louth
A6102 South Gainsborough Market Maltby Mablethorpe
Dronfield Anston A1 Dunholme Rasen le Marsh
20 19 Retford A156 Saxilby A46 Wragby A158 73 A16 Alford
Chesterfield Worksop Bardney A1028 Ingoldmells
Clay Cross Sutton Staveley A614 Tuxford North Horncastle Spilsby le Marsh Burgh
Matlock in Ashfield Bolsover NOTTINGHAMSHIRE Hykeham Lincoln Woodhall Spa Skegness
Alfreton Mansfield 85 Waddington A15 Coningsby Wainfleet
DERBYSHIRE Kirkby 86 Leadenham Billinghay Sibsey All Saints
Ripley in Ashfield Sherwood Newark- Balderton A17 Wrangle A52
Ashbourne Heanor Forest on-Trent Sleaford
Belper A61 Eastwood Arnold Long A1121 Boston
Brailsford Ilkeston Nottingham Bennington Boston Deeps
Derby West Swineshead Sutterton THE
Burton Castle Bridgford Bingham Grantham Gosberton WASH
upon Trent Donington Long A453 A52 74
Swadlincote Shepshed Eaton A606 72 A607 A1 Pinchbeck Welland King's
Ashby de Coalville Melton Morton Spalding A151 Holbeach Lynn
la Zouch Mountsorrel Mowbray Bourne A1101
M42 Ibstock Syston RUTLAND 94 Market Deeping The Fens Wisbech
Tamworth LEICESTERSHIRE Oakham A16 Stamford PETERBOROUGH NORFOLK
A5 Atherstone Leicester A47 A6003 Downham
Hinckley Oadby Uppingham Peterborough March Market
Nuneaton M69 Wigston A6 Rockingham Welland A43 Whittlesey A141 Southery
M6 Bedworth Market Harborough A427 Corby A6005 A1(M) Littleport
Coventry Rugby Lutterworth Geddington Ramsey Chatteris CAMBRIDGESHIRE
A4171 Kenilworth 137 M45 83 NORTHAMPTONSHIRE Rothwell A6116 Thrapston Sutton Ely
Kettering Raunds A14 Huntingdon Earith A10 A142
Wellingborough Higham Ferrers St Ives Fordham

©Bartholomew Ltd, 2002

Map 7

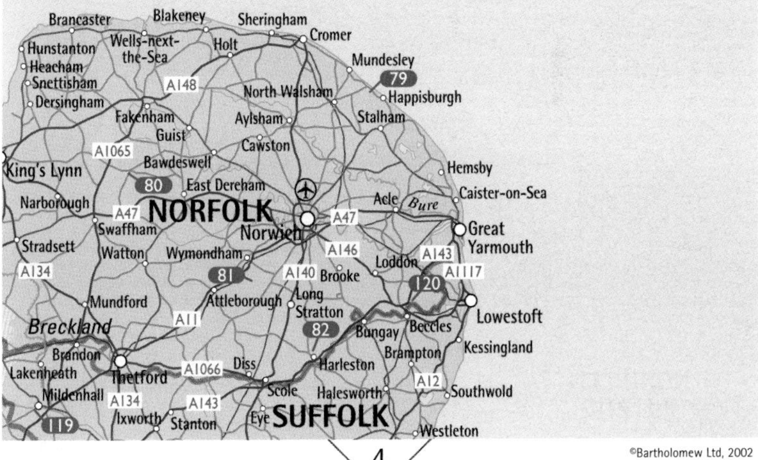

Brancaster Blakeney Sheringham
Hunstanton Wells-next- Holt Cromer
Heacham the-Sea Mundesley
Snettisham A148 79
Dersingham North Walsham Happisburgh
Fakenham Aylsham Stalham
Guist
A1065 Cawston
Bawdeswell
King's Lynn East Dereham Hemsby
Narborough A47 NORFOLK Acle Bure Caister-on-Sea
Swaffham Norwich A47
Stradsett Watton Wymondham A146 Great
A134 81 Loddon A143 Yarmouth
Mundford A140 Brooke 120 A1117
Breckland A11 Long Beccles Lowestoft
Brandon Attleborough Stratton Bungay Kessingland
Lakenheath Thetford A1066 Diss 82 Brampton
Mildenhall A134 A143 Scole Harleston A12 Southwold
119 Ixworth Stanton Eye SUFFOLK Halesworth Westleton

4

©Bartholomew Ltd, 2002

Map 8

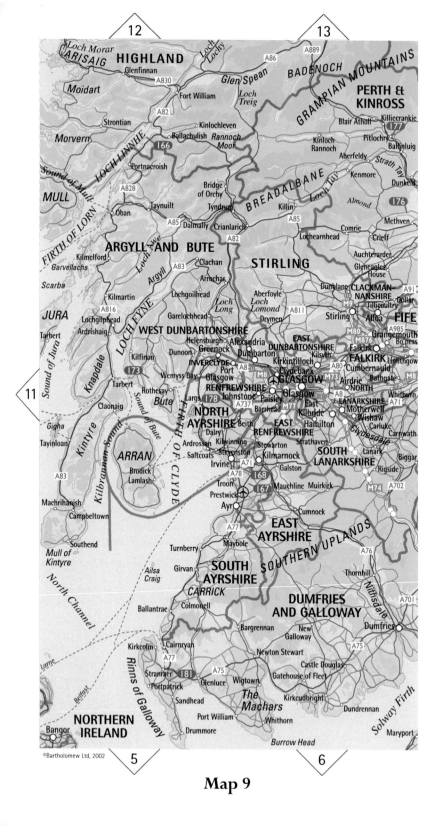

Map 9

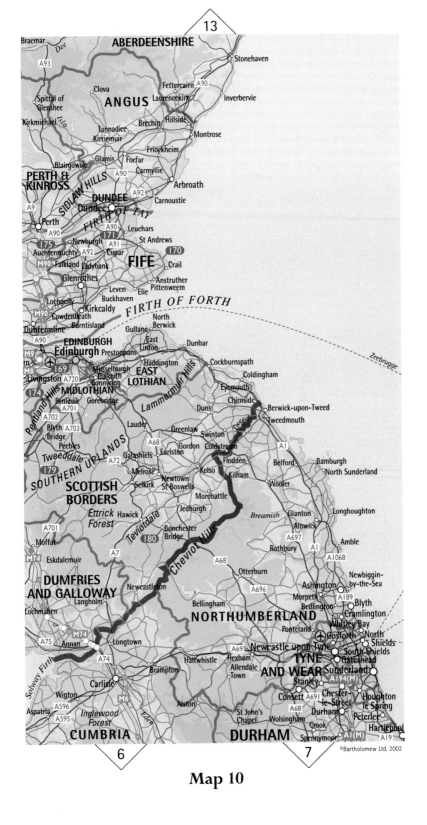

Map 10

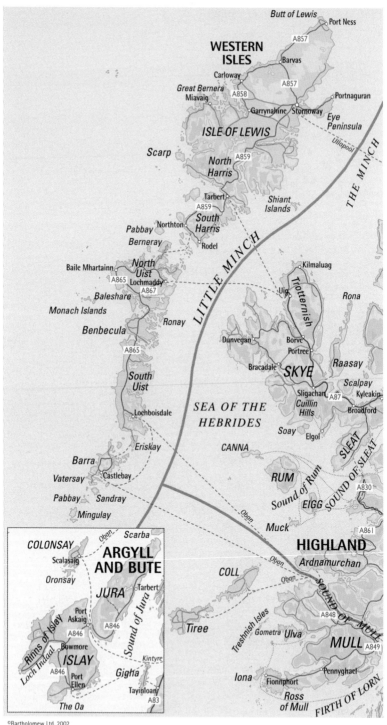

Map 11

©Bartholomew Ltd, 2002

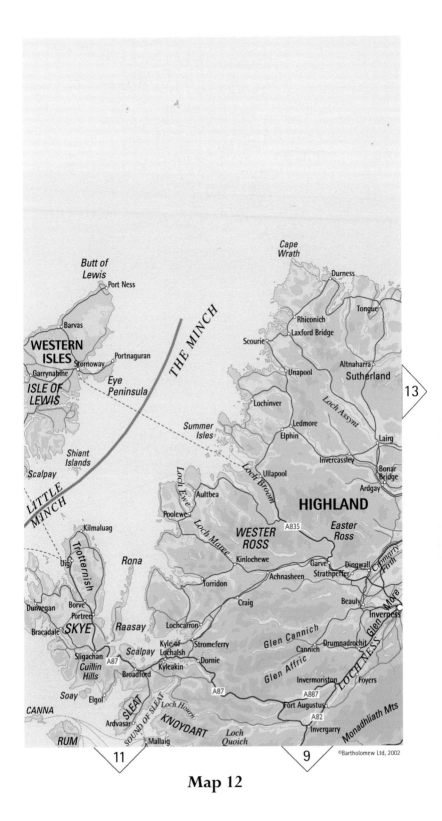

Map 12

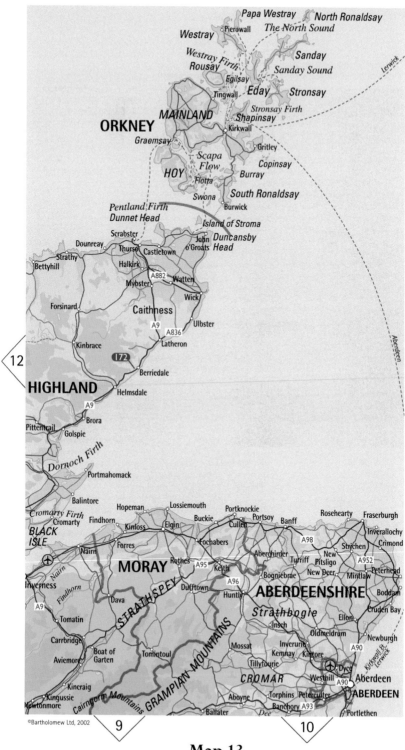

Map 13

"Pleasures newly found are sweet
When they lie about our feet"

WORDSWORTH

Photography by Mark Bolton

ENGLAND

"Come into the garden Maud
For the black bat, night, has flown"

TENNYSON

THE OLD RECTORY

Patrick & Gillian Mesquita
The Old Rectory,
Stanton Prior, Bath, Bath & N.E. Somerset BA2 9HT

tel   01761 471942
fax   01761 470662
e-mail g.coles_remedi@btinternet.com

It is said there was once a monastery on this site; only the medieval carp pond remains. But other connections between garden and the religious life have been made: the pleached limes planted 20 years ago by Gillian and Patrick down the drive from the neighbouring 11th-century church are now mature, and the more recent knot garden incorporates the church's original rose window mullions. Everything in this garden has been created from scratch over the last two decades. The apple and pear arches blossom simultaneously, and have been underplanted with clematis – 'Victoria', 'Gipsy Queen', 'Perle d'Azur' and 'Huldine' – that scramble up through the branches and provide a continuous profusion of flowers. Espaliered apples screen a productive kitchen garden, source of the fresh fruit and jams at the breakfast table. Friends know of Gillian's passion for gardening, and she is often given a present of a rare shrub, or encouraged by her favourite nurseries to try out something unusual. She is currently wondering what new project she might take on next; her knot garden has been such a success that she is quite tempted to create another.

rooms	2: 1 twin, 1 double, both with bath.
price	£60. Single occ. £35.
meals	Good food available locally.
closed	Occasionally.
directions	A4 to Bristol; at end of dual carriageway, A39 for Wells. Through Corston, left to Stanton Prior. Next to church.

Gillian's soft colours and traditional country style suit perfectly the pretty, Georgian house with views of garden and hills. The oldest parts date from pre-Reformation times and the house has been added to since; both Queen Anne and Regency extensions have a bedroom for guests. Huge Georgian French windows in dining and drawing rooms open straight onto the terrace: to breakfast here on a sunny summer morning is a special treat. Huge hospitality, a gorgeous house in a Duchy of Cornwall village, and Bath just a 15-minute drive. Bliss. *Minimum stay two nights.*

GREY LODGE

Jane & Anthony Stickland
Grey Lodge,
Summer Lane, Combe Down, Bath, Bath & N.E. Somerset BA2 7EU

tel	01225 832069
fax	01225 830161
e-mail	greylodge@freenet.co.uk
web	www.greylodge.co.uk

An encyclopaedic knowledge of plants and a collector's delight in finding new treasures have inspired Jane and Anthony's south-west-facing terraced garden. The main structure was laid out when the house was built in the 1860s, and their most cherished inheritance, a magnificent *Robinia pseudacia*, was probably planted then. For 34 years they have been adding to the garden's attractions, planting the series of borders with labour-saving in mind, since they do most of the work themselves. It's a garden that's great fun to explore because of its sloping lay-out and secret paths. The large lawn at the upper level leads to another – and another. A vine planted on the main terrace wall in 1973 now covers 14 yards of wall in three tiers and a fan-trained apricot nestles beside it. Jane caught the climbing rose bug some years ago, hence the very large 'Paul's Himalayan Musk'. There are more than 70 old roses and it is obvious that plants with scented leaves and flowers are much loved. The soil is free-draining alkaline, so sun-lovers like cistus, hebe, euphorbia and phormium have been chosen for the more open areas. Play boules or soak up the sun and scents on the main lawn, chat to your hosts about special plants, discover botanical treasures. A true garden-lover's garden with interesting plants to enjoy in every season.

rooms	3: 2 twins/doubles, 1 family, all with shower.
price	£60–£70. Single occ. £35–£40. Self-catering available.
meals	Excellent local pubs.
closed	Rarely.
directions	From A36, about 3 miles from Bath, on Warminster rd, take uphill road by lights & Viaduct Inn. 1st left for Monkton Combe. After village (0.5 miles on) house 1st on left.

You are in a conservation area, yet just five minutes from the centre of Bath. And the views: breathtaking from wherever you stand. The steep valley rolls out ahead of you from most of the rooms and from the garden comes a confusion and a profusion of scents and colours – it's a glory in its own right. The friendly and likeable Sticklands are conservationists too and have a Green Certificate to prove it. Breakfasts are a feast: bacon and eggs, cereals, home-grown jam, kedgeree. Jane will tell you all about excellent local gardens to visit.

2 COMBE ROYAL CRESCENT

Charmian Smith
2 Combe Royal Crescent,
Bathwick Hill, Bath, BA2 6EZ, Bath & N.E. Somerset

tel   01225 312549
fax   01225 312549

A six minute drive from the centre of elegant Bath and all its doings, yet you are 500 feet up, overlooking woodland and assailed by birdsong, not traffic noise – so park your car (securely) and walk or bus to town. Inside is immaculate and you will be graciously cared for by Guy and Charmian with delicious meals and comfortable rooms. Plain white walls, beautiful rugs and furniture and an eclectic mix of paintings show off their good taste - bedrooms are sunny and large, one with a four-poster and both with stunning views. Wide bookcases are packed with interest, colours are muted and soft, nothing glares. You may decide not to leave at all ...

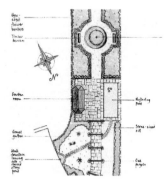

rooms	2: 1 double, 1 twin, both with bath/shower.
price	£65. Single occ. £40.
meals	Dinner £22.
closed	Never.
directions	From Bath follow signs to University. At top of Bathwick Hill, just before junction with North Road, very large gate on right between stone walls.

A rare opportunity to see a brand new garden. Looking out from the main terrace of the house you would be hard put to guess you were so close to the centre of Bath. The site is bounded by woods and mature gardens. This newly-created long and narrow garden, designed by Nick Williams-Ellis, has been carved out of the hillside, and is intended to provide an interesting variety of spaces along its length as well as being fairly maintenance-free for two retired gardeners. From the terrace, you drop down a flight of steps to the garden, which runs at right angles to the house. There is a central walkway with simple oak framed arches to be covered by climbers, a water feature issues into a rill, which in turn flows into a long reflecting pool, overlooked by a garden room. A Judas tree forms the centrepiece of a box-edged flower garden, with seats in both sun and shade. At the far end, backing onto the old stone boundary wall, a miniature fruit and vegetable garden with raised beds and a greenhouse complete the picture. Charmian will no doubt plant her favourite mauves, lilacs and pinks, and plenty of colour in pots will soften the edges and add vibrancy to the cool, stone terrace next to the house. *Widcombe Hill Association.*

HOLLYTREE COTTAGE

Julia Naismith
Hollytree Cottage,
Laverton, Bath & N.E. Somerset BA2 7QZ

tel	01373 830786
fax	01373 830786

Meandering lanes lead you to this 17th-century cottage - quintessentially English with roses round the door, a grandfather clock in the hall and an air of genteel tranquillity. Julia has updated the cottage charm with Regency mahogany in the inglenook dining room and sumptuous sofas in the sitting room. Bedrooms have long views over farmland and undulating countryside; behind is a conservatory and the sloping, south-facing garden. Do ask your hostess about Bath (just 20 minutes away) - she worked in the Holburne Museum and knows the city well.

rooms	3: 1 double/family (1 single let to same party), 1 twin, 1 single, all with bath/shower.
price	£60-£70.
meals	Dinner £18.
closed	Rarely.
directions	From Bath or Warminster A36 to Wolverton. Opp. Red Lion Pub turn for Laverton. 1 mile to x-roads & on toward Faulkland Wellow down hill 80 yds. House on left.

Twenty years of trial and error have gone into creating this cottage garden which slopes gently down from the house to fields below and which complements the house perfectly. It has everything you could want in an open, informal country garden. Very good trees and shrubs including a tamarisk, a white-flowering amelanchier and a soft pink *Magnolia stellata* have been introduced over the years. A tall laburnum flowers profusely in season and Julia's collection of prunus have been carefully planted so that they flower in succession in spring time. A series of irregular beds have been dug and planted with skill and flair, providing colour and interest from a wide variety of good plants. Julia is a keen member of her local horticultural society and buys many treasures at their plant sales, including clematis from the late Betty Risdon who ran the famous Rode Bird Gardens nearby and who was a leading member of the Clematis Society. Fish swim in the little pond, surrounded by water-loving plants, and for fresh vegetables and fruit, there is an immaculate kitchen garden edged with recycled railway sleepers. The small conservatory is absolutely packed with the more tender plants, a perfect spot to sit and enjoy the colour and interest outside. The position is delightful and the garden has been designed to make the most of its glorious views. *Rode Horticultural Society.*

THE OLD MANOR

Mrs R A G Sanders-Rose
The Old Manor,
Whitehouse Green, Sulhamstead, Reading, Berkshire RG7 4EA

tel   0118 983 2423
fax   0118 983 6262
e-mail rags-r@theoldmanor.fsbusiness.co.uk

A young, developing garden with 10 acres which are being transformed into a mix of the formal and informal, and views across open farmland in a deeply rural corner of Berkshire. One gorgeous feature is already in place: a beautifully worked, elaborate knot garden in the form of two roses, its little box hedges set among pristine gravel. Another is a long pergola heavy with roses and honeysuckle. There are as many family associations in the garden as there are inside Peter and Rosemary's home. One is the eye-catching stately sorbus avenue which was planted to celebrate their daughter's wedding; edged by tall, waving, uncut grasses, it leads you to a shady, creeper-covered bower with countryside beyond. Roses clamber up the façade of the house and the wide, open, sunny patio guarded by two bay sentinels in containers is a lovely place to sit and enjoy the view while a fountain splashes. An intimate side patio is bounded by flowers and hedges, with an arch covered in golden hop and honeysuckle. Deer abound, so Rosemary chooses plants which they dislike! Specimen trees are being planted across the 10 acres and, beyond the tall enclosing hedge sheltering the large croquet lawn, an avenue of ancient oaks bears witness to the centuries-old history of the manor. A handsome garden in the making and one which grows with interest all the time.

rooms	2 doubles both with bath.
price	£70. Single occ. £50.
meals	Dinner inc. wine £12.50.
closed	Christmas & New Year.
directions	From M4 junc. 12 for Newbury. Follow signs to Theale station, over r'way to lights. After 500 yds, turn right. Keep on country road for 0.75 miles, then left at x-roads. Entrance straight ahead.

Time-travel through Rosemary and Peter's luxurious house, part 1600s manor, part 1950s, part 1990s. The drawing room, with deep sofas, is modern and the cosy breakfast room is beamed. Bedrooms, one with a four-poster, are in the old part of the manor, with beamed ceilings and every comfort - one has a whirlpool bath. Family pictures give a homely touch and guests are treated as friends. Delicious dinners - both Rosemary and Peter are excellent cooks - are served at the long dining table sparkling with silver. Prepare to be pampered.

QUAKERS

Mrs Mary Bailey
Quakers,
Lower Hazel, Rudgeway, Bristol BS35 3QP

tel   01454 413205
e-mail marybailey@quakerbox.freeserve.co.uk

A lovely, peaceful, creeper-clad home - yet you are conveniently
close to the M4/M5 and just 12 miles from Bristol city centre.
Mary's natural generosity and courtesy make people feel
immediately at home: tea, cake, scones and home-made jam on
arrival, and muffins or Welsh cakes for breakfast. Bedrooms are
cottagey, adorned with chintz and sweet-smelling garden flowers
when in season. French windows in the dining room open to the
garden on warm days, and, with her inside knowledge of other
private gardens in the area, Mary may well be able to arrange
personal visits.

rooms	3: 1 twin, 2 singles, sharing bathroom for members of same party.
price	£60. Single occ. £30.
meals	Good pubs and restaurants near.
closed	Very occasionally.
directions	M5 junc. 15, A38 north to Thornbury. Over traffic lights, 1st left down Hazel Lane.

Quakers has been Mary's home for 42 years. For more than half that time her potential as a gardener lay almost dormant as she devoted her full attention to her family; then, 15 years ago, things began to change. The family lawn reduced in size as planting doubled, the few existing shrubs and beds were rationalised. Slopes and banks that children had rolled down became herbaceous borders, and the donkey paddock was turned into a wildlife area with a pond and interesting trees. The acre of garden was never designed on paper but rather evolved, following the ground's natural contours. And curve it does, up behind the house, against a happy backdrop of well-established native woodland trees. Mary chooses her plants for colour, cutting, scent and year-round interest. The vivid stems of willows and dogwood brighten the winter, early bulbs, hellebores and heathers herald the spring, and the brightness of the borders continues right into the autumn until the foliage starts to turn. The garden opens for charity, and Mary has been the National Gardens Scheme's county organiser for several years; it must be like having a second family. *NGS.*

THE BUNCH

Francis & Panna Newall
The Bunch,
Wotton Underwood, Aylesbury, Buckinghamshire HP18 0RZ

tel   01844 238376
fax   01844 237153
e-mail newallf@btconnect.com

Built in the 18th century for the Duke of Buckingham as staff
cottages for the estate, these five have been knocked into one,
long and low, cosy home. Francis and Panna are much travelled
and have a great interest in people, education and development;
you will be graciously looked after. The drawing room is hugely
comfortable and stylish, with a dark polished floor, old rugs and
plenty of squashy sofa seating. Dinner is eaten in the warm red
dining room and breakfast in the slate-floored conservatory. The
downstairs bedroom is beamed and large with lovely views of
the garden; the other twin is smaller but equally comfortable.

rooms	2: 1 twin with bath; 1 twin with private bath.
price	From £50. Single occ. from £30.
meals	Dinner £20.
closed	Easter, Christmas & New Year.
directions	At Kingswood on A41 for Wotton & Brill. At next 2 T-junctions left, & left again at sign saying Wotton only. First house on right with mushrooms at gate.

Mixed borders around an immaculate lawn and a series of rooms divided by neat hedging – about three acres in all. Mature trees stud the lawn including old, propped-up apple trees with 'Rambling Rector' and 'Bobby James' romping through the branches, a mulberry and a weeping pear. The bird theme is strong: woven willow ducks and peacocks and a tennis hut whose back wall has been painted with pheasants; from here there is a gorgeous view across to distant hills. Pots, urns and statues abound, there's a Whichford Pottery greyhound on a brick plinth with a blue wooden bench curving around it, looking down a mown path towards the house. The tennis court has roses growing up the outside wire (mostly 'Canary Bird', of course!) and lawsoniana bushes cut into pear-drop shapes. A little formal garden has low lonicera hedges, there's a wild pond shaded by mature trees with a waterfall trickling down old stones and a seat where you can admire more willow birds. The vegetable garden is immaculate and productive – not much has to be bought from outside – and the cutting garden always yields something colourful for Panna's perfect arrangements. Seeds and cuttings are grown in the hot and cold greenhouses; again, this means they have to buy very little. Last, but not least, are the aviary and pens: canaries, bantams, guinea fowl and golden pheasant are much loved and highly vocal. Waddesdon Manor and Claydon House are near. *NGS.*

THE MOUNT

Jonathan & Rachel Major
The Mount,
Higher Kinnerton, Chester, Cheshire CH4 9BQ

tel   01244 660275
fax   01244 660275
e-mail   major@mountkinnerton.freeserve.co.uk
web   www.bandbchester.com

Here is peace indeed - "Our guests seem to oversleep", says
Rachel. Britain at its best with a fruitful kitchen garden, scented
conservatory, a tennis court, croquet lawn and a genuinely warm
welcome from Rachel. She's an avid reader, there are books
everywhere, as well as her embroidered tapestry designs. The
house is furnished in elegant, traditional style and the proportions
of the light-filled drawing room and the big, high-ceilinged
dining room feel just right. The bedrooms too are light and large
and your hosts like to treat their visitors as family guests.

rooms	3: 2 twins/doubles both with bath; 1 double with shower.
price	From £50. Single occ. by arrangement.
meals	Good village pubs within walking distance.
closed	Christmas-3 January; last two weeks of August.
directions	From Chester, A55 west, then A5104 to Broughton. Left at r'bout to Pennyffordd on A5104. Through Broughton & over A55. 1st left to Kinnerton down Lesters Lane. On right.

A haven for garden buffs, bookworms and birdwatchers – you might catch sight of careering young sparrow hawks testing their wings overhead. Some old and very beautiful trees date back to the building of the house in 1860 while the front garden's acre outline was set out in the early 1950s. Rachel has worked wonders with grounds which were once simply open lawns and trees; the garden has developed gradually and naturally over the years, reflecting her, and Jonathan's, growing interest and commitment to gardening. Their 2001 project was the re-designing of the beech-hedged kitchen garden. Its formal structure contrasts happily with the more informal mood elsewhere. The front garden's croquet lawn, overlooked by trees, takes you down steps past stone pineapples into the cool seclusion of woodland, with huge 'Paul's Himalayan Musk' and 'Francis E Lester' roses soaring dizzily up a tall conifer. Roses, clematis and hydrangea sparkle on The Mount's façade as house-martins flit in and out of nests beneath the eaves. Another recent addition is a pond to one side of the house – a mass of bullrushes, foxgloves and iris which is perfect for wildlife. Behind the house the planting is more open and free, decorated with new beech hedges to give shape and form. The handsome pergola is clad in wisteria underplanted with lavender, a charming combination. A young arbour of willows is settling in nicely. A lovely garden in perfect harmony with the handsome Victorian house. *NGS*

LANDEWEDNACK HOUSE

Peter & Marion Stanley
Landewednack House,
Church Cove, The Lizard, Cornwall TR12 7PQ

tel   01326 290909
fax   01326 290192
e-mail landewednackhouse@amserve.com

The view of garden to church to sea to headland is heart-stopping
and the ever-changing light casts a spell over the landscape. The
dining room is illuminated by fire and candle; the yellow drawing
room, with wooden floors and deep sofas, is perfect. Cascading
drapes, immaculate linen, a regal four-poster and a luxurious
half-tester - the bedrooms are exquisite. Marion speaks with
passion and humour of her piece of England. Swim in the
sheltered, heated pool or breathe deeply of clean Cornish air
while walking the three minutes to the sea. Irresistible.

rooms	3: 1 four-poster, 1 double, 1 twin/double, all with bath/shower.
price	£80-£96. Single occ. £49-£56.
meals	Dinner £28.
closed	Christmas.
directions	From Helston, A3083 south. Just before Lizard, left to Church Cove. Follow signs for 0.75 miles. House on left behind blue gates.

The position is simply stunning and Marion and Peter have gardened assiduously to complement the garden's glorious outlook. This is Cornwall at its mildest and Marion has taken much inspiration from the exotic gardens at Tresco. It's a few degrees cooler than the Scilly Isles, a helicopter flight away, so Marion cannot use the full palette Tresco employs, but nonetheless you will be green with envy. The lushness and range of tender plants which thrive wonderfully in these carefully nurtured, delightfully informal grounds is impressive. Opposite the front door you'll find Cornwall-loving camellias and rhododendrons underplanted with masses of spring flowers, a row of box 'soldiers' standing to attention on the path. Rosarians will love the rose garden edged by lavender and a pretty hedge of the rose 'Ballerina'. Below the tall garden wall is a deep herbaceous border packed with colour and interest and, near the house, a stunning 'hot' garden of spiky architectural plants with dramatic foliage. Tomatoes, vegetables and flowers for the house flourish in a neat vegetable garden with a Victorian greenhouse. A lily pond in a sheltered tree fern hollow can be viewed from the veranda of the summer house… guests are always reluctant to leave. *NGS, Cornwall Garden Society, Cornwall Garden Trust.*

CARWINION

Mr & Mrs Anthony Rogers
Carwinion,
Mawnam Smith, Nr Falmouth, TR11 5JA, Cornwall

tel	01326 250258
fax	01326 250903
e-mail	jane@carwinion.freeserve.co.uk
web	www.carwinion.com

Originally a small farmhouse built in 1790, this rambling
manor was enlarged in the 1840s shortly after the garden
was originally designed and planted. The manor has the faded
grandeur and collections of oddities (corkscrews, penknives,
magnifying glasses) that successive generations hand on.
Your charmingly eccentric host will introduce you to his
ancestors, his antiques, his fine big old bedrooms - and he
and the tireless Jane serve "a breakfast to be reckoned with".
The self-catering wing has a fenced garden to keep your
children in and Carwinion dogs out.

rooms	3: 1 double, 2 twin/doubles, both with bath.
price	£60. Single occ. £35. Self-catering £175-£300 p.w.
meals	Dinner available, also available locally.
closed	Rarely.
directions	Left road in Mawnam Smith at Red Lion pub, onto Carwinion Road. 400 yds up hill on right, sign for Carwinion Garden.

If an inquisitive, errant dinosaur were to come rustling out of the great stands of bamboo or soaring gunnera, you honestly wouldn't be surprised. These 14 acres are a ravishing homage to leaf, foliage, wildness... a heavenly place of trees, ponds, streams. No wonder that Jane, who has done so much for these grounds in recent years, calls it an "unmanicured garden". At the end of the 19th century, Anthony's grandfather planted the first bamboos in this gorgeous valley garden leading down to the Helford River. Today Carwinion has one of the finest collections in Europe, more than 160 species with wonderful leaf and stem forms... the Bamboo Society of Great Britain flock here for annual get-togethers. The lushness soars impressively to the sky - don't miss the 20-foot pieris. Jane has made a series of paths to lead you through one breathtakingly romantic area after another, a palm sheltering under a tall beech tree, a banana tree thriving in the mild atmosphere. Tree ferns soar and, in a final flourish at the foot of the garden, Jane has transformed an old quarry into an enchanting fern garden. Camellia lovers will be knocked out by the walled garden where the renowned camellia grower John Price has now established his Towan Camellias business, offering more than 300 varieties and 100 types of hydrangea. Magic everywhere. *NGS, Good Gardens Guide.*

TRIST HOUSE

Graham & Brenda Salmon
Trist House,
Veryan, Truro, Cornwall TR2 5QA

tel   01872 501422
fax   01872 501211
e-mail graham@tristobs.ndo.co.uk

History lurks in this five-acre garden, as Brenda and Graham have found since they've been unwrapping its secrets over the last eight years. The outer reaches of the garden were very overgrown when they arrived, and in hacking through the jungle they have made unexpected discoveries. No fewer than 12 rockeries, so fashionable in Victorian times, have come to light – the largest being 25 feet high and designed to resemble the Matterhorn, with a small lake below it. The process of clearing has caused spring flowers to proliferate, and a woodland rose garden has been created above the recently uncovered dell garden. Meanwhile the original Italian terraces, croquet lawn and herbaceous borders immediately around the house have been embellished with new features. Imaginative themed walks create a formal feel: a 150-foot-long rose pergola intersects the north walk lined with magnolias and azaleas, a hydrangea walk is backed with cherry trees, and a canal leads to a small pond. An abundance of tender plants suited to the Cornish climate are grown here: Brenda propagates many of her own plants and also sells them on open days (Sundays and Tuesdays, April-September). Come and see for yourself just how sympathetically new ideas can blend with conservation of the historic. *NGS, Cornwall Garden Society.*

rooms	4: 2 twins, 2 singles, sharing 2 bathrooms.
price	£50.
meals	Available locally.
closed	Very occasionally.
directions	First drive on right past Post Office Stores in Veryan.

Built in the 1830s by the vicar responsible for laying out the gardens, the house overlooks the formal parts of the garden sloping away to the north and west. Large and beautifully proportioned rooms with tall windows make it a sunny and light house; comfortably and traditionally furnished, there's also a wide range of paintings, many by local artists. The Salmons used to run the Old Rectory residential adult education college at Fittleworth in Sussex, so you can be sure not only of a comfortable but also an interesting stay. Graham's an astronomer and loves to show visitors the Meade 10" telescope in his observatory.

THE WAGON HOUSE

Charles & Mally Francis
The Wagon House,
Heligan Manor, St Ewe, St Austell, Cornwall PL26 6EW

tel   01726 844505
fax   01726 844525
e-mail thewagonhouse@macace.co.uk
web   www.thewagonhouse.com

The 18th-century wagoners would be amazed if they could see the Wagon House today. Spotless bedrooms upstairs in what used to be the joiner's workshop, and, where the wagons rolled in, five huge windows through which the morning light streams (and the dawn chorus). There's tea in the cheerful sitting-room on arrival, and plenty of advice from Charles and Mally on local gardens and pubs to visit. Across the drive, courses in botanical art and photography are held in the Saw-Pit Studio where, as you would imagine, the walls are lined with fascinating paintings and photographs.

rooms	2 twins sharing bath/shower.
price	£70. Single occ. £40.
meals	Good local pubs and restaurants.
closed	Christmas & New Year.
directions	From St Austell for Heligan Gardens. Follow private drive towards Heligan House. Left before white gate-posts, keep left past cottages, left after The Magnolias, follow drive to house.

The Wagon House lies next to the world-famous Heligan Gardens, just over the wall from the Sundial Garden; Charles and Mally would be the first to admit that most people are coming to visit next-door's garden rather than their own! However, their small plot will give huge encouragement to those who are just starting out with a long-neglected patch. They have eradicated all brambles and nettles, and unearthed a Mini car door from the flower bed in the process – together with some nice slate slabs. Now they are developing a garden which includes plants that thrive in the Cornish coastal climate: hydrangeas, cordylines, griselinias and phormiums, as well as a crinodendron and a grevillea. In spite of Heligan's popularity, the Wagon House sits in a private spot undisturbed by visitors; stroll 400 yards up the tree-lined drive and you arrive at the Gardens. Charles is a garden photographer and Heligan tour-guide while Mally is a botanical artist, so both are closely involved with Heligan and can provide fascinating insights. They are involved with the Eden Project too, so you really are perfectly placed for a horticultural stay.

TREGOOSE

Anthony & Alison O'Connor
Tregoose,
Grampound, Truro, Cornwall TR2 4DB

tel   01726 882460
fax   01872 222427

At the head of the Roseland Peninsula, Tregoose is a handsome, late-Regency country house surrounded by rolling countryside. In the drawing room, where a log fire is lit on cooler evenings, a beautiful Chinese cabinet occupies one wall and in the dining room is a Malayan inscribed silk screen - a thank you present from the days of Empire. Upstairs the comfortable bedrooms have antique furniture, views onto the glorious garden, and pretty bathrooms. The Eden Project and Heligan are nearby. *Children by arrangement.*

rooms	3: 1 four-poster with bath; 1 twin with bath & shower; 1 double with private bath & shower.
price	From £40.
meals	Dinner £24. BYO wine.
closed	Christmas & Easter.
directions	A30 for Truro, left for Grampound Rd. After 3 miles, right onto A390 for Truro. After 200 yds, right where double white lines end. Pass between reflector posts to house, 200 yds down private lane.

This is open under the National Gardens Scheme. Alison, who grew up in Cornwall, is an NDH and has created a lovely garden with a wide variety of plants. Five fat Irish yews and a tumbledown wall were the starting point, but having reconstructed the walls to create a sunken garden, things started to look up. The L-shaped barn was a good backdrop for planting, so in went cotinus and yellow privet, flame-coloured alstroemerias, show-stopping *Crocosmia solfaterre* with its bronzey leaves and apricot yellow flowers, and blue agapanthus for contrast. The sunken walled garden protects such tender treasures as *Aloysia citrodora*, leptospermum, and, pièce de résistance, *Acacia baileyana purpurea*. Palm-like dracaena, Monterey pines and cypresses and the Chusan palm do well, and you can't miss the spectacular magenta blooms of the 30-foot *Rhododendron arboreum* 'Cornish Red'. The woodland garden displays more muted colours, scented deciduous azaleas, and the white July-scented rhododendron 'Polar Bear'. The potager supplies produce for dinners and flowers for the house, and Alison can supply almost any information about Cornish plants and gardens. *NGS, Cornwall Garden Society*.

CREED HOUSE

Lally & William Croggon
Creed House,
Creed, Grampound, Truro, TR2 4SL, Cornwall

tel   01872 530372

In Lally and William's lovely house and garden there's a
comforting sense of all being well in England's green and
pleasant land - although Lally grew up in India and met
William in Malaysia where they spent 10 years. St Crida's
Church rises on tip-toes above treetops while the murmur
of a lazy stream reaches your ears. Inside the 1730s house,
shimmering wooden floors are covered with Persian rugs
and light pours into every elegant corner. Breakfast at
the mahogany table can turn into an early morning
house-party, such is Lally's sense of fun and spontaneity.
The big guestrooms - with extra large beds - exude taste
and simplicity.

rooms	3: 1 twin/double with bath/shower; 2 twin/doubles with private bathrooms.
price	£70-£80. Single occ. by arrangement.
meals	Available locally.
closed	Christmas & New Year.
directions	From St Austell, A390 to Grampound. Just beyond clock tower, left into Creed Lane. After 1 mile left at grass triangle opp. church. House behind 2nd white gate on left.

Here is one of Cornwall's loveliest gardens, a tribute to the enormous amount of hard work, dedication and brilliant plantsmanship devoted to these stunning seven acres. Lally and William came here in 1974 to find a Miss Havisham of a garden with a lawn like a hayfield edged in brambles, and the rest an impenetrable jungle with glimpses of 40-ft high rhododendrons, magnolia and huge stands of gunnera. There clearly had been a garden here once upon a time. Today this jungle has been transformed into a fine, gentle, old-fashioned rectory garden. Along the way they discovered many exciting buildings including a cobbled yard with a sunken centre and a summer house which they have carefully restored. The mass clearance also encouraged long-dormant snowdrops and daffodils to bloom in their thousands. The tree and shrub collection is outstanding; rhododendrons, camellias, azaleas and magnolias do brilliantly and secret paths leading from the gently sloping lawns lure you deep into the decorative woodland. So much to admire and enjoy, such as the circular lily pond, the swamp garden with its candelabra primulas and mecanopsis, and the lower stable yard with its alpines and sun loving plants on its raised wall beds. Lally and William are delightful, enthusiastic and very knowledgeable and their pleasure in their masterpiece is totally infectious. So close to Heligan and the Eden project. *NGS County Organiser, Good Gardens Guide.*

OLD DE LANK FARM

John & Marcia Castle
Old De Lank Farm,
St. Breward, Bodmin, Cornwall PL30 4ND

tel   01208 851366
fax   01208 851829
e-mail olddelankfarm@aol.com

It is thought that the origins of this 13th-century hall house were ecclesiastical. It was added to in the early 19th century, and the Castles have completely restored the period Regency look: one guest commented that it was like living in a Jane Austen set! Slate flagstones with Oriental rugs on the ground floor, an oak-panelled drawing room and a classic Regency dining room with open or granite inglenook fireplaces. History is blended with every modern comfort upstairs: new period bathrooms have roll-top baths and/or power showers, and pretty bedrooms have leaded windows and generously proportioned, very comfortable beds.

rooms	3: 1 double with bath; 1 double with shower; 1 twin/double with bath/shower.
price	From £60. Single occ. £40.
meals	Supper £12.50. Dinner £22.50. Picnics available.
closed	Very occasionally.
directions	10 minutes from A30 taking Blisland & Breward turning. Precise directions given at time of booking.

Newly-planted rhododendrons lead you down the drive to the handsome Cornish granite house tucked in snugly at the bottom. Its lines are softened by well-established creepers and climbers, with wisteria across the front of the house and roses around the front door. Agapanthus, camellias and olive trees are grouped in pots on the front patio, surrounded by lavender, hydrangeas and herbs, making a colourful welcome for the arriving visitor, particularly in spring. A new raised pond in a granite block surround blends easily with its ancient surroundings, and is a lovely spot for drinks before dinner. You eat well: Marcia is a great cook and published cookery writer, and visitors love her dinners. John is a talented builder having done all the house restoration himself. He is in the process of creating a barbecue terrace and herb garden above the kitchen patio so that Marcia can have her herbs close to hand: standard bay trees in pots already stand sentinel outside the kitchen door. The Castles are thoughtful hosts: if like most of their visitors you wish to see the Eden Project, they very obligingly hold tickets so that you won't have to queue.

HORNACOTT

Jos & Mary-Anne Otway-Ruthven
Hornacott,
South Petherwin, Launceston, Cornwall PL15 7LH

tel   01566 782461
fax   01566 782461
e-mail otwayruthven@btinternet.com

The house is named after the hill and the peace within is as deep as the valley. You have utter privacy, a private entrance to your own fresh, elegant suite: a twin-bedded room and a large, square, high sitting room with double doors giving onto the wooded valley. There's a CD player as well as music, chocolates and magazines and you can have tea in the rambling garden that wraps itself around the house. Jos and Mary-Anne really want you to enjoy your stay; you will. Butcher's sausages and free-range eggs for breakfast. Perfect.

rooms	1 twin with bath/shower; sitting room & adjoining single for child available.
price	£70. Single occ. £45.
meals	Dinner £20. BYO wine.
closed	Christmas & New Year.
directions	From Launceston, B3254 for Liskeard. Through Daw's House & South Petherwin, down steep hill & last left before little bridge. House first on left.

A dynamic garden where lots has been happening in recent years as Jos and Mary-Anne work their way from one area to the next. The garden is about one-and-a-half acres of sloping ground with shady spots, open sunny lawns and borders and many shrubs. A stream tumbles through the garden after heavy rain and trickles quietly by in the dryer months of summer; its banks are being cleared and water-loving plants introduced. Elsewhere, clearance is underway, too, and by opening up long-hidden areas, wild flowers have been given space and light to thrive. A charming pergola with its own seat has been built at one end of the garden to add vertical interest and a touch of formality. The recent loss of some mature trees near the house has been a blessing in disguise – it has created open spaces where there was once too much shade. Jos, a kitchen designer, and Mary-Anne have planted rhododendrons, azaleas, camellias and many flowering shrubs and everything is being designed to blend with the peaceful setting and the backdrop of grand old trees. A collection of David Austin roses has been introduced – his are the only ones which seem to do well here, says Mary-Anne. There's plenty of colour too, with varied colour themings from one border to the next.

BICTON MILL

Richard & Mariebel Allerton
Bicton Mill,
Bicton, Nr Liskeard, Cornwall PL14 5RF

tel   01579 383577
fax   01579 383577

Richard says, self-deprecatingly, that Bicton Mill deserves a mention for its national collection of weeds... but then one man's weeds are another man's wild flowers. Richard and Mariebel have made their large, river- and leat-bound garden a perfectly harmonised blend of the wild and the informal. The long, park-like, luxurious lawn with its pretty bridge is edged by mature trees and gently flowing water; sea trout linger and, if they're not careful, are skillfully caught by Richard, a keen game fisherman. Mariebel knows her plants and has added scores of delightful touches and displays, especially in the terraced garden above the house with its bountiful planting and summer flowers. Do explore this part of the grounds – you'll find carved stonework which hints at the ancient history of this secluded, utterly peaceful valley, and added interest like the huge cider press near the front door that has been transformed into a raised bed. A hefty pergola groans with vigorous climbers like 'Kiftsgate'; 'Rambling Rector' spirals up the hillside. Across the little lane good shrubs and trees have been planted to create a separate garden – a sort of introduction to the main event. Spring time is particularly magical here, with bluebells giving hazy displays in wilder areas. Later, autumnal drifts of windflowers shimmer like flamingoes. Don't listen to a word Richard says about weeds... this is a place of beauty and he and Mariebel have done much to enhance the valley that they love.

rooms	2: 1 double with shower; 1 double with private bathroom.
price	£50–£60. Single occ. by arrangement.
meals	Packed lunch from £5. Excellent pubs/restaurants within 7 miles.
closed	Rarely.
directions	On A388 Callington-Launceston, left at Kelly Bray (opp. garage) to Maders. 400 yds after Maders, left to Golberdon & left at x-roads. After 400 yds, right down lane. 0.75 miles on, by bridge.

An old corn mill with the original waterwheel now in the kitchen and with views down the garden to the salmon/sea trout river from the bedrooms. Richard is a keen fly fisherman and can fix up rods for visitors. Mariebel is a professional portrait painter who taught for many years; she's still happy to teach individuals or groups. Bicton is informal, comfortable and relaxed. Meals are eaten in the huge farmhouse kitchen or in the impressive slate-floored dining room/sitting room. The Lynher Valley is unspoilt and enchanting, with lovely walks all round. *Children by arrangement.*

BARN CLOSE

Anne Robinson
Barn Close,
Beetham, Cumbria LA7 7AL

tel   01539 563191 mob 07752 670658
fax   01539 563191
e-mail anne@nwbirds.co.uk
web   www.nwbirds.co.uk

An unusual entrance: you find yourself in a wide hall running the length of the house. Erected on the original site of an ancient stone barn, the handsome 1920s building has been a happy family home and is furnished simply but gracefully. With just two rooms (the lovely twin has a south-west-facing view of the garden) Anne is able to give her visitors lots of personal attention, and she certainly provides very good value. The Wheatsheaf pub, a short stroll through the village of Beetham, provides excellent food and this is a perfect base for exploring the Lake District.

rooms	2: 1 twin with bath/shower; 1 single with private bath/shower.
price	£50. Single occ. £25–£30.
meals	Supper £15.
closed	Christmas.
directions	Exit M6 junc. 35 for 4 miles. A6 north to Milnthorpe & Beetham. Left before bridge; right at Wheatsheaf pub & church. Right at end of village, over cattle grid. House at end of drive.

There is something in this garden to interest the visitor at any time of the year. Fantastic displays of snowdrops, aconites and bluebells in the spring, a swathe of autumn colour from the surrounding mature trees, and a large herbaceous border that looks stunning in June and July. Mike organises birdwatching holidays round the local area but you need not go very far: the garden itself attracts many birds. Over the last 10 years nearly 80 different species have been seen in the grounds (or flying over), including a number of rarities like the hawfinch. Anne has kindly planted teazels, acanthus, grasses and anything with seedheads that might appeal to the birds but no doubt they are equally – and ungratefully – keen on her productive vegetable garden and fruit trees. The pond has been supplemented with water irises, candelabra primulas and water lilies: wildlife flourishes here, particularly dragonflies, and there are many resident butterflies. This is a beautiful unspoiled part of Cumbria, with good walks round the Morecambe Bay estuary, famous for its huge flocks of wading birds, and Arnside Knott with its butterflies and exceptional views of the Lake District peaks. *RHS, HPS, Lakeland Horticultural Society, Cumbria Gardens Trust.*

HORSLEYGATE HALL

Margaret Ford
Horsleygate Hall,
Horsleygate Lane, Holmesfield, Derbyshire SI8 7WD

tel   0114 289 0333

Margaret and Robert are dedicated, skillful, knowledgeable gardeners and their talents are abundantly clear from the moment you arrive. Margaret is a true plantsman who knows and loves her plants; Robert is the garden architect. He has added delightful touches, including a pergola fashioned from the iron pipes of the old greenhouse heating system and fences made from holly poles. Exploring the garden is enormous fun – there are so many surprises. The sloping site includes a woodland garden, hot sun terrace, rockeries, pools, a fern area, a jungle garden, mixed borders and an exquisite ornamental kitchen garden. The Fords are keen on evergreen shrubs and have an interest in euphorbias. They have a particularly unusual collection of herbaceous perennials and are always on the lookout for fresh treasures to add to their collection. Quirky statuary peeps out at you in unusual places and all around the garden are strategically placed seats where you can soak up the varied displays. The overall theme is one of informality, with walls, terraces, paths and well-planted troughs hidden from each other. Lovely in spring, gorgeous in the full flower of summer, and good autumn colour and winter interest, too, from their huge collection of shrubs. *NGS*

rooms	3: 1 double with bath/shower; 1 family, 1 twin sharing bathroom & wc.
price	£45–£50. Single occ. from £30.
meals	Available locally.
closed	23 December–4 January.
directions	From M1 junc. 29 A617 to Chesterfield; B6051 to Millthorpe. Horsleygate Lane 1 mile on, on right.

Wake up to the sounds of hens, ponies and doves as they cluck, strut and coo in a charming old stableyard outside. The house was built in 1783 as a farmhouse and substantially extended in 1856; the garden was once home to the hounds of the local hunt. The house is elegant yet relaxed and full of antique country furniture and subtle colours. Breakfast is served in the old schoolroom and is a feast of organic eggs, honey, home-made jams and garden fruit from Margaret's superbly maintained kitchen garden. Glorious setting... and place. *Children over five welcome.*

CRESSBROOK HALL

Bobby & Len Hull-Bailey
Cressbrook Hall,
Cressbrook, Nr Buxton, Derbyshire SK17 8SY

tel   01298 871289
fax   01298 871845
e-mail stay@cressbrookhall.co.uk
web   www.cressbrookhall.co.uk

A magnificent William IV property built on the precipice of a
spectacular limestone gorge. Beyond the formal gardens and 30
acres of parkland there are panoramic views over the River Wye
and to the green hillside of Brushfield beyond. Inside, sympathetic
renovation is complete - you'll marvel at the ornate, delicate
plasterwork on the ceilings. Imposing though it is, this former
mill owner's house Buzzes with family life. Four generations of
Hull-Baileys live here and Bobby cares for guests and family
alike with efficient kindness.

rooms	3: 2 doubles, 1 twin, all with bath and/or shower.
price	£75-£105.
meals	Packed lunch available.
closed	Christmas & New Year.
directions	From Ashford-in-the-Water, B6465 to Monsal Head. Left at Monsal Head Hotel, follow valley to The Old Mill, fork left. Left, at lodge building with white fence & 'Private Drive' sign.

A fascinating project in garden archaeology. Huge efforts have been made to restore the stately 1835 grounds of the Gothic/Elizabethan-style mansion, magnificent in its spectacular setting. The gardens were originally designed and made by Edward Kemp who trained under Joseph Paxton – of Crystal Palace fame – at nearby Chatsworth House. A neat touch of history in reverse is that the gardener who helped Bobby in the early stages of the great scheme has now moved on to Chatsworth. The Hull-Baileys have Edward Kemp's original design and planting plan and their first idea was to replicate it in all its details. An ambition too far, Bobby says now, but their compromise, to interpret the original, is working well. Kemp capitalised on the position by creating the terrace gardens from which you may gaze down to the river below and across to the countryside beyond. The garden is utterly of its time, with elegant balustrades, a parterre tapestry, lawns so emerald green you hesitate to walk on them. Each of the beds has been restored to its original outline. Bobby comes from a family of keen gardeners and says modestly that she was the only one who didn't show an early interest and isn't a gardener by nature. She's catching up fast. She and Len have chosen good perennial plants for many of the formal beds and a judicious selection of annuals to adorn others. The result is a brilliant period piece.

GREENSWOOD FARM

Mrs Helen Baron
Greenswood Farm,
Greenswood Lane, Dartmouth, Devon TQ6 0LY

tel   01803 712100

A lovely, low Devon longhouse painted cream and covered in wisteria; stone flagging, deep window sills, and elegant furniture. But this is a working farm and there is no stuffiness in Helen and Roger – this is a warm and cosy place to relax and enjoy the gorgeous valley that is now their patch. Bedrooms are feminine but not namby-pamby: huge mirrors, colour-washed walls and pretty curtains are fresh and clean, old pine chests give a solid feel and the views are special. Organic beef and lamb are reared on the farm and breakfast eggs come straight from Sally Henny Penny outside – buy some to take home, if you can drag yourself away.

rooms	3: 2 doubles, 1 twin, 2 with bath, 1 with shower.
price	From £50. Single occ. £35-£40
meals	Dinner from £15.
closed	December 23–January 1.
directions	A381 for Dartmouth. At Golf & Country Club right to Strete. Sign after 1 mile.

R oger has a huge interest in forestry and countryside management (he recently worked on the new cycle track from Ashprington to Totnes) and Helen adores growing flamboyant and colourful flowers – she also arranges them skillfully for the house. When they moved to Greenswood five years ago they inherited a garden planted some 20 years ago, on a boggy field with a stream running through the middle. There were some mture shrubs and trees, somewhat overgrown and needing attention. South-facing and completely sheltered from any wind as it lies in a dip, the garden now sweeps down from the house in a long hollow via three large ponds fed by a stream running down the middle. Enlarged and landscaped, it has been designed to reflect the contours of its hilly, wooded outer borders. Planting has evolved, as it should, over time – there are now perfect beds and borders, packed with spring bulbs, primroses, rhododendrons and azaleas. Many pathways and older beds have been discovered and restored. Water lovers such as the gigantic *Gunnera manicata*, white irises, ferns and grasses hug the ponds while there are delightful secret pathways through borders full of colourful planting and large shrubs. Future plans include restoring the waterfall from the second to the third pond which they recently uncovered, and developing the planting. The final pond is on level ground, hidden from the house and reached by a line of tall poplar trees. Birdsong, wind in the trees and absolute peace.

WADSTRAY HOUSE

Philip & Merilyn Smith
Wadstray House,
Wadstray, Blackawton, Devon TQ9 7DE

tel   01803 712539
fax   01803 712539
e-mail wadstraym@aol.com

Wadstray, a solid, early Georgian Grade II-listed country house, was originally built as a gentleman's residence for a merchant trading in the nearby seafaring town of Dartmouth. Everything here has an air of substance. The bedrooms have balconies, or canopied beds, or sea views. There are open fires in the dining room and a fine library for rainy days. There is the mood of a secret garden with a self-catering orangery with its own creeper-clad ruin... and behind it all a long valley view bridged by a distant strip of sea.

rooms	3: 1 double, 2 twins, all with bathroom.
price	From £60. Single occ. £45.
meals	Available locally.
closed	Christmas Day & Boxing Day.
directions	From A38, A384 for Totnes. Follow signs for Totnes, A381 to Halwell; left by Old Inn pub. At T-junc, left onto A3122. House 0.5 miles past Golf & Country Club, on right.

Merilyn and Philip are both passionate about their eight-acre garden, always planning new features and displays to add to Wadstray's charms. When they came in the early 1990s, both house and garden needed major renovation but, on the plus side, they inherited plenty of mature planting; this was the work of Viscount Chaplin, a leading member of the Horticultural Society. He planted vigorously and well in the early 1950s, hence the profusion of good shrubs and trees including magnolia, camellias, azaleas and rhododendrons. The garden is open and sunny, with lovely valley views which they have improved by extending the lawn and moving a ha-ha fence to open up the vista even further. By the house, with its colonial veranda, Merilyn has created a gorgeous herbaceous border which blooms in profusion in summer. Spring displays get better all the time thanks to a continuing programme of bulb planting. Woodland areas have been slowly cleared to give more light, older shrubs pruned back to encourage vigorous growth. Lots of good hydrangeas – Merilyn and Philip are gradually adding to their collection because they do so well here. A new acer glade has now been established to give autumn colour. Beyond the lawn is a wildflower meadow leading to a wildlife pond and a walled garden which attracts alpinists from miles around who come to buy plants from the specialist nursery. *Devon Gardens Trust, NCCPG.*

BROOK

Bee & Peter Smyth
Brook,
East Cornworthy, Nr Totnes, Devon TQ9 7HQ

tel   01803 722424

Needing to escape to a more peaceful spot three years ago, Peter and Bee had the luck to find Brook tucked away down by the river near Dittisham. Lucky, not only because Brook happens to be so picturesque, but also because the previous owner had planted a particularly interesting collection of specimen trees and shrubs. At least one is flowering – such as eucryphia, drimys, or a Chilean flame tree – during each month of the year, and the garden boasts one of the largest hoherias in the country. The brook after which the house is named flows through the three-acre garden, and Peter has recently planted a colourful bog garden with thalictrum and arum lilies, and a larger pond area. This is an immaculately conceived and maintained garden, from the colourful herbaceous beds either side of the front path, to the well-kept lawns and the array of nasturtiums, geraniums and agapanthus in pots around the terrace. The white wicker chairs in the shade of an old apple tree on the lawn look really inviting: a blissful place to sit over a cup of tea when you arrive. The Smyths also run a commercial camellia nursery nearby which you are welcome to visit. *RHS, The International Camellia Society.*

rooms	1 twin with private bathroom.
price	£50. Single occ. £30.
meals	Available locally.
closed	Very occasionally.
directions	A381 to Dartmouth; stay in left-hand lane for Ashprington, Tuckenhay & Cornworthy. Right for East Cornworthy. Last house on right.

With only one bedroom available for guests, the Smyths will make you feel as welcome as personal friends. The pretty bedroom looks south over the garden and east with uninterrupted views over fields; the floral decoration reflects the garden outside and matches the bright, sparkling bathroom. Although not technically a conservatory, the breakfast room was built with wide windows to open up the view over the garden to the south and west, and the doors fold back to open onto the terrace. With an attractive contemporary check sofa and chairs, it is a very pleasant place to sit, read and relax. Dittisham and the river Dart are a short walk away.

KINGSTON HOUSE

Elizabeth Corfield
Kingston House,
Staverton, Totnes, Devon TQ9 6AR

tel   01803 762 235
fax   01803 762 444
e-mail admin@kingston-estate.co.uk
web   www.kingston-estate.co.uk

Gracious and grand, the impeccably-restored former home of a wealthy wool merchant with all the trappings intact. A rare marquetry staircase, an 18th-century painted china closet, marble works, original baths, galleried landings and oak panelling to gasp at. But it's not austere – the bedrooms are steeped in comfort and cushions, a fire roars in the guest sitting room (formerly the chapel) and food is fresh, local and home-grown. Rugged Dartmoor is to the north, Totnes minutes away and walks from the house through the gentle South Hams are spectacular.

rooms	3: 2 doubles with bath; 1 twin/double with private bath.
price	From £130. Single occ. from £85.
meals	Dinner £35.
closed	23 December-7 January.
directions	At Buckfastleigh A384 Totnes road for 2.5 miles. Left to Staverton. At Sea Trout Inn left fork, for Kingston. House 1 mile on left.

Elizabeth's love of wildlife has made restoring the garden a hard task – she is adamant that no pesticides be used – but most of the estate was in need of a complete overhaul when she arrived. Now it is perfectly renovated and opens for the National Gardens Scheme three times a year: a rosy walled garden with peaches, pears, greengages and nectarines intertwined with roses and jasmine, beech hedging with yew arches, a formal rose garden, box topiary, a dear little summer house edged with lavender, an orchard with rare apples, and, in the South Garden, an avenue of pleached limes leading to a wild woodland. Elizabeth is also a stickler for historical accuracy – some of the outline of the garden was revealed by uncovering the original slate 'keepers' which edged the formal beds and borders, and new projects include three baroque gardens with patterned gravel and box hedging, all meticulously researched to be in keeping with the house. The vegetable garden is productive and neat with a nod to the contemporary – unusually shaped twigs and branches are used as natural sculptures for supporting beans and sweet peas. The whole place is an absolute gem for purists and nature lovers alike. *NGS.*

DODBROOKE FARM

Judy Henderson
Dodbrooke Farm,
Michelcombe, Holne, Devon TQ13 7SP

tel   01364 631461
e-mail judy@dodbrooke.freeserve.co.uk
web   www.dodbrookefarm.com

You come for the glory of the setting and the unpretentiousness of it all, not for huge luxury or sterile scrupulousness. The 17th-century longhouse has a gorgeous cobbled yard (laid by Judy), a bridge across to the island (shades of Monet) and goats. The family produces its own moorland water, all its fruit and vegetables and they even make cheese. The rooms are in simple country style, the attitude very 'green' – hedge-laying, stone wall-mending – and the conversation fascinating. You can wander through two acres of young woodland, too.

rooms	4: 2 twins, 2 singles, sharing 1 bathroom.
price	£50. Single occ. £23–£25.
meals	Dinner occasionally available, £12.50.
closed	Christmas.
directions	From A38 2nd Ashburton turn, towards Dartmeet. After 2 miles, left to Holne. Pass church & inn. After 250 yds, right; after 150yds, left to Michelcombe. Left at foot of hill.

Twisting lanes and a steep hill lead to secluded Dodbrooke Farm in its rural valley setting. Since John and Judy moved here from Kent 17 years ago – they farmed and grew fruit – they have made the most of the glorious natural beauty all around. Dartmoor looms above distant trees and a rapid stream winds its way through this charmingly informal garden – a magnet for birds and other wildlife. A little island, reached by a wooden bridge, is now a secret garden planted with rhododendrons, hydrangeas and camellias which thrive in the acid soil. Wild flowers grow in profusion and are cherished, Muscovy ducks waddle and swim in the sparkling stream. Trees grow well here so John and Judy have created their own arboretum in an adjacent field and dug out a pond. A little orchard produces apples, plums and soft fruit and a very productive organic kitchen garden supplies the house with most of its vegetables. Two cider orchards provide the fruit for freshly-made apple juice and traditional cider. As Judy says, they're not fussy about garden plants but they are utterly devoted to making the very most of the setting. On bright spring days, masses of daffodils bloom; in summer, the acid-lovers come into their own. Perfect peace with the soothing sound of running water in a fabulous setting.

CORNDONFORD FARM

Ann & Will Williams
Corndonford Farm,
Poundsgate, Newton Abbot, Devon TQ13 7PP

tel   01364 631595
e-mail corndonford@btinternet.com

Come to be engrossed in the routines of a wild, engagingly chaotic haven. Ann and Will are friendly, kind and extrovert; guests adore them and keep coming back. There is comfort, too: warm curtains, a four-poster with lacy drapes, early morning tea. Gentle giant shire horses live at the shippon end where the cows once stood, and there's medieval magic with Bronze Age foundations. A wonderful place for those who love the rhythm of real country life – and the Two Moors Way footpath is on the doorstep. *Children over 10 by arrangement.*

rooms	2: 1 four-poster, 1 twin, sharing bathroom.
price	£50-£60. Single occ. £25-£30.
meals	Available locally.
closed	Christmas.
directions	From A38 2nd Ashburton turn for Dartmeet & Princetown. In Poundsgate pass pub on left & take 3rd signposted right for Corndon. Straight over x-roads, 0.5 miles further & farm on left.

Climb and climb the Dartmoor edge with views growing wider and wilder all the time until you reach the stone-walled lane and the sturdy granite buildings of Corndonford Farm. Roses and wisteria clamber up the rugged façade, softening the ancient strength of the house. At jam-making time the air is filled with the sweetness of an enormous pan of bubbling strawberries. Ann's jewel-like little farm garden has an arched walk of richly scented honeysuckle, roses and other climbers which leads to her very productive vegetable and soft fruit garden – the source of the berries. She knows her plants and has created a small, cottagey garden in complete harmony with its surroundings. There's a rockery and a little gravelled patio just outside the house which has been planted with charming cottage flowers. Above is a lawn edged by deep borders absolutely packed with colour and traditional cottage garden plants, including salmon-pink rhododendron, cranesbill and lupins. Do take the very short walk along the lane to Ann's second garden, known locally as the "traffic calmer". Here, by the roadside, she has planted loads of rhododendrons and shrubs in a delightful display – and it really does encourage even the most hurried motorists to slow down. The views are breathtaking, the setting wonderfully peaceful, the garden as informal and welcoming as Ann and Will themselves.

THE OLD RECTORY

Rachel Belgrave
The Old Rectory,
Widecombe in the Moor, Newton Abbot, Devon TQ13 7TB

tel 01364 621231
fax 01364 621231
e-mail rachel.belgrave@care4free.net

The jolly former home of the vicar of Widecombe with its famous fair and "Uncle Tom Cobbley and all", the house feels peaceful and calm. One of Rachel's hobbies is sculpture so although the decoration is traditional – wooden floors, pretty curtains, good furniture and family portraits – there are glimpses of well-travelled bohemianism. The dining room is iron-oxide red, there are tapestries from Ecuador and Peru and vibrant colours glow in the comfortable bedrooms. Pretty bathrooms are sparkling with unusual tiles and original ceramic sinks and there are long views from deep window seats – pick up a book and soak it all in.

rooms	2: 1 double with shower; 1 twin/family with private bath/shower.
price	From £40.
meals	Dinner available.
closed	November–March.
directions	From A38 Exeter to Plymouth road towards Bovey Tracey. Follow signs to Widecombe.

Rachel has been "potty about gardening" since she was a child. After moving here from London six years ago, she has used her artistic talent to create an organic cottage garden with a twist. Wanting the garden to reflect the symmetry of the house and then merge into the Dartmoor landscape, she has developed what was just a field and a sloping lawn. Herbaceous borders hug the sides and are crammed with old favourites and many British wild flowers. Half-way down is a sunny terrace for lounging, a border of scented roses and a heather bank reflecting the Moor. Then down through two labyrinth paths mown into the grass to a little stone circle and an open meadow which borders the woodland garden. The walled garden bursts with soft fruit and apple trees and a willow tunnel takes you to an old pond and bog garden fed by a stream and surrounded with varieties of primula, iris and other bog plants. Lovely arty touches everywhere – peep-holes through hedges, secret places, benches cut into the bottoms of old trees, willow structures and plenty of room for her sculptures. Rachel was told she couldn't grow roses on Dartmoor but her successes are everywhere, from the ramblers she loves to the old scented varieties that go so well with the Georgian house.

THE CIDER HOUSE

Mrs Sarah Stone
The Cider House,
Buckland Abbey, Yelverton, Devon PL20 6EZ

tel   01822 853285
fax   01822 853626
e-mail sarah.stone@cider-house.co.uk

Big mullion windows and an artistic interior - an enchanting
former refectory of a medieval abbey. In the dining room the
Stones' artist daughter's paintings hang on hessian walls; in the
kitchen a red medallion design scintillates on a white-painted
wooden floor. Upstairs, sunny-coloured wallpapers and a double
room that overlooks the parterre and the marvellous view down
the valley beyond. The larger twin has an arched window recess
and looks onto the tower in the courtyard and the island of
camellias and azaleas that greets you on arrival. Sarah's home-
made muesli with fresh fruit is a breakfast favourite.

rooms	3: 1 double, 1 twin, both with private bath; 1 extra twin with shared bath.
price	£60. Single occ. £40.
meals	Good local pubs & restaurants.
closed	Christmas & New Year.
directions	To Plymouth on A38 for Tavistock. At Yelverton follow signs for Buckland Abbey, at x-roads right for Buckland Monachorum. 1st left to granite gateposts down drive to courtyard.

As the fortunes of next-door Buckland Abbey changed, so did the history of The Cider House – it transmuted from monastery refectory to cider barn to private house. In a subtle reference to Sir Francis Drake's association with the Abbey and his achievement in bringing a water supply to Plymouth, a narrow leat runs across the terrace in front of the house. By the time the Stones arrived in 1980, the National Trust had acquired the Abbey and subsequently most of its surrounding property; keen gardeners both, Sarah and Michael found the framework of old buildings and walls a perfect setting in which to create their garden. They have chosen plants sympathetic to the environment – species plants where possible – and have avoided 'modern' colour combinations. White-scented *Wisteria venusta* twines up an arch in a purple berberis-edged parterre. Down the tree-shaded side of a long walk an interesting woodland border has gradually taken shape. In contrast, beyond a wisteria-covered barn, a hot border is set against a sunny wall. Pretty wrought-iron gates incorporating spider and bird designs lead through to the summer house in the wild garden, a place in which to dream. But the place that will make your jaw drop is the walled kitchen garden – an unbelievable treat. *NGS.*

TOR COTTAGE

Maureen Rowlatt
Tor Cottage,
Chillaton, Nr Tavistock, Devon PL16 0JE

tel	01822 860248
fax	01822 860126
e-mail	info@torcottage.co.uk
web	www.torcottage.co.uk

Your final approach to the house is along a half-mile, tree-lined track that's so long you'll wonder if you've taken the wrong turning. Your persistence is rewarded with a sudden burst of light and colour as you arrive at this lovely hideaway home. Birds sing, dragonflies hover over ponds and buzzards patrol the skies in that lazy way of theirs. Maureen has created this idyllic corner from what was no more than a field with a stream running through it. She has managed to make use of leylandii in such a way that even its staunchest opponent would approve, and shaped it into a perfectly-manicured 20-foot-high L-shaped hedge which effectively shields the heated swimming pool and adds welcome privacy. A series of paths and steps lead you to new delights – flowers, shrubs and plants chosen for leaf texture and colour and all beautifully maintained. There are secret corners, too, particularly by the stream and in a dappled wood with its very own, wonderfully slug-free hosta garden. Two of the cleverly converted outbuildings used for bed and breakfast have their own little gardens. Natural woodland and a recently made path up the wooded hillside are bonuses. A year-round fairytale garden – from the first wild flowers of spring to the icy white of winter frosts.

rooms	3: 2 doubles, 1 twin/double, all with bathroom & private garden or conservatory.
price	£130. Single occ. £89. Discount for longer stays.
meals	Restaurant nearby.
closed	Christmas & New Year.
directions	In Chillaton keep pub & PO on left, up hill towards Tavistock. After 300 yds, right (bridlepath sign). Cottage at end of lane.

Luxury touches at every turn – as if the rare solitary stream-side setting of this longhouse wasn't enough. Maureen pampers you imaginatively: champagne on occasions, toiletries, bedside bags of truffles, soft towels and robes in huge bedrooms with log fires - one with its own conservatory, the other two with private terraces. Outdoors, a swimming pool is colourfully lit at night. Renowned for inspired vegetarian and traditional cooking, Maureen serves breakfast in the (fountained) sunroom. She is gregarious yet unobtrusive. Moors, not fairies, at the bottom of the garden. But there is magic here... *Minimum stay two nights.*

TOR DOWN HOUSE

John & Maureen Pakenham
Tor Down House,
Belstone, Okehampton, Devon EX20 1QY

tel   01837 840731
fax   01837 840731
e-mail info@tordownhouse.co.uk
web   www.tordownhouse.co.uk

A truly glorious garden, but I would expect nothing less of a theatre designer with an RHS certificate and a painter: John uses his design skills in the garden and Maureen paints pictures which you can buy from the walls. They are not only gifted but generous, and love to share their considerable knowledge. They've been here for eight years and created much from scratch: planted hundreds of trees, thousands of bulbs, mixed hedging and rambling roses, a wildflower meadow and a pond garden which sweeps down to an orchard. A boules terrace is bounded by a hornbeam hedge which will eventually enclose it, hard structures include a formal wrought-iron pergola (designed with help from Rosemary Verey) through which the views are stunning, and some elegant metal gates with a weather vane. There must be some magic in the soil because everything is huge: eight-foot-high red hot pokers, a 12-foot pieris and a 40-foot holly tower over waist-high herbaceous borders and bursting shrubs. A smooth "cream tea lawn" at the front of the house is a more formal area, the perfect spot to relax – perhaps with one of John's many gardening books. As both gardeners obviously have such a good eye for shape, it's no surprise that these four acres seamlessly flow into the surrounding fields: charms of goldfinches descend on Knapwood seed, deer graze, buzzards peep and it all looks entirely natural and uncontrived. Clever... *RHS, HPS.*

rooms	2: 1 four-poster with shower; 1 four-poster with bath.
price	£70. Single occ. £45.
meals	Good pubs and restaurants nearby.
closed	Christmas & New Year.
directions	Exit A30 to Belstone. In centre of village, right after red phone box. After 0.75 miles cross cattle grid. Next house on left.

The 14th-century, Grade II-listed, thatched Devon longhouse within Dartmoor National Park was recently home of author Doris Lessing. Its history goes on and on... enchantingly pervasive in the architecture, interiors, gardens - and atmosphere. Sleep resplendent in four-posters in low-ceilinged, beamy rooms, all with views of the very English country garden whence come copious fresh flowers. Your hosts are adventurously well-travelled and interesting. Just one field away lies the moor with all its wild treasures.

SILKHOUSE

James Clifton
Silkhouse,
Drewsteignton , Exeter , Devon EX6 6RF

tel   01647 231267

Heavenly. No other word. James has created a masterpiece in his valley garden, a place of so many delights and such glorious informality and plantsmanship that even on a cold, wet June morning it was hard to tear oneself away. Black swans glide on the large pool fed by the stream which runs through the garden, a pair of amiable turkeys gobble on the lawns and nut-hatches bully more timid birds at the bird table. And that's before you have discovered the wonderful contrasts in every corner. The garden is mature and informal and in perfect harmony with the architecture of James's home and with the charm of this hidden, wooded valley. Lovely roses climb up the façade, good shrubs thrive everywhere and herbaceous borders are piled high with colour and leaf. One secret place leads to another, with shaded, private sitting places; reflect and become overwhelmed by the natural beauty which surrounds you. James calls this a cottage and pond garden but it is much, much more. It's an exquisite celebration of nature, from the rare breeds of poultry and decorative pheasants to the fabulous collection of plants he has introduced so skillfully over the past 20 years. An all-weather tennis court is secreted away and you'll even find a table-tennis table under a tree. And you can stay in these grounds – there's a little gipsy caravan complete with its own double bed!

rooms	3: 1 double with bath & private sitting room; 1 double, 1 twin, both with bath.
price	£50-£60. Single occ. £30-£35.
meals	Dinner, 4 courses, £15-£18. Light supper available.
closed	Rarely.
directions	M5 junc. 31 onto A30 for Okehampton. 10 miles on, left for Cheriton Bishop. 4 miles on, 1st left after going over dual carriageway. Through tunnel & immed. right; follow lane to bottom of hill.

A dazzling, eclectic style energises the long, rambling 16th-century longhouse, named by Huguenots who wove silk here. Fine furniture, lovely pictures, but not slick or pristine - there's a deeply bowed ceiling in the Boat Room so don't forget to duck. Dine or breakfast in the beamed, low-ceilinged dining room beneath a vast brass chandelier; rest or read by a large granite fireplace with views of the garden. A wonderful, relaxed place for laid-back people; James is charming.

REGENCY HOUSE

Mrs Jenny Parsons
Regency House,
Hemyock, Cullompton, Devon EX15 3RQ

tel   01823 680238
e-mail jenny.parsons@btinternet.com

Lovely Regency-proportioned rooms with stripped and varnished floors and rugs downstairs. Both the music room and the drawing room with its woodburning stove have floor-to-ceiling windows overlooking the lake at the bottom of the garden, and Jenny would love more visitors to play the grand piano. She also adores collecting pictures and there are some interesting contemporary paintings and hunting prints around. Large, comfortable and light bedrooms are decorated in classic pale creamy colours, still with the original Georgian shutters. You have breakfast in the dining area of the huge farmhouse kitchen warmed by the Aga.

rooms	2: 1 double with bath; 1 single with private bath.
price	£70. Single occ. £40.
meals	Dinner £20.
closed	Rarely.
directions	M5 junc. 26 for Wellington. Left at roundabout; left at x-roads to Hemyock. Right at top of hill. Left at x-roads. In Hemyock take Dunkeswell/Honiton Road. House 500m on right.

Jenny was in the middle of her horticultural and garden design courses at Bicton when she moved here 11 years ago, so she put her increasing knowledge to immediate good use as she licked the jungle she had bought into shape. Nowadays she rarely buys vegetables: the large south-facing walled kitchen garden has not only been brought back into full production but is also decorative. Plum trees are fanned against the wall, and at the top a bench looks down a central espaliered apple walk. On the other side of the house an artistic son's fern sculpture attracts admiring comments, and nearby Jenny has planted a colourful bog garden around a little dew pond. However, her favourite area remains her spring garden by the drive with its *Anemone blanda* and bulbs, *Exochorda macrantha* and epimediums. There's restoration work going on along the fast-moving stream where a mid-19th century race and waterfall are being rebuilt. Further upstream the drive passes through a newly cobbled ford, which already looks 200 years old. It's a bit like the Good Life at Regency House: not only the garden interests her visitors but also her little Dexter cattle, Jacob sheep and Berkshire pigs. The sausages you get for breakfast will be home-grown. *NGS.*

LOWER HUMMACOTT

Tony & Liz Williams
Lower Hummacott,
Kings Nympton, Umberleigh, Devon EX37 9TU

tel   01769 581177
fax   01769 581177

How did Tony and Liz manage to create a garden and complete
the massive renovation and decoration of their delightful home all
at once? Fireplaces were opened, decorative ceiling panels added,
new bathrooms installed and wooden columns and panelling set
into the fabric of the house. Bright, fresh colours, antique
furniture and charming decorative touches with pretty papers
greet you. There are fresh fruit and flowers in bedrooms and a
deeply inviting king-size bed in one. Dinner is superb: organic
and traditionally reared meats, local fish, organic own vegetables,
free-range eggs and home-made cakes, biscuits and jams.

rooms	2 doubles, both with bath.
price	£58. Single occ. £29.
meals	Dinner £20.
closed	Occasionally.
directions	From M5, A361 to Tiverton. There, B3137 3 miles on, B3042 to Eggsford, right for A377. 5 miles on, B3226. 1 mile on, right for Kings Nympton. Through to x-roads, straight over, house 0.5 miles on left.

Enthusiastic gardeners, Tony and Liz are making a fascinating garden in the seven acres around their new home – a Georgian farmhouse on a warm, south-facing site. It's a lovely mix of the classically formal and gently informal, a wide wildflower meadow and two acres of natural parkland wood. They have only been here since mid-1999 and the work they have put into the grounds is stupendous. Within a year they have transformed what was, until recently, no more than a field. By the house is a half-acre landscaped and charmingly designed formal garden with a spring-fed pool, a lime walk, handsome borders, a pergola for roses and wisteria, and yew hedges already taking shape. In direct line with the front door a bold, straight grassy avenue has been cut, leading you down the gentle hillside; then a side path leads you to the woodland which Tony and Liz are restoring and re-planting, encouraging wild spring flowers to reappear. There are also wildlife ponds with ducks, dragonflies, fish and dipping swallows. They are keen plant collectors, so there are new plants everywhere, along with trees, spring bulbs, herbaceous beds – they have made more than 4,000 plantings in their first 12 months alone. They love and encourage wildlife and you'll find an abundance of birds, even a tawny owl. A wonderful garden in an unspoilt setting.

COURT HALL

Charles & Sally Worthington
Court Hall,
North Molton, Devon EX36 3HP

tel   01598 740224
e-mail sworthington@onetel.net.uk

Sally's family home was largely demolished in 1954; when she
and Charles arrived 30 years later they built an extension that
combined the best of the old with the convenience of the new.
In the drawing room under the gaze of Sally's ancestors the most
striking feature at the far end is the great oak fireplace sporting
a carving of Charles I on horseback. In contrast, the dining area
in the modern kitchen is light and bright, and leads out to some
secluded seating on the hornbeam-framed lawn. Bedrooms in the
Victorian end upstairs are simply and comfortably furnished.

rooms	3: 2 doubles, 1 twin all with bath.
price	£64. Single occ. £42.
meals	Supper £15. Dinner £25.
closed	December–March.
directions	A361 for S. Molton; right to N. Molton. There, right up drive next to Old School building.

Surveying the garden as you advance up the drive you observe parkland, formal double pleached hornbeams around a lawn, and, at the front of the house, a little box-hedged gravel garden. Sedate surroundings for a handsome house, you might think, but you're in for a surprise. Those pleached hornbeams become an avenue, which, if you follow it, lead you to a secret door in a wall some way from the house. Open that door, and you're into a breathtaking tropical riot of jungly conservatory planting: a profusion of abutilon, passion flower, vines and prostanthera. Recovering the senses, you descend spiral wrought-iron steps. The swimming pool below emerges into the open air; intensively planted around with magnolias, geraniums, campanulas, cistuses and a huge fig tree, the effect is positively Mediterranean. A glimpse of colour through the avenue of pleached hornbeams draws you through into a flower garden: orange and lemon trees, camellias and sweetly scented rhododendrons fill the top of the garden, and a rose arch leads you down onto a lower lawn. The large vegetable garden is a testament to the Worthingtons' love of cooking for their guests, and fresh produce in season is always on the menu. *RHS*.

CERNE RIVER COTTAGE

Nick & Ginny Williams-Ellis
Cerne River Cottage,
8 The Folly, Cerne Abbas, Dorchester, Dorset DT2 7JR

tel   01300 341355
e-mail enquiries@cernerivercottage.co.uk
web   www.cernerivercottage.co.uk

As immaculate inside as out. Bedrooms are light, bright and
prettily but unfussily furnished; books and fresh flowers abound.
The twin has a view over the village to the famous Cerne Abbas
Giant, and the double overlooks the garden. There's a lit fire in the
sitting room if it's cool, and breakfast under the apple trees if it's
balmy - with local produce, much of it organic. Ginny - whose
paintings grace the dining room - is the daughter of the Salmons
in Cornwall who ran a residential adult education college, so
relaxed, friendly, and effortless hospitality runs in the blood.
No bookings starting Sunday.

rooms	2: 1 double with shower; 1 twin with bath.
price	£50-£54. Single occ. £30.
meals	Pubs in village.
closed	Christmas.
directions	A352 from Sherborne or Dorchester. At Cerne Abbas turn into village at x-roads signed Sydling/Village Centre. House signed on right before red phone box.

This must be one of the prettiest B&Bs in this book; no wonder Nick and Ginny find tourists wandering in from the village taking photographs of their garden. It's a picture-book setting: the River Cerne flows through the middle of the walled third of an acre, the creamy thatched 18th-century house invites you up the curved gravel path. Nick is a garden designer and Ginny paints, and the effects they've created look totally natural and uncontrived. The curved path edged with Dutch lavender is beautifully pointed with clipped box cones at each end, two white bridges over the river are framed against the dark foliage of yew, with a huge chestnut tree behind, and an ancient apple tree on the lawn shades a white table and seats. A shady bog garden beyond the stream sports a massive gunnera – and primulas, *Iris sibirica* and marsh marigolds in spring. The river is home to trout and moorhens, and you may be lucky enough to catch sight of water voles – an increasingly endangered species – feeding on the water weed. Cerne Abbas is a beautiful village in unspoiled rolling countryside, Cerne River Cottage an idyllic base from which to explore it all.

LYTCHETT HARD

David & Elizabeth Collinson
Lytchett Hard,
Beach Road, Upton, Poole, Dorset BH16 5NA

tel   01202 622297
fax   01202 632716
e-mail lytchetthard@ntlworld.com

One fascinating acre adjoins a reeded inlet of Poole harbour and their own SSSI where, if you're lucky, you'll spot a Dartford Warbler among the gorse. The garden has been created from scratch over the past 30 years and carefully designed to make the most of the views over heathland – haunt of two species of lizard – and water. Liz is a trained horticulturalist and she and David have capitalised on the mild weather here to grow tender plants; copious additions of compost and horse manure have improved the sandy soil. These tender treasures thrive gloriously and are unusually large – you're greeted by a huge phormium in the pretty entrance garden by the drive; cordyline and hibiscus do well, too. Acid-lovers are happy, so there are fine displays of camellias and rhododendrons among hosts of daffodil and tulips once the sweeps of snowdrops have finished. Three borders are colour-themed, each representing a wedding anniversary: silver, pearl and ruby. Kitchen gardeners will be knocked out by the seriously good vegetable garden. Play croquet on the large lawn, explore the private woodland where David has created winding paths, relax in the shade of the gazebo or in the warmth of the working conservatory, admire the many unusual plants or simply sit back and enjoy the colour and interest around you... and that shimmering view. *RHS*.

rooms	3: 1 four-poster with bath & shower; 1 twin with bath; 1 double with shower.
price	£42–£66. Single occ. in double £25.
meals	Dinner £12–£18.
closed	Occasionally.
directions	From Upton x-roads (0.5 miles SE of A35/A350 interchange), west into Dorchester Rd, 2nd left into Seaview Rd, cross junc. over Sandy Lane into Slough Lane, then 1st left into Beach Rd. 150 yds on, on right.

The house takes its name from the place where fishermen brought their craft ashore, in the unspoilt upper reaches of Poole harbour. The three guest bedrooms all face south and make the most of the main garden below and the views beyond. Elizabeth and David's green fingers conjure up a mass of home-grown produce as well as flowers - vegetables, jams, eggs, herbs and fruit; the food is fabulous. Guests can linger in the antique oak dining room; there are log fires and a lovely, huggable pointer called Coco.

THE DAIRY HOUSE

Paul & Penny Burns
The Dairy House,
Stowell, Nr Sherborne, Dorset D79 4PD

tel   01963 370754
fax   01963 370237
e-mail paul.burns@totalise.co.uk

Paul is the gardener. When he was 12 years old he helped to landscape his parents' garden and was smitten. Here he has created a number of garden rooms, each distinctive but connected by a series of paths and walkways through woodland and under arches. Collecting unusual things for the garden is also a hobby – the potting shed windows were the lavatory windows from Salisbury workhouse – 50p each! The terrace just outside the house has stone flags from the dairy which lead to the first path, past an old sundial and then through a pergola tunnel covered in white rambling roses. A lawned area is interspersed with many herbaceous borders, a beautiful wrought-iron and wood archway leads to the woodland garden with hundreds of new trees. As the path continues through the woods the sunlight breaks through the tree canopy to reveal the woodland floor of periwinkle and hardy geraniums and then there are just fields in every direction. A pond is guarded by yellow flag irises and wild ducks, and there is a 200-yard-long herbaceous border leading back to the house flanked by a stream which is the first tributary of the River Yeo. Soft fruit bushes for the kitchen are planted informally and many birds thrive here including greenfinches, goldfinches and wrens. A fascinating and artistic place to wander and ponder. *HPS.*

rooms	2: 1 family with private bath/shower; 1 twin with shower.
price	From £45.
meals	Dinner £12.
closed	Occasionally.
directions	From A303, south on A357, right at sign to Stowell by lodge on left. After 1 mile pass church, after 800 yds first two-storey house on left.

An 18th-century stone house with original Welsh roof slates (though Penny and Paul bought it covered in thick snow so didn't realise until the thaw) which belonged to the dairyman of a nearby farm. Penny is an artist so the house is crammed with paintings, prints, books and her wonderful tapestries. It's all huge fun – no stuffiness - with squashy sofas, gleaming wood, pretty china, a roaring open fire and coloured walls. Bedrooms are soft: lovely linen, a mish-mash of styles but always something beautiful to look at and colourful Spanish tiles in the bathroom. Food is fresh and home-made, with vegetables and salad from the garden in season.

YEW TREE HOUSE

Mrs Dickinson
Yew Tree House,
Mill Green Road, Ingatestone, Essex CM4 0HS

tel   01277 352580

Eight years ago there was nothing here at all, just the 'bones' of what was the old kitchen garden to a large estate and two of the original walls. Elizabeth, with a design course under her belt, planned the beds, the borders, the terrace and all the planting, and then sent Tony out with his shovel! Not an easy task as he kept digging up the old foundations to the greenhouses – bucket loads of bricks were carted away – but all is now perfect. A long shingle driveway to the front is bordered by a yew hedge and a lovely bed full of shrubs and trees including a maple, a rubinea and an Italian 'pencil' cypress. Clematis, roses and honeysuckle add colour, scent and height. From the back of the house a large terrace of old York stone leads down to the lawn and colour-themed beds; little paths are edged with low box hedges and cones (immaculate!), and there are some good specimen trees. Trellises – covered in roses and other travellers – provide structure and a perfect frame for the large cypress standing centre-stage, though future plans are to replace this and open up the view. A little pond with a water feature is surrounded by irises and a castor-oil plant, a blue border is filled with alliums, hydrangea and the purple climbing rose 'Violette', and an old wisteria clambers along the fence and pergola. A huge bay sits in the centre of the vegetable parterre with an obedient audience of sweet-smelling herbs peppered up with nasturtiums and sweet peas in the summer. *RHS*.

rooms	3: 2 doubles with bath; 1 single with private bath.
price	£80. Single occ. £50.
meals	Supper £15. Dinner £25.
closed	Christmas & New Year.
directions	From A12, B1002 to Ingatestone. After church left into Fryeming Lane. At T-junc. right. House 300 yds on right.

Elizabeth is a natural home maker (she used to teach home economics) who loves sewing, cooking and gardening, so you'll be well looked after in this spick-and-span 60s house. The fabrics are exquisite and the colour schemes muted; soft beiges, pale greens, light oak furniture and some lovely antiques – all gleaming and groomed. Bedrooms and bathrooms get the same treatment: a super mix of old and new and sumptuously comfortable with fresh flowers, huge baths, ladder radiators and proper modern lighting. Naturally the food is excellent. Tuck in to an early supper or go for a three-course dinner – there's a very good bed to sink into afterwards.

LITTLE BROCKHOLDS FARM

Antony & Anne Wordsworth
Little Brockholds Farm,
Radwinter, Saffron Walden, Essex CB10 2TF

tel   01799 599458
fax   01799 599458
e-mail   as@brockholds99.freeserve.co.uk
web   www.brockholds.co.uk

An Elizabethan jewel in a superb rural setting. Exposed timber ceilings, open fireplaces, nooks and crannies: this 'farmhouse' trumpets its history at every turn. The two-acre garden has old-fashioned roses and a pond that attracts many birds. The Wordsworths (yes, they are related to the poet) are engaging and solicitous people, who delight in their guests. Anne, an excellent cook, serves home-grown organic vegetables with dinner and the hens and bantams provide organic eggs for breakfast served in the Aga-warm kitchen. The perfect retreat from London and so close to Stansted airport, Cambridge and the Imperial War Museum at Duxford.

rooms	2: 1 double with bath; 1 twin with private bath.
price	£80. Single occ. £50.
meals	Dinner £25. Supper £18.
closed	Never.
directions	From Saffron Walden B1053 (George St) to Radwinter. Right at church & 1st left after 1 mile, at grass triangle on sharp right-hand bend. Signed from here.

Antony and Anne are justly proud of the fact that they care for their immaculate garden by themselves, with no outside help. The attention to detail is there at every turn, from the box-hedged formal rose garden at the front, to the less constrained charm of the enclosed garden to the rear. "Antony's in charge of the Surrey-striped lawn and razor-sharp edges," says Anne, "and I manage the long grass." There are cowslips in her grass, and, over the last two years, bee orchids have begun to appear. Their beloved old-fashioned roses give a sensational display in June and July: 'Blush Noisette' and 'Zephirine Drouhin' flank the octagonal summer house, and now a recently planted rose walk leads up towards the orchard. There's also a rose arch leading into the enclosed garden; hedged and walled it creates a shady haven for foxgloves, hellebores and violas. Away from the house a natural pond attracts wildlife, while the bog border beside it is themed yellow and blue with ligularia, loosestrife and irises. A wonderful garden, but you may be even more fascinated by the source of your breakfast eggs: Millefleur and Porcelaine Barba d'Uccles. The names are as pretty as the bantams themselves. *NGS.*

MOUNT HALL

Sue Carbutt
Mount Hall,
Great Horkesley, Nr Colchester, Essex CO6 4BZ

tel   01206 271359
fax   01206 273154
e-mail suecarbutt@yahoo.co.uk

A Queen Anne listed house ...immaculate. There are two upstairs rooms, light and airy and all with garden views, but it is the ground floor annexe with its own entrance that Sue enthuses about most. She particularly enjoys welcoming the disabled, and also families and dogs – indeed, there is even a door out to a separate secure garden for visiting dogs. Here there are twin zip-link beds, two futons for families, a huge sofa and masses of lovely books to browse through. An ideal centre for touring, or useful for that first or last stop for European travellers coming through Stansted or Harwich.

rooms	2: 1 twin with bath; 1 single with bath & shower. Annexe: 1 twin/double, 2 futons, with shower.
price	£60-£70.
meals	Good food available locally.
closed	Very occasionally.
directions	A134 through Gt. Horkesley to Rose & Crown pub, left (London Rd). 1st left marked West Bergholt; 2nd drive on left.

The drive sweeps you around and up to the handsome pillared and stuccoed front porch. Mount Hall is a listed Queen Anne house overlooking a wide lawn flanked by mature trees and shrubs. Sue has a great interest in trees and the many well-established varieties act as a dramatic backdrop to the labour-saving foliage plants which speak for themselves through their different shapes and shades of green and yellow. This is a place for retreat, very tranquil, with plenty of seats under trees, or by the pool. The walled pool garden is totally secluded and private, a haven of peace watched over by a huge eucalyptus, and again, Sue prefers calm, cool and subdued colours in her planting. A beautiful evergreen tapestry border is of year-round interest in muted greens; elsewhere greys and whites, pale blues and silver predominate, most of the plants coming from the Beth Chatto Gardens only eight miles away. The pool was an erstwhile swimming pool: the formal rectangular shape has been kept, but it is now teeming with wildlife. Nicknamed her "gosh" pool after her visitors' first reactions, the fish and frogs have bred and multiplied well since its conversion 18 months ago. So peaceful, yet you are only four miles from the edge of the Dedham Vale, and close to the oldest recorded town of Colchester. *HPS.*

NEIGHBROOK MANOR

John & Camilla Playfair
Neighbrook Manor,
Nr Aston Magna, Moreton-in-Marsh, Gloucestershire GL56 9QP

tel   01386 593232
fax   01386 593500
e-mail info@neighbrook.com
web   www.neighbrookmanor.com

Ample space for everyone to feel at ease – and you do so in luxury and style. You are on the site of an extinct medieval village, mentioned in the Domesday book; until 1610 this was the village church. The hall and ground floor are stone-flagged, with rugs for colour, and there are delightful touches of exotica everywhere. One bedroom is massive. The gardens, set in 37 acres, are simply beautiful, with a trout lake, tennis court, pool and wonderful views. John and Camilla are wickedly funny and easy-going. Our inspector didn't want to come home. *Children over seven welcome.*

rooms	3: 2 doubles both with bath; 1 single with private bathroom.
price	£85. Single £48.
meals	Supper available. Excellent pub and restaurant nearby.
closed	Rarely.
directions	4 miles north of Moreton-in-Marsh on A429, left to Aston Magna. At first building, immed. right; house 0.75 miles on right 0.5 miles down drive.

When they bought Neighbrook 18 years ago the place was so run down it took a bulldozer three days to hack its way through the jungle. An old edifice that housed German prisoners-of-war was unearthed – now hidden behind a graceful circle of clipped conifer topped off with an attractive urn (John's idea: he is a designer by profession and has won a prize at Chelsea). Unearthed medieval stones were used to create a raised herb bed in the courtyard. There are over 8,000 newly-planted trees in these 37 acres, and a trout lake, daily poached by heron. And, of course, an acreage of lawn. John devotes up to 16 hours a week to mowing it: up the long drive, round the lake, through the orchard (which contains three tall perry pear trees). Such a sweeping, generous garden, with Gloucestershire views to every side, and lots of fun too: croquet lawn at the front, herbaceous border to the side, topiary at the far end, white roses peeping behind, a swimming pool hiding behind hornbeam and beech… and, for children, a tree house, a 'death' slide and a rustic playground. The house is covered with climbing roses; its stone makes the perfect backdrop. John puts in an enormous amount of work to keep the place ticking over and Camilla picks the flowers – beautifully.

MILL DENE

Wendy Dare
Mill Dene,
Blockley, Moreton-in-Marsh, Gloucestershire GL56 9HU

tel   01386 700457
fax   01386 700526
e-mail wendy@milldene.co.uk
web   www.milldene.co.uk

Breakfast on Wye smoked salmon and scrambled Cotswold Legbar eggs, home-made marmalade and local honey in the sunny, plant-filled conservatory and you may see a heron fishing for trout in the mill pond or the electric flash of a kingfisher. The beamed bedrooms have brightly painted or papered walls - William Morris in one. Barry ran Unwin Seeds and each bedroom is named after a plant and has its own little original painting for an Unwin packet. Dressing gowns on doors, sparkling bath/shower rooms and, in the large green living room with its huge inglenook fireplace and warm wooden floors, Wendy's home-bred white Birman cats.

rooms	3: 1 twin/double with bath; 1 twin/double with shower; 1 double with private bathroom.
price	£65-£80. Single occ. £55-£70.
meals	Available locally.
closed	Occasionally.
directions	A44 at Bourton-on-the-Hill follow signs to Mill Dene Garden & Blockley. 1.3 miles down hill left, again at brown sign. Mill 50 yds on right.

Wendy knew almost nothing about gardening when she and Barry bought their tumbledown mill as a weekend retreat from London life 35 years ago. Today Mill Dene's two acres are a magical celebration of plantsmanship and design with the constant, soothing murmur of water from the mill stream. The mill's original garden was a third of its present size and Wendy began her horticultural efforts with a patio by the house. She caught the bug, was inspired by Rosemary Verey's Barnsley House and took gardening classes. She has devotedly extended and improved the garden ever since. All is informal but very carefully planned to make the most of the setting which is perfect for Wendy's frequent sculpture exhibitions. There is now a sequence of enchanting displays in the sharply sloping, terraced grounds, including a fantastical shell-decorated grotto by the stream. Admire the closely planted beds and borders, her dye plant collection, a little camomile lawn, a bog garden, a smart potager and a cricket lawn for play. Corridors of plants lead you up from the sparkling mill pond to the more open areas above with their Cotswold views. Fragrances everywhere – Wendy is devoted to scented plants and even in darkest winter some delicious scent will come wafting your way. Fragrance, enough interesting plants to satisfy the most demanding plantsman, clever design and a superb setting. *NGS, Good Gardens Guide.*

CLAPTON MANOR

Karin & James Bolton
Clapton Manor,
Clapton-on-the-Hill, Nr Bourton-on-the-Water,
Gloucestershire GL54 2LG

tel   01451 810202
fax   01451 821804
e-mail   bandb@claptonmanor.co.uk

Look over the garden wall as you breakfast on home-made
jams and enjoy long views over the valley. The 16th- and 17th-
century manor house has a flagstoned hall, huge fireplaces,
sit-in inglenooks and Cotswold stone mullioned windows. One
of the bedrooms has a secret door that leads to a stunning,
surprising fuchsia-pink bathroom. The other, though smaller,
has wonderful views of the garden. An easy-going and lovely
house with owners to match - both were featured in *The English
Garden* in May 2000.

rooms	2: 1 double with bath/shower; 1 twin/double with bath.
price	From £70. Single occ. £45.
meals	Available locally.
closed	Christmas.
directions	From Cirencester, A429 for Stow. Right at Apple Pie House Hotel & on to Clapton. There, down hill & left at green-doored 3-storey house. Manor on left of church.

When James abandoned his hectic life in the City and moved with Karin to the Cotswolds, he longed to become a garden designer. Today he's a respected historian and successful garden designer, and it shows. They have created a delightfully informal – with a formal touch or two – gently sloping, L-shaped, one-acre garden wrapped around their 16th-century manor. The garden is a series of compartments defined by old Cotswold stone walls and hedges of yew, hornbeam, box and cotoneaster, while overhanging trees give welcoming shade on hot summer days. Many good plants have been introduced in an overall design planned for all-year interest, with sparkling displays of rare snowdrops and narcissi and a wide variety of hellebores and species peonies. Summer sees masses of old roses such as the late-flowering 'Primrose Warburg' and, in late summer and early autumn, the double borders with their perennials come into their own. Rose arches over a new path are packed with colour and scent, rosa 'Cedric Morris' scrambles through a walnut tree, the climber 'Mrs Honey Dison' covers the children's Wendy house and clematis flowers among apple tree branches. A lovingly designed garden where the Boltons' four children, three dogs and many chickens romp, grown-ups can relax and garden-lovers enjoy a fine collection of plants in a beautiful setting.

HAMPTON FIELDS

Richard & Jill Barry
Hampton Fields,
Meysey Hampton, Cirencesterf, Gloucestershire GL7 5JL

tel   01285 850070
fax   01285 850993
e-mail richard@hampflds.fsnet.co.uk

Richard and Jill Barry are making a garden as exciting and as individual as their incredibly ambitious conversion of a derelict barn into a beautiful home. Friends thought they were mad when they left their village house with its gorgeous garden for the empty three acres and abandoned stonework of Hampton Fields... now they've changed their minds. This is dynamic, naturally evolving large-scale country gardening of a very high order. Not a single sheet of graph paper was used; instead the design flowed in a naturally evolving process. Jill loves old roses, herbaceous perennials, interesting shrubs with good leaf features and attractive trees. She and Richard have introduced thousands in a series of fascinating areas which culminate in fan-shaped avenues of the decorative pear *Pyrus calleryana* 'Chanticleer'. You arrive to a riot of self-seeding hollyhocks and other sun-lovers thrusting through gravel and will find it easy to relax in the well-planted sunken garden with its charming fountain and hexagonal pond. Beyond lie lawns, attractive herbaceous borders and an orchard underplanted with climbing roses. There are roses, too, on trellises, walls and arches, mingling with intoxicatingly scented honeysuckle. The garden's water level rises and falls alarmingly and the natural pond in the main garden can become a sheet of flood water; Richard and Jill have met this challenge and many more by trial and error and with great imagination.

rooms	3: 1 double with bath; 1 twin, 1 double sharing bath & shower.
price	£64–£70. Single occ. by arrangement.
meals	Excellent pubs nearby.
closed	Christmas, New Year & Easter.
directions	From Cirencester A417 for Lechlade. At Meysey Hampton x-roads left to Sun Hill. After 1 mile left at cottage. House 400 yds down drive.

In a delightfully unspoilt area of the Cotswolds, this attractive, long stone house sits in splendid, peaceful isolation. Lovely high windows in the central part give onto the views and from the soft green-painted conservatory you can admire the garden that the Barrys have so lovingly created. Inside, the décor is fresh - so are the flowers - the furniture and books old, the charming owners happy and proud to have you in their home. Beds are incredibly comfortable with excellent sheets and pillows.

WINSTONE GLEBE

Shaun & Susanna Parsons
Winstone Glebe,
Winstone, Cirencester, Gloucestershire GL7 7LN

tel   01285 821451
fax   01285 821451
e-mail   sparsons@winstoneglebe.com
web   www.winstoneglebe.com

Susanna, who has been looking after guests for 10 years, will create traditional favourites like kedgeree as an alternative to the conventional English breakfast. You eat well in fine surroundings - the striking green dining room's long table is surrounded by an eclectic mix of art and furniture. A blazing open fire will lure you into the drawing room of this Georgian former rectory. There's garlanded wallpaper and a desk in the main double and a delightful wardrobe hand-painted by designer Sarah Baxter in the twin. Across the courtyard is a surprise - a large, cheerful, very modern three-bedded room.

rooms	3: 1 double with bath; 1 twin, 1 double, both with private bathroom.
price	£60-£72. Single £40-£46.
meals	Packed lunch & lunch available. Dinner £22.
closed	Occasionally.
directions	Winstone 6 miles NW of Cirencester off A417. In village follow signs to church. House just short of church on left on sharp bend by Public Footpath sign.

A Cotswold garden with aristocratic bones. It was laid out by Dame Sylvia Crowe, author of *Garden Design* (1958) — a mover and shaker of her time and a founder member of The Institute of Landscape Architects — in a rather formal manner with stone walls and a barrier yew hedge. Shaun and Susanna — the gardening fan — moved here in the mid-1970s inheriting only Michaelmas daisies and a red hot poker. Now all is transformed. The bones are softened with luscious herbaceous borders and wilder areas where spring flowers give vivid colour. A recent addition is a little arboretum of unusual trees in a paddock opposite the house. In an impetuous and utterly vindicated moment of inspiration, she recklessly shoved one shaky drystone wall into the field below to create a ha-ha and opened up the view to the Saxon church. Horses in the field now lean across the ha-ha to nibble spring flowers, but Susanna is good-humoured about it. Daughter Harriet, who discovered a love of gardening while working for Rosemary Verey at Barnsley House, now studies at Kew. She pops back bearing unusual treasures to add horticultural interest and help her mother achieve an easy, colourful mood which suits the time-worn architecture of their home. Relish the intimate view to the church and, on clear days, the glorious panorama of the Marlborough Downs.

MILLEND HOUSE

John & April Tremlett
Millend House,
Nr Newland, Coleford, Gloucestershire GL16 8NF

tel   01594 832128
fax   01594 832128
e-mail apriljohnt@aol.com

Deep in the Forest of Dean, just three miles from Lower Wye Valley and in an AONB. Lots of curiosities here in the Tremletts' 1750 stone house and all sorts of amusing ups and downs and in and outs because it's built on a hill; the architectural solutions to this challenge are all part of its charm. The rooms are bright and cheerful and the original semicircular cupboard in one of the doubles is a gem. A friendly, family home with hosts whose love of plants and gardens is infectious. Excellent walking, cycle tracks and good golf courses nearby.

rooms	3: 2 twin/doubles both with bath; 1 double sharing bathroom.
price	From £50. Single occ. £32.50.
meals	Dinner £20–£25.
closed	Occasionally.
directions	On A466 in Redbrook, to Newland & Clearwell. 0.5 miles past Newland, bear left for Coleford. 300 yds on, 2nd house on right. Park in orchard on left, not in front of house.

Nature's Garden – that's what they call the Forest of Dean – and you have to agree with the sentiment. Here you have a plant-lover's garden overlooking the valley to Newland. Whichever way you approach the house, you enjoy a glorious drive. April was a flower demonstrator for the NAFAS (National Association of Flower Arranging Societies) for 25 years so, as you'd expect, she's chosen interesting foliage and plants with strong form and texture. The two-acre garden she and John have made over the past 35 years is packed with gems. One acre is woodland with mostly deciduous forest trees, one gloriously smothered with the rampant rose 'Treasure Trove'. Explore the winding woodland walk which in turn entices you up to the head of the hill and then down past delightful, informal arrangements. A wide variety of shrubs and perennials in a series of profuse descending displays and some intimate touches too, like the tiny Italian garden with its formal stepped area, the little Japanese garden at the start of the woodland walk and small-scree bed garden. The kitchen garden is just as attractive. This garden is occasionally open for charity. *NGS.*

DRAKESTONE HOUSE

Hugh & Crystal St John Mildmay
Drakestone House,
Stinchcombe, Dursley, Gloucestershire GL11 6AS

tel   01453 542140
fax   01453 542140

The hauntingly atmospheric Edwardian landscaped grounds would make a perfect setting for open-air Shakespeare – rather apposite since it's said that young Shakespeare roamed the hills around Stinchcombe. Hugh's grandparents laid out the grounds, influenced by a love of Italian gardens and admiration for Gertrude Jekyll. When Hugh and Crystal moved here, the garden was distressed and needed attention, particularly the magnificent topiary. The beautifully varied, lofty, sculptural yew and box hedges, domes and busbies dominating the view from the house are restored to perfection, creating a series of garden rooms with a backdrop of woodland. Paths and a romantic Irish yew walk invite you to wander as you move from one compartment to the next. By the house, a pergola is covered with wisteria in spring and rambling roses in summer, near displays of lovely old roses underplanted with lavender. Crystal describes these two acres as informally formal or formally informal – she can't quite decide which. But it's that elegant Edwardian design with its Mediterranean mood which makes Drakestone House so special. The best moments to enjoy the grounds are on sunny days when the shadows play strange tricks with the sculptured hedges and trees... expect Puck or Arial to make a dramatic entrance at any moment!

rooms	3: 2 twins, 1 double; 1 with private bath/shower, 2 with shared bathroom.
price	£68. Single occ. £44.
meals	Dinner £17.50. BYO wine.
closed	December-January.
directions	From Stinchcombe B4060 to Wotton-under-Edge. Up long hill, house at top on left, gateway marked.

A treat: utterly delightful people with wide-ranging interests (ex-British Council and college lecturing; arts, travel, gardening) in a manor-type house full of beautiful antiques and furniture. The house was born of the Arts and Crafts movement - the architect was Oswald P Milne and the two thatched cottages in the grounds were designed by Ernest Gimson - and remain fascinating: wood panels painted green, a log-fired drawing room for guests, quarry tiles on window sills, handsome old furniture, comfortable proportions... elegant but human, refined but easy.

BOYTS FARM

John & Sally Eyre
Boyts Farm,
Tytherington, Wotton-under-Edge, Gloucestershire GL12 8UG

tel   01454 412220
fax   01454 412220
e-mail jre@boyts.fsnet.co.uk

Sally's sunny two-acre garden suits this tall, rugged, handsome 16th-century stone farmhouse. Nothing whacky, no new-wave effects, instead a pleasant series of well-tended formal and informal areas setting off both house and its position against a wooded hillside. Originally laid out in the 1930s, the garden's present form was created in the 1950s/60s by a previous owner. The centrepiece is a long Italianate garden which follows a long lawn edged with lush herbaceous borders to a cool, hedge-enclosed canal. Across is a strait-laced rose garden of the old school built around a square pool. A young arboretum is springing up near water features including a deliciously water-lily-choked pool and then the ha-ha draws the eye across fields to the southern tip of the Cotswolds. The enclosed orchard is an oasis of dappled light that gleams with spring flowers, hot areas around the house are generously planted and Sally's potager-like vegetable garden is a charming blend of the functional and the decorative. She grows colourful, as well as standard, veggies and herbs and a clever touch is added by a pair of diamond-shaped lavender beds. Boyts is not a plantsman's garden — although there are many good plants; instead, it is a warm, welcoming, generous traditional English country house garden which treats its architecture and surroundings with respect. *NCCPG, the Gloucestershire Gardens and Landscape Trust.*

rooms	2: 1 double, 1 twin, both with bath.
price	£70. Single occ. £40.
meals	Pub within walking distance.
closed	21 December-2 January.
directions	At M5 junc. 16, A38 for Gloucester. After 6 miles, Tytherington turn. From north, leave M5 exit 14 & south on A38 for Bristol. Tytherington turn after 3 miles.

Views of the garden everywhere, whether from wide staircase or rooms. The guest sitting room is scented with wood fires and the dining room has a fireplace, oil paintings and large mahogany table. The windows are mullioned and there's a strong sense of country life, from the sound of horses outside to horsey prints indoors. One delightful eccentricity is the perfectly preserved 30s bathroom with fishy wallpaper. Flagged floors, panelled walls and a spotless interior complete a ravishing picture. Lovers of both horses and gardens will be utterly at home.

MARSH BARN

Tony & Lindy Ball
Marsh Barn,
Rockbourne, Fordingbridge, Hampshire SP6 3NF

tel   01725 518768
fax   01725 518380

Seagrass matting, Moroccan rugs, antiques and a woodburning stove all contribute to the easy atmosphere in this terrifically light and sunny 200-year-old barn. Lindy, who speaks French and lets out her French holiday home in the Lot, organises garden tours for foreigners. You can relax on the terrace overlooking her pretty well-tended English garden with cornfields beyond, admire the waterfowl on the pond or saunter to the pub past the thatched cottages of this chocolate-box village. Golf, riding, fishing and antique shops nearby. *Children over 10 welcome.*

rooms	3: 1 double with shower; 1 twin with private bathroom; 1 studio double with shower (separate entrance across courtyard).
price	£50-£70. Single occ. from £35.
meals	Excellent pub in village.
closed	Christmas & New Year.
directions	From Salisbury, A354 for Blandford, through Coombe Bissett. After 1.5 miles, left to Rockbourne. Through village, 200 yds after 30mph zone, house signed on left. After 50 yds, gravel drive on right.

When Tony and Lindy arrived here eight years ago there wasn't much to shout about – a lawn, a terrace and a clump of tall conifers. Not that this would faze Lindy, who has gardened passionately for 40 years and has made or restored seven gardens from similar beginnings. Where to start? There were few trees anywhere near the house and they wanted height so their first job was to erect nine tall brick pillars with a timber cross-piece now beautifully covered in wisteria, solanum, honeysuckle and roses – the perfect framework for the gravel courtyard behind. The addition of curving, mixed borders planted with shrub roses, perennials and small flowering trees has given the garden shape and form for every season. More trees have been planted in the far corner where laburnum arches tempt you to wlk along the box-punctuated path through the conifers to see the sheep grazing near the small, landscaped lake. Other features such as a pole-and-rope pergola, Lutyens-shaped brick steps and another arch, this time with ivy, mean that there is plenty of structure to be shown to advantage in the winter. The lawn must also be mentioned – it is perfect, smooth and beautifully shown off by the gently curved borders which undulate in and out of it. Lindy's bookshelves are groaning with gardening books and she knows her patch of Hampshire well – a perfect base for garden lovers.

MIZZARDS FARM

Harriet & Julian Francis
Mizzards Farm,
Rogate, Petersfield, Hampshire GU31 5HS

tel   01730 821656

Wow! The central hall is three storeys high, its vaulted roof open to the rafters - a splendid spot for bacon and eggs. This is the oldest (and medieval) part of this lovely, rambling, mostly 16th-century farmhouse; this room also comes with a huge fireplace and a stone-flagged floor, softened by a large Persian rug. A four-poster in the master bedroom has switches in the bedhead to operate curtains and bathroom light... the sumptuousness continues with a multi-mirrored, marble bathroom, an upstairs conservatory for tea, a drawing room for concerts, croquet in the grounds and a covered, heated pool. Fabulous.

rooms	3: 1 double with bath/shower; 1 double with bath; 1 twin with bath & shower.
price	£62–£72. Single occ.£45–£50.
meals	Available locally.
closed	Christmas & New Year.
directions	From A272 at Rogate for Harting & Nyewood. Cross humpback bridge; drive signed to right after 300 yds.

The Francis family have derived huge pleasure from this garden – set in a deeply rural part of Hampshire – for more than a quarter century. A series of sweeping terraced lawns flow down to a peaceful lake and woodland stream. Not only is there a heated and covered swimming pool (that you, too, may use) but there's a chess set beside it, its squares painted on a concrete base, its wooden pieces two feet high. Stroll across the terrace on the other side of the house, peer round the box parterre, and you find a croquet lawn. And if you'd like a quiet spot from which to watch others play – or you wish to read – just make for the gazebo at the end of the lawn. When deciding to create a garden from a field, Harriet deliberately chose not to divide the area into rooms, but, wisely, to keep the natural vista to lake and stream. Over the years she has developed a series of colour co-ordinated borders, terraces and island beds. Today the garden plays host to a series of charity concerts; members of the audience bring their own picnics and everyone is served with strawberries and cream. A mini-Glyndebourne in a fine garden in Hampshire.

BROXWOOD COURT

Mike & Anne Allen
Broxwood Court,
Broxwood, Leominster, Herefordshire HR6 9TJ

tel   01544 340245
fax   01544 340573
e-mail mikeanne@broxwood.kc3.co.uk

Your expectations, as you arrive through the original arched clock tower into the courtyard, are high. Although the house is a modern surprise, it is filled with antiques and fittings from an earlier mansion, including original library bookcases and polished parquet floors. The bedrooms are charming, with colourful curtains, good furniture and, in the larger of the twins, a huge and ornately-edged padded bedhead and views across to the Black Mountains. Anne, a *Cordon Bleu* cook, uses local produce and fruit and vegetables from the organic garden. They are amusing, relaxed hosts.

rooms	3: 1 double, 2 twins, all with bath/shower.
price	£66–£80. Single occ. £40–£60.
meals	Dinner £25.
closed	Usually in February.
directions	From Leominster for Brecon. After 8 miles, just past Weobley turn, right to Broxwood & Pembridge. After 2 miles straight over x-roads for Lyonshall. After 500 yds, left over cattle grid.

A dichotomy: 30 majestic acres of lawns, soaring yew hedges, a 19th-century arboretum, a great avenue of Wellingtonia, cedar and other giants, and ornamental lakes all set around a mid-1950s home. Anne reveals that the family's Victorian mansion was here until her father, defeated by spiralling costs, had the original Court demolished and re-built his family home in the recycled stone. The grounds were originally designed by William Nesfield in 1858 but have needed total restoration. Mike left ICI so that he and Anne could return to Broxwood to help bring back the grounds to their former glory. They assembled a squadron of the latest motorised equipment to make their grand dreams a reality. Overgrown stands of laurel were ripped out, lawns restored, paths re-opened, huge rhododendrons disciplined and lakes cleared. The recent final touch was decorating the formal rose garden, sheltered by dizzily tall yew hedges, with two drystone slate urns by master craftsman Joe Smith. Anne's Roman Catholic ancestry explains the follies and the names of the avenues – St John's with its St Michael's Walk – and the little Our Lady's Chapel, St Joseph's Hut and Abbot's Pool. Only the occasional screech of white and common peacocks breaks the peace of one of the most unexpected parkland gardens of all.

THE OLD VICARAGE

Guy & Amanda Griffiths
The Old Vicarage,
Leysters, Leominster, Herefordshire HR6 0HS

tel   01568 750208
fax   01568 750208
e-mail guy.griffiths@virgin.net

This is one of the three remaining 'tranquil' areas of England (says
the CPRE), 18 acres of which are the grounds and garden of this
17th-century farmhouse. Victorian additions brought generous,
high-ceilinged spaces. Antiques, old paintings and large, high beds
with crisp white linen add to the comfort. Guy not only grows the
fruit and veg but also bakes the bread. Amanda loves cooking and
sharing meals with guests around the dining table. Wonderful,
and in a very lovely, surprisingly undiscovered, corner of England.
Children over 12 welcome.

rooms	2: 1 twin with bath; 1 double with bath/shower.
price	£70. Single occ. £45.
meals	Packed lunch. Dinner £25, inc. wine and pre-dinner drink.
closed	Occasionally.
directions	1 mile south of A4112 between Tenbury Wells & Leominster. On entering Leysters from Tenbury Wells, left at x-roads. Ignore sign to church. House on left, through wooden gate (after postbox in wall).

Guests have been known to join in the weeding, so infectious is the enthusiasm of Amanda and Guy for their garden with its handsome lawns and mature trees. The couple couldn't garden in Guy's service days but he took early retirement from the RAF and, once work on the house was complete, they relished turning next to the garden. Their best legacy was the collection of fine mixed deciduous and evergreen trees; Victorian maps describe the grounds as a Plantation, and Victorian diarist Francis Kilvert records playing croquet here in 1871. Over the years the Plantation had become overgrown; areas were choked by brambles or hidden under laurels, so a cut-and-burn programme began. Today Amanda and Guy are brimming with plans big and small and putting them into practice. Borders are being extended, raised beds re-planted, new shrubs introduced and saplings added to the orchard with its collection of traditional varieties of English apples and other fruit. Guy is determined to be self-sufficient in fruit and vegetables and is developing his two kitchen gardens, one by the all-weather tennis court. Above all, they are striving successfully to make these grounds blend naturally and elegantly with the surrounding pastureland.

Rose & Leslie Wiles
Lower Bache House,
Kimbolton, Nr Leominster, Herefordshire HR6 0ER

tel   01568 750304
fax   01568 750304
e-mail leslie.wiles@care4free.net

A large painted sign of a Black-Veined White on the main road beckons you down high-hedged, narrow lanes to the utter peace and seclusion of Rose and Leslie's home and garden. Leslie is a butterfly-lover — he has his own butterfly house and hopes to help re-introduce the lost Black-Veined White — and their favourite plants, like red valerian, are encouraged in this charming, informal cottage garden. The whole place is undergoing major changes; a formal pond, a herringbone-bricked herb garden and steps to the private nature reserve and wooded valley below are just the start. A garden room with reclaimed oak-framed windows is to be added to the valley side. The little orchard is being extended with new trees and the series of beds are a mass of cottage garden favourites, such as red, pink and white foxgloves. Tall busbies of box stand guard in the pretty lawned side garden, overlooked by screens of taller conifers to bring intimacy. Through an archway, a new woodland glade has been planted: a feast of snowdrops, bluebells, foxgloves and other shade-loving wild flowers. Part the side branches of a large, sweet-smelling philadelphus and you open a natural door to the sunny front garden where a pond glints with swooping dragonflies. The Wiles encourage birds and wildlife: an owl box has been built on a gable, swallows swoop in and out of the eaves, doves, swifts and chattering starlings nest in the roof every year. A delightful, natural garden and a place of real tranquillity.

rooms	4 suites (2 doubles, 2 twins), each with sitting room & bath/shower room.
price	£67. Single occ. £43.50.
meals	Dinner £16.50–£24.50.
closed	Rarely.
directions	From Leominster, A49 north but turning right onto A4122, for Leysters. Lower Bache, then signed. Look for white butterfly.

An utterly fascinating place. The 17th-century farmhouse, cider house, dairy, granary and 14-acre nature reserve are perched at the top of the small valley; the views are tremendous. In the huge dining room is the old cider mill, and dinner may feature home-smoked fish or meat and home-made bread. Much of what they serve is organic – all the wines are. One room is across the courtyard, the other three in the granary annexe; they are all timber-framed, compact and well thought out and have their own sitting rooms. *Children over eight welcome.*

THE MALT HOUSE

Louise Robbins
The Malt House,
Almeley Wootton, Herefordshire HR3 6PY

tel   01544 340681

If the thing you like least about being in a B&B is creeping around on eggshells knowing you are in somebody else's home then rejoice! For here is your very own gorgeous house with private door from the garden, a beautiful drawing room (yes, it's even beamed) with a log-burning stove and comfortable, squashy chairs in the palest of colours, and a dining room with whitewashed walls and an old Welsh settle. Flagstoned steps lead up to the bedroom and bathroom - just as exquisite and filled with goodies and fresh flowers. The only time you'll remember it isn't yours is when you're served a delicious organic breakfast or dinner. Perfect.

rooms	1 double with bath, drawing room & dining room.
price	£80. Single occ. £50.
meals	Dinner £20.
closed	Occasionally.
directions	From A480 to Kington, left to Almeley, follow lane 2 miles, past cricket green in village. Right at T-junc, half a mile, pink house opposite Quaker Meeting House.

Louise is a designer and her strong sense of colour, texture and shape is as dazzling in the garden as it is in the house. She has been here for two years, specifically seeking a garden which already had "its integrity intact". She has added and extended large beds to the lawn at the back of the house, clearing trees and changing the structure. The beds are edged with low box hedging, immaculately groomed, yet containing a mass and profusion of cottage planting. Louise is passionate about seeking out rare plants, especially herbaceous perennials. Almost the entire digitalis family is invited and lots of old roses – including the striped 'Ferdinand Pichard', 'William Lobb' and sweet-scented 'Fantin-Latour' – also grace the party. Varieties of euphorbia, salvia, rubus and ligularia rub shoulders with evening primrose and the single-petalled kerria. Roses also climb and scramble over the many arches dotted about to give height, along with fruit trees. In a secluded corner stands a 200-year-old yew with bench seat; also a formal display of large box balls and *Viburnum tinus* standards. At the front of the rose-covered house is a pea gravel area, rows of large Mediterranean-style terracotta pots and the orchard: just under an acre of old apple, plum, pear and damson – the perfect roaming ground for the two donkeys. A well balanced garden – formal structure, informal planting. In case you haven't yet guessed what Louise's favourite flowers are – try roses! *RHS, HPS*.

BOLLINGHAM HOUSE

Stephanie & John Grant
Bollingham House,
Eardisley, Herefordshire HR5 3LE

tel   01544 327326
fax   01544 327880
e-mail bollhouse@bigfoot.com

A Georgian jewel in a delightful, lofty – 600 feet above sea level – setting. When they arrived, John and Stephanie carefully studied the garden around the house, absorbed its possibilities, assessed where it needed rejuvenation and set to work with huge gusto. The result is a well-considered four-acre country garden. Their master plan was to create gardens within a garden, always with labour-saving ideas in mind. The gardens at the front of the house are a formal introduction to the stunning views, and terraced front lawns sweep down to meet the sight of the Wye Valley and the Black Mountains. Beyond is a wildflower meadow divided into two terraces, one of which is guarded by a magnificent, ancient sweet-chestnut tree. The old walled garden is approached through a specially commissioned Millennium iron gate which leads to a perfumed avenue of old roses and a sequence of formal parterres. There's a Moghul-influenced area edged by a rectangular rill that contrasts with the silent pool. The rill and other water features use modern pump technology to create yesterday's classic effects. A well-stocked fish pond leads to a long bog garden planted with willow and water-loving plants including a gigantic gunnera, and to the shady shrubbery restored and thinned to give rhododendrons and azaleas room to sparkle. The final flourish behind the house and its 14th-century barn – decorated as a splendid party hall – is a motte-and-bailey topped with an ancient water tower and dovecote.

rooms	2:1 double, 1 twin, both with private bathroom.
price	From £60. Single occ. from £30.
meals	Packed lunch £3.50. Dinner £20.
closed	Christmas.
directions	From A438 Hereford/Brecon road towards Kington on A4111 through Eardisley. House 2 miles up hill on left, behind long line of conifers.

From the sofa in your sybaritically comfortable bedroom you can gaze out on the Malvern Hills and the Black Mountains. In spite of the grandeur of this Georgian house it feels like a real home with large rooms graciously furnished. Fascinating features and furniture everywhere: a timbered frame wall from the original 14th-century house, wide elm floorboards upstairs and a dining room table reputed to be an Irish 'coffin table' which John found in Dublin. Your hosts are delightful and Stephanie's Aga cooking is excellent.

WINFORTON COURT

Jackie Kingdon
Winforton Court,
Winforton, Herefordshire HR3 6EA

tel   01544 328498
fax   01544 328498

The staircase, mentioned in Pevsner's, is 17th century. Most of the house was built in 1500 and is breathtaking in its ancient dignity, its undulating floors, two-foot-thick walls and great oak beams. Take a book from the small library and settle into a window seat overlooking the gardens. There is a guest sitting room too, festooned with works of art by local artists. Candles feature all over the house. The two four-postered bedrooms verge on the luxurious; so does the double. Gorgeous.

rooms	3: 1 double, 1 four-poster, both with bath; 1 four-poster suite with bath.
price	£56–£76. Single occ. £43–£53.
meals	Available locally.
closed	Christmas.
directions	From Hereford, A438 into village. House on left with large green sign & iron gates.

A delightful little walled garden greets you at this beautiful, half-timbered, early 16th-century house. The path is edged with profuse purple and green sage studded with perennial geraniums, walls carry climbing roses and borders bloom. When Jackie arrived, all the grounds were down to grass with some mature trees and with fine views across the Wye Valley to the Black Mountains – there's a lovely walk to the river from the house. She took heaps of cuttings and potted up plants from her previous home, created borders, planted vigorously and transformed her big new garden. The sunny courtyard behind the house has a fruit-covered fig tree and mature magnolia, with spiky cordylines in containers, cherubs on walls and a fountain brought from Portugal. Beyond lies her open, terraced garden dominated by a huge weeping willow, with an ancient standing stone on a ley line shaded by a tall horse chestnut, emerald-green lawns, flower-packed beds and, below, a stream being developed into a small water garden. She has even planted the edge of the parking area with colourful sun-lovers thrusting through the gravel. Jackie aimed to make an interesting, informal, open sunny garden to complement Winforton Court's dreamy architecture, and that's what she has achieved. Guests love it here – regulars come bearing gifts to add to her collection, and are sometimes generously given cuttings so a little bit of Winforton Court will grow in their garden and give them pleasure for years to come.

DARKLEY HOUSE

Jill & Malcolm Ainslie
Darkley House,
Norton Canon, Herefordshire HR4 7BT

tel   01544 318121
fax   01544 318121
e-mail darkley@freeuk.com

All is bright and fresh in the guest rooms in the house and converted barns and stables (the latter divided into B&B and self-catering). The house and outbuildings date back to the 16th and 17th centuries and the ground-floor Garden Room in the house has its own sitting room and garden. The dining room has beamed walls, scroll-carved panels from an old oak cupboard and a large old bread oven. The light-filled conservatory is the perfect vantage point from which to drink in the views of garden and countryside.

rooms	6: 2 doubles, both with private bathroom; 1 twin with shower; 1 twin with bath; 2 doubles, in converted stables, sharing bathroom. Self-catering cottage available.
price	From £50. Single occ. £30.
meals	Available locally
closed	November-mid-March.
directions	From Hereford A480. At Norton Canon take lane to Norton Wood & Hurstley. Follow through disused r'way arch, sharp bend, past cottages on right. Single track driveway on left.

Malcolm and Jill began this garden in 1990 and within five years it was featured on BBC TV. Little wonder. The planting is outstanding and the design a clever blend of formal, informal and wild. All this and romantic views to the Black Mountains. Wander through the wild meadow where campion sparkles among tall meadowsweet and waving grass, dream in the shady orchard where tea is served under a canopy of trees smothered in rambling roses or watch dragonflies hover over the wild pond. Many schoolchildren have enjoyed visits discovering the perfect natural environment. The more formal features should be admired, too – a large brick-columned pergola weighed down by roses, the rose arch, the lawns edged by beautifully planted, irregular borders. Jill adores clematis and has a collection of more than 150 varieties and has constructed a walk through them all. Maturing hornbeam, yew and beech hedges create a series of areas as you move from one part of the garden to the next – the delight of discovery carries you through. Every hedge, pond, border, maturing specimen tree and inch of the lawn has been nurtured by the Ainslies and the sheer variety is breathtaking. There are more than 4,000 trees – again planted by the Ainslies – in these magnificent seven acres. The effect of all that hard work is clear. *NGS, Good Gardens Guide, RHS, Clematis Society.*

HALL END HOUSE

Angela & Hugh Jefferson
Hall End House,
Kynaston, Ledbury, Herefordshire HR8 2PD

tel   01531 670225
fax   01531 670747
e-mail khjefferson@hallend91.freeserve.co.uk

All the grandeur you could ask for from the moment you enter. The airy hall has a handsome staircase leading to wide landings and the bedrooms upstairs. They are large and elegant, with rich curtains, comfortable beds and immaculate new bath/shower rooms. The dining and drawing rooms echo the mood of classic English elegance. A friendly welcome from a couple who have devoted an enormous amount of care and energy to the restoration of both house and garden. There are, too, the farm's own lamb, pork and free-range eggs to enjoy. *Children over 12 welcome.*

rooms	2: 1 double with shower; 1 twin with bath/shower.
price	£75-£80. Single occ. £50.
meals	Dinner £25. BYO wine. Good food also avaible locally.
closed	Christmas & New Year.
directions	From Ledbury, A449 west. Right for Leominster on A4172. 1 mile on, left for Aylton. 1.25 miles to junc. Left, towards Nat'l Fuschia Collection. Past to junc. with Hallend Farm, keep left, drive 1st right.

A particularly special treat for garden lovers is to visit a garden in the making, particularly one with plans as ambitious as those Angela is developing with the help of talented young designer Josie Anderson from Cheltenham. What was, until not so very long ago, a run-down farmyard is being transformed into a large, elegant, feature-packed, open sunny garden. It perfectly complements the grand listed Georgian farmhouse which Angela and Hugh have restored, brilliantly, over the past two years. A neglected pond in front of the house has been cleared and planted with water-loving beauties and a second has been created nearby so that as you approach up the drive you see the house in reflection. So much to enjoy once you arrive: a designer kitchen garden, a herb garden, a pretty box parterre, a formal rose garden with the finest roses, a croquet lawn to add green and space. Angela loves flowers and her beds and borders are starting to brim with the most beautiful plants. There's a summer house in which you can unwind and a large conservatory where you can linger and gaze at the splendours outside. On a sunny day, enjoy a swim in the striking L-shaped heated swimming pool lined in the deepest blue. The setting, in 411 acres of farmland, is a delight. Views everywhere – of woodland, open countryside and parkland – in one of the loveliest corners of Herefordshire.

HOMESTEAD FARM

Joanna & Iain MacLeod
Homestead Farm,
Canon Frome, Ledbury, Herefordshire HR8 2TG

tel   01531 670268
fax   01531 670210
e-mail imacleod@btopenworld.com

Prepare to be thrilled. A Roderick James oak-framed modern
building blistered onto a 16th-century keeper's cottage: huge
ceilings, light, airy and with soft views over cider orchards and
hop fields. Inside is stylish – featured in *Beautiful Homes* – with
creative use of colour, attractive pictures and books, open
fireplace and a gob-smackingly gorgeous drawing room. Bedrooms
are unfussy: pale yellow cord carpet, aqua-blue tongue and
groove panelling round a bath, vertical beams, dazzling light and
a designer feel. A 'New England' deck outside and balcony above
cunningly melt a 500 year age difference into nothing at all.

rooms	2: 1 double, 1 twin both with bath.
price	£60. Single occ. £40.
meals	Dinner £20.
closed	Christmas, New Year & occasionally.
directions	A438 west from Ledbury, north on A417 for 2 miles. At UK garage right to Canon Frome. After 0.75 miles right in front of red brick gates; house at end of track.

An enchanting mix of terrace, sunken garden, vegetable garden, a field with a folly, a lake, mown paths, matrix-planted trees as windbreaks and the fabulous long distance views. All totally created by Iain and Joanna, who arrived clutching some pots from their old home and began with the terrace, flagstoned with a rectangular pond and a bubbly fountain. Along paths and across the garden are mounded metal arches planted with roses and clematis, a rope swag (once the Mallaig ferry's rope) is blue-smothered in 'Prince Charles' clematis and bushes of white *spinosissima* roses. This is a copy of Rosemary Verey's potager at Barnsley (without the box edging); here, too, a great honeysuckle hedge, a greenhouse with a fanned nectarine and an abundant vine, a fruit cage with 'Autumn Bliss' raspberries and wild strawberries grown from seed. The field is mown with paths, cut for hay in the autumn, and contains a thousand trees planted for the millennium. Some trees are planted as a shelter belt, some in avenues and Iain's "folly" is a circle of pleached rowans with a stockade of 20 young oaks – donated by the architect to replace those cut down for the house. Views are created everywhere; across the length of the field towards the lake there's another avenue of *Malus coronaria* 'Charlottae' alternating with bird cherries. Two thousand snowdrops have been planted and there are plans for a carpet of bluebells – never mind June, spring will be busting out all over. *RHS*.

NORTH COURT

John & Christine Harrison
North Court,
Shorwell, Isle of Wight PO30 3JG

tel   01983 740415
fax   01983 740409
e-mail   sawdays@northcourt.info
web   www.northcourt.info

North Court's astonishing 15 acres have developed over the last four centuries into a garden of significant historical interest, and a paradise for plantsmen. The Isle of Wight remains warm well into the autumn, and in its downland-sheltered position the garden exploits its micro-climate to the full. Able to specialise in such exotics as bananas and echiums, the Harrisons have developed a sub-tropical garden, while higher up the slope behind the house there are Mediterranean terraces. There's such extensive variety here: the chalk stream surrounded with bog plants, the knot garden planted with herbs, the walled rose garden, the sunken garden, the one-acre kitchen garden – and a Himalayan glade and a maritime area. All this represents a collection of 10,000 plants, some occasionally for sale – how do they do it? Modest John, the plantsman, says it is the good soil and atmosphere that allows everything to grow naturally and in profusion: "I just allow the plants to express themselves." But that is only half the story – he has left out the back-breakingly hard work and committment that have gone into it. They are both extremely knowledgeable too – he is a leading light in the Isle of Wight Gardens Trust, and Christine has been the NGS county organiser for the Island. Between them they have done a huge amount to encourage horticultural excellence in the area and deserve a pat on the back. *NGS, Good Gardens Guide, RHS, Isle of Wight Gardens Trust.*

rooms	6: 3 doubles, 3 twins, all with bath/shower.
price	£50–£65. Single occ. £37–£40.
meals	Light meals available.
closed	Christmas.
directions	From Newport, into Shorwell, down a steep hill, under a rustic bridge & right opposite thatched cottage. Signed.

Think big and think Jacobean - built in 1615 by the then deputy governor of the Isle of Wight, North Court was once the manor house of a 2,000-acre estate. Extensively modified in the 18th century, the house has 80 rooms including a library housing a full-sized snooker table (yes, you may use it), and a 32-foot music room (you may play the piano, too). Bedrooms are large, in two separate wings, but although it all sounds terribly grand, this is a warm and informal family home - and your hosts more than likely to be found in gardening clothes. Autumn is an excellent and less busy time to visit.

WORPLES FIELD

Sue & Alastair Marr
Worples Field,
Farley Common, Westerham, Kent TN16 1UB

tel   01959 562869
e-mail marr@worplesfield.com
web   www.worplesfield.com

Sue is likely to greet guests in her wellies and gardening clothes at her home above a steep valley. You are only 22 miles from central London, yet immersed in much of historical, geological and architectural interest. The house was built in the 1920s by a local architect in a style typical of the area and period. Bedrooms are light, towels soft and colours restful; the bedrooms that share the bathroom have a lovely view. Relax in the garden room full of scented plants, and Sue will spoil you with home-made treats.

rooms	3: 1 twin with private bathroom; 1 twin, 1 double sharing bathroom.
price	£50. Single occ. £40.
meals	Available locally.
closed	Christmas & New Year.
directions	A25 eastbound, 1st left (after sign for Westerham & red stripes on road) into Farley Lane. House at top on left.

Is the sensually undulating lawn just an example of modernistic landscaping? Not a bit of it. Worples is a corruption of 'wurples', Kentish for ridge-and-furrow; the wave-like lawn patterns around which Sue has built her garden are far from modern, and hugely intriguing. Sue is a garden designer and it shows. She makes interesting use of large garden 'furniture' – a traditional Shepherd's hut here, a little 100-year-old summer house from Alastair's grandmother's garden there. And that is just the start. In 1997 she began a serious re-design of these three-acre grounds with their beautiful views across the valley; no corner is untouched by her flair and her plans are starting to bear fruit. The new orchard is underplanted with bulbs, the wildflower meadow is beginning to blossom, the trees and fine shrubs she has introduced are fleshing out beds and borders. There's a lily-pad shaped pond for frogs, newts and damselflies and an avenue planted with winter-flowering cherries and azaleas. The original sunken garden just below the house is being lovingly re-designed into a 'planet' garden with sparkling surprises. The vegetable garden has been transformed into an ornamental potager. Every feature enhances the view and entrances. Each season is a delight in this young garden. *RHS, Society of Garden Designers, Westerham Horticultural Society.*

ROCK FARM HOUSE

Mrs Sue Corfe
Rock Farm House,
Gibbs Hill, Nettlestead, Maidstone, Kent ME18 5HT

tel   01622 812244
fax   01622 812244
web www.rockfarmhousebandb.co.uk

Plantsmen will be happy bunnies here. In the Seventies, when her children were young, Sue ran a nursery at Rock Farm that built up a considerable reputation. It closed in 2000, but her collection of interesting plants continues to be celebrated in her own garden. She knows from experience what plants grow best in these alkaline conditions, and they perform for her. The evergreen *Berberis stenophylla* provides a striking backdrop to the large herbaceous border – 90-foot long and, in places, 35-foot wide. Bulbs grown along the hedge are superceded by herbaceous plants; as these grow, the dying bulb foliage behind is neatly hidden from view. The oriental poppies in May herald the riot of colour that lasts from June to September, and, to encourage wildlife, cutting down is delayed until January. The bog garden that lies below the house is filled with candelabra primulas, trollius, astilbes, day lilies, gunnera, lythrum, filipendulas and arum lilies: a continuous flowering from April to July. In a further area – around two natural ponds – contrasting conifer foliage interplanted with herbaceous perennials is set against a backdrop of Kentish woodland; superb groupings of hostas and ferns grow in shady areas. It is a delightful spot on hot days. *NGS, Good Gardens Guide.*

rooms	3: 1 double, 1 twin both with shower; 1 twin with private bath/shower.
price	£60. Single occ. £35.
meals	Available locally.
closed	Christmas Day.
directions	From Maidstone A26 to Tonbridge. At Wateringbury lights, left B2015. Right up Gibbs Hill; first right down drive, past converted oast house on right. Farm next.

A delightful Kentish farmhouse, with beams fashioned from recycled ships' timbers from Chatham dockyard. Bedrooms are simple, traditional, exquisite, one with a four-poster bed. Walls are pale or pure white, bedheads floral, furniture antique; the bedroom in the Victorian extension has a barrel ceiling and two big windows that look eastwards over the bog garden to the glorious Kentish Weald. Stairs lead down into the dining room with its lovely old log fire. Free-range eggs from the farm, home-made jams and local honey for breakfast.

MAYCOTTS

David & Debbie Jolley
Maycotts,
Matfield, Tonbridge, Kent TN12 7JU

tel   01892 723983
fax   01892 723222
e-mail debbie.jolley@dial.pipex.com

The original oak-framed Wealden hall house dating from 1472 was considerably renovated in 1910, when it was tile-hung, and leaded windows and big oak doors were added. Huge Tudor inglenooks, low beamed ceilings in the dining room and two double bedrooms, original creaky oak floorboards and Georgian doors upstairs. The Edwardian proportions of the twin bedroom and the drawing room below are quite different with high ceilings and tall windows: the drawing room is beautifully done up and has a period satinwood fireplace. All bedrooms look over the garden and are elegantly furnished.

rooms	3: 1 twin with private bath; 2 doubles with private or shared bath.
price	From £70. Single occ. from £45.
meals	Good pub within walking distance.
closed	Christmas
directions	M25 junc. 5 to A21 south. At roundabout left to B2160 for Matfield. At Standings Cross pub left. 250m left to Maycotts Lane. 1st house on right after 30mph sign

Since gaining distinction and a prize for her Diploma in Garden Design in 1990, Debbie's horticultural career has blossomed. Having run a successful garden design business, she is currently organising and teaching garden courses at West Dean College. Now she and David have restored their own garden to some of its former glory of the 1940s and 50s, and added their own touches. A Victorian shrubbery has been rejuvenated with winter shrubs and early spring plants and bulbs. The recently created gravel garden in its own sheltered microclimate features Mediterranean and late-flowering plants. Based on a previous owner's layout, the serpentine-edged borders of old-fashioned roses and perennials draw the eye down to a hedge through which you find a potager. Here, blocks of vegetables are interspersed with flowers, bowers of hazel and willow sprout forth, and roses and honeysuckle romp up a central four-pillared arch – all formally designed but growing riotously. The whole garden positively buzzes with energy like its creator, but away from the house and beyond the nursery area, David has created a more informal conservation area where wildlife is attracted to the restored ponds, stream and an orchard. *NGS, Society of Garden Designers, RHS, HDRA, Brenchley & Matfield Horticultural Society.*

MOUNT HOUSE

David & Margaret Sargent
Mount House ,
Ranters Lane, Goudhurst, Kent TN17 1HN

tel   01580 211230
e-mail davidmargaretsargent@compuserve.com

An oast house in the garden, a Grade II Wealden part-brick, part tile-hung former farmhouse. This is an intimate, charming corner of High Weald countryside which David and Margaret have worked hard to embellish both indoors and out since they moved here in 1983. The garden is almost two acres with a fine layout, thanks to a previous owner's friendship with garden writer Christopher Lloyd. The planting, however, was a little past its best and needed attention. Everything changed in one terrifying crescendo with the Great Gale four years after David and Margaret arrived. Mature trees were torn aside, the garden blasted, but they turned adversity into advantage, using newly-opened areas to introduce new shrubs now reaching handsome maturity. The long, open lawn has a new circular lily pond surrounded by herbaceous beds leading to a little stream and tiny valley. Interesting initiatives with plants are everywhere: there's a growing collection of old-fashioned roses and a drive heavily planted with spring flowering bulbs. The herbaceous borders near the house set off the architecture nicely, giving floral detail and contrast with the tree planting at the far end of the garden. David recently took early retirement from the City and his growing enthusiasm and skill in gardening is reflected everywhere. A professional kitchen gardener would be hard put to equal the efforts that go into the partially walled kitchen garden and it has stunning cutting flower beds.

rooms	2: 1 double with private bathroom; 1 twin with bath.
price	From £55. Single occ. by arrangement.
meals	Available locally.
closed	October–March.
directions	On A21, 5 miles south of Tunbridge Wells, left onto A262 for Goudhurst. 2 miles on, right into Bluecoat Lane, for Kilndown. At minor x-roads, right into Ranters Lane. House 1st on right.

A mini-library of very good garden books awaits you outside the bedrooms so you can mug up before or after Sissinghurst and other local delights in this garden hotspot of Kent. Breakfast in style beneath a brass candelabra in a dining room decorated with striking, very effective American blue-flowered paper. Bedrooms are pretty and pristine, one in Colefax & Fowler floral, the second in gentle shades of pale - and there are cut flowers from the garden in season, too. Enthusiastic hosts, in a friendly family home.

DEACONS

Jane Wilson
Deacons,
High Street, Cranbrook, Kent TN17 3DT

tel   01580 712261
web   www.oasts.com

Jane once farmed fruit and cattle; the superb naïve pictures of
bucolic cows remind her of her days in an old beamed farmhouse.
Today she is a charmingly informal hostess, her home is elegant,
pristine Regency, with good furniture, cosy bedrooms - one with
bold floral wallpaper - and comfy beds. Staffordshire dogs peer
down from the tops of cupboards and shelves. Eat breakfast
looking over the garden from the dining room, or watch life go
by on the historic High Street from your own little sitting room.

rooms	2: 1 twin, 1 single, sharing bathroom.
price	£55-£60. Single occ. £27.50-£30.
meals	Dinner/supper available; also available locally.
closed	December-February.
directions	From A229 left fork for town centre. Near left into High Street. House approx. 300 yds on left.

A small, lawned, bordered and railed front garden by the stuccoed High Street façade, a long-walled town garden behind the red-brick rear frontage – two utterly different worlds. Jane has gardened assiduously since she moved from country to town 20 years ago. Until she came to Deacons, she had a four-acre farm garden with woodland. It was, she says, quite a culture shock, but she has adjusted well and learned the very different discipline of creating an urban sanctuary by working ever-deeper borders around the lawn. She has skilfully broken up the stern rigidity of a typical rectangular back garden space by introducing curving edges, tall growing shrubs to give height and a bed dividing the lawn into two areas. Strong focal features include a large urn on a noble pedestal. She adores old-fashioned roses and always asks friends and family to add to her collection on important birthdays and celebrations. Another passion is for clematis – Jane has dozens and reckons that there is hardly a day in the year in which at least one clematis is not in bloom, from the subtle charm of winter's evergreen *Clematis cirrhosa* to the showier blooms of summer. Walls and fences have been carefully planted to soften the surroundings and give extra privacy. Good plants jostle for attention, colour is everywhere. Delightful.

BOYTON COURT

Richard & Patricia Stileman
Boyton Court,
Sutton Valence, Kent ME17 3BY

tel   01622 844065
fax   01622 843913
e-mail richstileman@aol.com

Higgledy-piggledy but immaculate. A truly handsome Grade II
listed house – 16th century brick-and-tile-hung, with Victorian
additions. The lighting is modern and the furnishings softly
comfortable. There's a sky-blue drawing room, an elegant green
dining room with a long view over the garden and stacks of
books. Richard and Patricia will give you breakfast here
(sausages with hops and other local produce) or you can eat
in the Aga-warmed kitchen looking out of French windows onto
a terrace. Soft colours in the bedrooms too – terracotta or cool
lavender - with pretty tiles in the sparkling bathrooms. Super
views from both.

rooms	2 twin/doubles, both with bath.
price	£70. Single occ. £45.
meals	Available locally.
closed	Christmas & New Year.
directions	From M20, junc. 8, A20. Right at r'bout onto B2163, left onto A274. In S. Valence left at King's Head. Through village with chapel on right. After 0.5 miles right at 1st x-roads; house on left past barn.

A stunning series of slopes and terraces that swoop southwards with breathtaking views over the Weald to Tenterden and Sissinghurst. A natural spring feeds a series of ornamental pools which splash down to a small lake, packed around with primulas and other damp-loving plants. The terrace outside the house has a formal feeling – four box-edged beds each with a Flower Carpet rose stand and underplanted with 'Queen Mother' roses – and an old bird bath in the centre. An attractive arch in the brick wall leads to the tennis court and a large bank of rock roses. One level below the drive is a box-edged parterre with knot-garden elements; Richard and Patricia's initials are clipped from box and helichrysum within two octagonal box beds. An octagonal pool with a fountain forms a striking centre piece. Steep steps – with the water flowing down the middle – lead to the next level: a rectangular pond full of fish and water-lilies, an iris bed with verbena for colour and several specimen trees planted in grass. Between the pond and below the house is a bog garden – a huge patch of arum lilies ("they grow like weeds"), *Salix eleagnos* and *Thalictrum aquilegifolium* flourish and to one side is a juniper bank, the other a mixed border. There's a grassy slope with paths mown through it, a new avenue of limes to be pleached and a little rose garden with a selection of David Austin repeat-flowering roses underplanted with hardy geraniums. Absolute perfection. *NGS*.

BUNKERS HILL

Nicola Harris
Bunkers Hill,
Lenham, Kent ME17 2EE

tel   01622 858259

The garden room is an inspiration: not technically a conservatory, but a room extended into the garden, with windows all round, and doors onto the terrace. Breakfast (with eggs from Nicola's chickens) and dinner are served in here among the pots of jasmine, mimosa and streptocarpus. Leading off it, the sitting room is low-beamed, and the oak panelling has decorative Tudor-style friezes: very cosy with a woodburning stove. A little sofa by the upstairs landing window is a sunny place for morning letter-writing, and the classic pale colours of the pretty bedroom give a bright welcome in the afternoons. Lots of good books to read.

rooms	1 twin, with private bath & shower.
price	£60. Single occ. £40.
meals	Dinner £20.
closed	Christmas & New Year.
directions	From M20 junc. 8, A20 east for Ashford. At Lenham, left to Warren St. On for 1 mile. Harrow pub on right. Bear left. After 300 yds, 3-way junc, sharp left. House 3rd on left.

From seats in different rooms in this treeful garden, you particularly notice the birdlife. The golden robinia framed against dark, spreading yew attracts many species to its bird feeder, and there are busy flutterings in and out of mature trees and shrubs all over the garden. The terrace is planted with pots of lilies, roses and fuchsia, and from here the eye is drawn down between yew hedges and two pairs of swelling conifers to the little white dovecot at the end. Behind it, the layers of white blooms on the massive *Viburnum plicatum* 'Mariesii' are the spring focal point. Down between mixed borders and a tapestry beech hedge dividing the garden into two halves, round a mound of wisteria, or behind a thicket of hydrangeas, rhododendrons and hollies, sits another bench in a sunny clearing. Scent rises from the border of shrub roses in this little secret garden: a 'Paul's Himalayan Musk' has dived up a silver birch, and 'Wedding Day' has taken over an old prunus. Nicola took over her mother-in-law's garden when she moved here: rather than make drastic changes she has gently nurtured and gradually developed her inheritance, and the garden reflects her quiet affection for it.

LITTLE MYSTOLE

Hugh & Patricia Tennent
Little Mystole,
Mystole, Nr Canterbury, Kent CT4 7DB

tel   01227 738210
fax   01227 738210
e-mail little_mystole@yahoo.co.uk

At last! A garden with which owners of smaller gardens can identify. Hugh and Patricia call their half-acre-plus a cottage garden, but they wear their experience and achievements lightly. It's actually more of a small country-house garden, in two parts. As you approach, a path passes between a mature herbaceous border and a curving rockery, then follows a long wall up to an old mulberry tree. This stands opposite the entrance to the walled garden, right by the house. White, scented 'Rambling Rector' frames the summer house in the corner, and 'Galway Bay' and clematis 'Perle d'Azur' romp up a wall. There's a cottagey and relaxed feel to this delightful planting and people are most happy sitting here in the comfy garden chairs. Hugh and Patricia love plants in pots, and their groupings by the house include white lacecap hydrangeas, fuchsias, an all-white display of pelargoniums, lobelia and impatiens and the softly pink 'Queen Mother' rose flanking the front door. They like groupings of the same colours: a pretty pink bed of hydrangeas and hardy geraniums lies under the dining room window. A secluded haven in an area of outstanding natural beauty, in the parkland, orchards and hop gardens of Kent.

rooms	2: 1 double with shower; 1 single in adjoining dressing room; 1 twin with bath & shower.
price	£75. Single occ. £43. Single £15.
meals	Occasionally.
closed	Christmas & Easter.
directions	A28 Canterbury to Ashford. Left to Shalmsford Street village; right at end at Bobbin Lodge Hill. Bear left at bottom; right at T-junc.; 2nd left to Mystole, signed Mystole Farm. House at end of lane.

A small, graceful Georgian house and much loved family home; the Tennents, your retired army hosts, have lived here for 35 years. A charming drawing room, especially for guests, is full of family photographs and looks onto the garden. Both bedrooms - prettily decorated with chintz - have lovely views of fields and woods; the double has an extra single bed in an adjoining dressing room, the twin has an alcove with a sofa by the window. Comfortable beds, soft pillows, fluffy towels and much gently courteous hospitality. The dogs, Scilla and Pippin, greet you with as much pleasure as your hosts. *Children over 10 welcome.*

HORNBEAMS

Alison Crawley
Hornbeams,
Jesses Hill, Canterbury, Kent CT4 6JD

tel   01227 830119
fax   01227 830119

Rolling hills and woodland, long views over luscious Kent, and a lovely garden that Alison has created entirely herself. This is a modern bungalow, a rare phenomenon in this book, a Scandia house brick-built from a Swedish kit. It is brilliant for wheelchair users and altogether easy and comfortable to be in, with floral-covered sofas and chairs and plain reproduction furniture. Alison is sweet, very much a 'coper' who used to live here with her disabled father. The house is so close to Dover that it is worth staying here for the night before embarking on the ferry fray.

rooms	2: 1 double with bath/shower; 1 twin with private bath/shower.
price	£70. Single occ. £35.
meals	Dinner occasionally available. Pubs within walking distance.
closed	Christmas.
directions	From A2 Canterbury-Dover, for Barham & Kingston. Right at bottom of hill, into The Street, Kingston to top of hill & right fork. 1st left on sharp right bend. 100 yds left into farm keeping right of barn.

Perfectly designed, brilliantly executed – Alison has come a long way since this garden was a field. She used to picnic here as a child, admire the view and dream about living here… The garden now completely surrounds the house and is bursting with plants. At the front are roses, camellias, lavender and acers in big pots; a blackthorn and hawthorn hedge is grown through with golden hop, vines and yet more roses. By the front gate is a spring bed, then a purple bed leading to a white-scented border of winter flowering clematis and magnolia trees. An immaculate herb garden is spiked with tall fennel, the vegetable garden has raised beds and a morello cherry tree, and the orchard is humming with fecundity from apples, plums and pears. Winter and autumn beds are filled with interest and colour from snake-bark maple, dusky pink chrysanthemums and corkscrew willow through to witch hazel and red-stemmed cornus. The huge herbaceous border is a triumph – colours move from pinks, purples and blues through apricots, creams and whites to the 'hot' end of yellows and reds – self-seeded intruders are soon dealt with. A little waterfall surrounded by lilies (yellow, pink and white) sits in the pond garden and rockery where hostas, ferns, astilbes, gunnera, bamboo and lilac compete for space. Look at the 'picnic' view, admire the delicate alpines in troughs and feel glad that someone who has achieved their dream is so happy to share it with others. *RHS, Barham Horticultural Society.*

LAKE HOUSE

Anthony Rickards Collinson
Lake House,
Capernwray, Carnforth, Lancashire LA6 1AL

tel   01524 734333
e-mail   edwina@mrscroc.demon.co.uk

A barn conversion built of old, local stone – but with a cosy, older feel. Inside is absolutely sparkling and filled with light from the lovely square hall to the cream and coral drawing room with good furniture and interesting original art. Coir carpets give a modern feel and the bedrooms are delightful: huge wooden beds, proper lighting, crisp linen, lemon colour-washed walls and power showers in large bathrooms. The only sound is birdsong and there are long views over the 100 acres of land. Edwina is a breath of fresh air and will look after you – but don't mind her going barefoot: she doesn't like shoes!

rooms	3: 1 double with private bath; 1 twin with bath/shower; 1 single with private or shared bath.
price	£70-£90. Single occ. from £40.
meals	Good food locally.
closed	Christmas & New Year.
directions	M6 junc. 35; A6 for Carnforth. At next r'bout right for Milnthorpe, then right for Borwick. Right at green for Docker Park Farm. Over r'way bridge & left. 0.5 miles past lodge; next on right over cattle grid.

Arabella Lennox-Boyd has designed these four acres – the beautiful original drawings are in the hall for you to pore over – but Anthony and Edwina have done the hard physical work. A lime tree avenue hugs the drive up to the house where hundreds of bulbs lurk until spring, including some unusual varieties of daffodil. The formal planting around the house includes beds of old-fashioned roses, scented viburnum, agapanthus and a verdant herb garden. The terrace has pergolas for height – clematis, roses, Virginia creeper and honeysuckle vie for attention – but the real stunner is the view to the lake. It is so peaceful with many specimen trees planted around it, a bluebell walk, sculptures – one of a highland cow which grazes happily alongside the real thing – and all that water: a great draw for wildlife including curlews, snipe and oyster catchers. Beyond are just acres of rolling countryside, perfect for walking and great for dogs. If you want to talk gardens Anthony is keen, or you'll find Edwina in the greenhouse "playing", as she calls it (but actually she knows exactly what she is doing) with all her seeds and neat rows of pots. A lovely, country garden.

THE RIDGES COACH HOUSE

John & Barbara Barlow
The Ridges Coach House,
Weavers Brow, Limbrick, Nr Chorley, Lancashire PR6 9EB

tel 01257 279981
e-mail barlow.ridges@virgin.net

You get a whole house to yourself here: a self-contained
converted Georgian coach house has been simply, comfortably
and prettily furnished. Original oak beams in the double room and
bathrooms upstairs. Where coaches once entered there's now a
large picture window in the half-panelled sitting room. French
windows from the dining room open out onto a patio in the
coach house's own bit of private garden. Your breakfast is cooked
for you on the range-type cooker in your kitchen, and you are
welcome to come and go at any time of day. The house can
also be rented for self-catering.

rooms	3: 1 twin/double with shower, 2 twins with private or shared bath.
price	£45-£55. Single occ. £32.50-£37.50.
meals	Excellent pub within walking distance.
closed	Very occasionally.
directions	M61 junc. 8 for Chorley, A6 for town centre, follow signs to Rivington & Cowling. House on right.

The story of Barbara's garden starts in the 70s when she used to help her mother with their garden centre in the back garden. The more she learned about plants, the more her interest grew: by the time her children had grown and flown she was hooked. Realising the potential of the garden, she began restoring and developing. Original apple trees lining the path were pruned, but otherwise you wouldn't recognise the back garden now: dense cottage garden planting demonstrates Barbara's eye for combinations of colour, form, and foliage. Through a laburnum arch, a lawned area is fringed with bright foliaged specimen trees cleverly positioned to shine against dark copper beech, holly and rhododendron. This shelter protects such tender plants as windmill palm and *Magnolia grandiflora*, and provides a lovely setting for a Victorian-style glass house used for entertaining. In a natural stream garden damp-loving plants such as rodgersia and gunnera grow down towards a pool, and a 'Paul's Himalayan Musk' runs rampant over trellis and trees. Recently an old buttressed wall has been uncovered to create a new, naturally planted quiet area, with scented plants and herbs to attract butterflies and bees. Barbara's horticultural achievement is to be admired and enjoyed. *NGS, Good Gardens Guide.*

GOADBY HALL

Victoria Westropp
Goadby Hall,
Goadby Marwood, Melton Mowbray, Leicestershire LE14 4LN

tel   01664 464202

Each room has panelling and an open fireplace, enough reason for wanting to sleep here. The panelling is painted in the plain, gentle colours that suit beautiful and traditional rooms; they're generous and faultless. It is a fine and grand house, done to the standards expected of the National Trust. High and ornate plaster ceilings, two handsome main staircases, floor-to-ceiling drapes and your own sitting room. There is even a lake – one mile long, no less – for you to row on and acres and acres of grounds divided into several gardens, some walled. A wonderful place to do your own thing.

rooms	2: 1 double, 1 twin both with bath.
price	£80.
meals	Available locally.
closed	Christmas, New Year & some weekends.
directions	From Waltham on the Wolds A607 for Eastwell; 1 mile, left for Goadby Marwood; after red phone box, 50 yds, right into Towns Lane; gates are 100 yds on left.

An important estate and garden, unique and glorious. Until two years ago it had fallen into a wild state, ivy and nettle clad with the great lakes silted up – a real secret garden which Vicky, like the handsome prince with his sword, has penetrated and is claiming back. Now when you walk out of the front door there is a great swathe of lawn down to an elegant iron gate, designed by Vicky: the entrance to the gardens. Turn left and you come to the formal walled gardens: an elegant rose garden with ancient sundial, the ladies' garden, the rose garden, the vegetable garden, the small orchard, the tennis court garden – all divided by neat paths and restored outbuildings including the original Victorian ice house. Then there is the children's garden, a perfect croquet lawn and Nanny's garden – but the best is yet to come... Semi-circular rosy brick steps lead down to the three vast lakes built by the Duke of Buckingham – a testament to 18th-century engineering with islands, bridges, a cherry walk, a kissing gate to open countryside, thousands of bulbs and new trees, a ha-ha, intricate iron gates and views to gently grazing horses. Lazy carp and trout trundle around in the sparkling water over which lilies and gunnera tower. Turn back and look up at the house – all is serene and the Sleeping Beauty is very much awake.

BAUMBER PARK

Clare Harrison
Baumber Park,
Baumber, Nr Horncastle, Lincolnshire LN9 5NE

tel   01507 578235
fax   01507 578417
web   uk.geocities.com/baumberpark/the house

Lincoln red cows and Longwool sheep ruminate in the fields around this rosy-brick farmhouse - once a stud that bred a Derby winner. The old watering pond is now a wildlife haven for frogs, newts and toads, bees drip honey, Maran hens conjure delicious eggs and Clare - a botanist - is hugely knowledgeable about the area. Bedrooms are light and traditional, not swish, with mahogany furniture, and there is a heart-stopping view through an arched window on the landing. Grass tennis court, guest sitting room with log fire, and dining room with local books. Very few cars on the roads so come for walking, riding and cycling.

rooms	3: 1 double with shower; 1 twin with private shower; 1 single with shared bath.
price	£50-£55. Single £25.
meals	Dinner, two courses, £10; three courses, £12. Light supper/high tea £7.
closed	Christmas & New Year.
directions	From Baumber follow road for Wispington & Bardney. House 300 yds on right.

If I were a bird I would go and live in this garden. Just over an acre of delicious smelling flowers, shrubs and hedges (sea buckthorn because the thrushes like the berries). "Scent is the thing," says Clare and even her favourite daffodil, 'Pheasants Eye', smells lovely. A formal gravel front bordered by lonicera hedges, leading under a solid pergola over which golden hop and honeysuckle battle for the sky, to lawn and large borders full of sweet-smelling roses, eleagnus, buddleja, sedum and a tiny pocket handkerchief tree – a third and final attempt to commemorate an anniversary! Beds are full, colourful and scented – thousands of bulbs pop up in the spring. There's a vast cherry tree underplanted with more bulbs, periwinkles and holly, a peony bed interplanted with sweet-smelling viburnum, a wildflower meadow and then a lovely arch through which peeps the open countryside. Few large trees have been planted so that the views are un-hindered and an old pond is planted around with native species only – for the wildlife, lucky things. A small quantity of interesting plants are for sale – propagated by Clare's fair hand.

THE OLD VICARAGE

Mrs Liz Dixon-Spain
The Old Vicarage,
Holbeach Hurn, Spalding, Lincolnshire PE12 8JN

tel   01406 424148
fax   01406 426676
e-mail lizds@ukonline.co.uk

One of Liz's sons is an artist and his work appears all over her lovely, relaxed home. Although her children are now grown up, a family atmosphere prevails and all is practical rather than frilly: a combination of antique and modern furniture, ethnic rugs, spider plants and bamboo, with squashy sofas in the drawing room. Bedrooms are sunny, covered in an eclectic mix of artwork and the twin has floral quilts with matching curtains and cushions. Liz is friendly and will spoil you with a good breakfast including home-made jam and marmalade.

rooms	2: 1 twin with bath; 1 double with private shower.
price	£50. Single occ. £30.
meals	Available locally
closed	Mid-December–mid-March.
directions	Off A17 north to Holbeach Hurn, past post box in middle of village, first right into Low Road. Old Vicarage approx. 400 yds on right.

Trained as a dress designer, Liz has swapped needle and thread for a spade and created the two-acre garden of her old family home from scratch. A large job to tackle on your own but Liz has now nurtured it into a fairly maintenance-free zone which only needs her time for two or three days a week. At first she wasn't quite sure how she wanted the garden to look, "definitely not too formal" though, so started from the house and worked outwards, reclaiming it bit by bit. The result is lovely. Some older trees were cleared – the stumps cleverly carved into a rustic seat or used as the edge to a flower border – but plenty of mature trees and shrubs form the backdrop including a 50-foot tulip tree. Ideas have 'grown' by themselves, like the wisteria which covered its arch and then shot up a nearby holly tree, giving a stunning display in late spring. Liz is always on the look-out for new plants but gives them a gentle start by re-potting them first in a mix of her homemade compost and soil and planting them out the following year – she very rarely loses anything. Grasses are a favourite, mixed in with colourful shrubs, roses, perennials and bulbs. There's plenty to explore and little surprises around every corner; a smooth croquet lawn, pond and bog garden, a wild and wooded area, a south-facing terrace beside the house and plenty of vegetables and fruit trees. Birds love it here – no chemicals are used – and the atmosphere is very special. *NGS, Lincolnshire Gardens Trust.*

Susan Collier
80 Bromfelde Road,
London SW4 6PR

tel   020 7720 4080
fax   020 7720 9311
e-mail susan@colliercampbell.com

If a weekend in a Victorian house just five minutes from Clapham North tube doesn't sound 'quiet and contemplative' then think again. Susan - a successful designer, but "not minimalist" - can give you just that. Sunny rooms with coir matting and painted floorboards are crammed with a fabulous collection of paintings, hundreds of books and gorgeous fabrics (some of her own designs) as curtains, throws and cushions. The bedroom - at the top of the house - is quiet, cosy and traditional with gay rugs, a pretty pink and green bedcover, plenty of cushions and tempting books. There's more: Susan is a superb cook and loves to entertain.

rooms	1 double with bathroom
price	£80.
meals	Family supper or candle-lit dinner available.
closed	Occasionally and Christmas.
directions	5 minute walk from Clapham North tube.

The Secret Garden. Surprises everywhere, but the biggest surprise of all is finding such a large, glorious and peaceful space in Clapham. This used to be parkland, which explains the many mature trees, but Susan has kept the backdrop and painted her own picture. The garden is now divided into three separate sections, cunningly concealed from one another with dense planting. By the house is a paved area; gravel paths, pots, and huge herbaceous borders on both sides are packed with plants which reflect Susan's love of form, design and colour. A beautiful greenhouse with the original wisteria and vines twisting around it lolls against the house and a tall bamboo and macleaya screen hide the next bit, a paved and gravel square. It contains an urban water feature made of London drainpipes, an elegant terracotta table in a seating area and more packed planting. A winding path meanders through the jungle to the final trumpet blast, a rectangular lawn – neat as a pin – under siege from all sides and above. The borders are enormous and tightly planted, wild as you like and brimming with delicious scents, "other people's trees" overhang giving a feeling of concealment and there are the lovely, tall trees of the original parkland – a towering holm oak is especially attractive. You can visit The Chelsea Physic, the Museum of Garden History, whip along to the RHS halls at Vincent Square for a show and be back at your haven in 20 minutes. Irresistible. *NGS*

Mrs Winkle Haworth
38 Killieser Avenue,
London SW2 4NT

tel   020 8671 4196
fax   020 8671 4196
e-mail winklehaworth@hotmail.com

Winkle is a gardener to the last tip of her green fingers. She is unusually devoted to gardening, garden details, design, collecting unusual plants and the pleasure of creating ever more displays. She wants her plants to look their best in a town setting and her devotion is the secret of this ravishing garden in Streatham's delightful conservation area. There are myriad lessons to be learned for town gardeners the moment you step into this south-facing plot. The simple, long rectangle of the garden's space has been magicked into three compartments, each with a character of its own, and each decorated with the finest plants. Certain items stand out: a lofty rose arch, water features, a carefully worked parterre. Deep, deep borders, a sequence of intimate areas, topiary to give form, sweet peas rising up rockets, wonderful old roses, mostly courtesy of Peter Beales, fine shrubs – a triumph. A blacksmith forged the Gothic garden seat where you sit surrounded by colour and scent. A pink wisteria adorns the back of the pretty Victorian house; old London bricks form patterns on the final terrace which creates the finale to the garden. Containers are stuffed with agapanthus and other beauties around the patio, a perfect place to relax in a heavenly garden. *NGS, Good Gardens Guide.*

rooms	2: 1 twin, 1 single sharing bathroom.
price	£80–£90. Single occ. from £50.
meals	Dinner £25.
closed	Occasionally.
directions	3 minute walk from Streatham station (15 minutes to Victoria); 15 minute walk from Balham tube.

The Haworths – early Streatham pioneers – have brought country-house chic to South London. Few people do things with as much natural good humour and style as Winkle. The house glows yellow, and you breakfast in the rug-strewn, wooden-floored, farmhouse kitchen - but can decamp in spring or summer to the spectacular garden. Bedrooms are big, grand and homely: more rugs, comfy beds, lamb's wool blankets, loads of books, waffle bathrobes, beautiful linen. Even the single is generous. All on a quiet residential street, and Streatham Hill station a three-minute walk; you can be in Victoria in 15 minutes. Brilliant. *Children over 12 welcome.*

Beatrice Fraser
57 Breakspears Road,
London SE4 1XR

tel   020 8469 3162
e-mail Bunzl@btinternet.com

If Beatrice has brought a wildly colourful new twist to B&B, her partner, New Zealander James Fraser, brings something different to modest-sized town garden design with his funky planting. He dreamed of creating a corner of South Island, New Zealand in South London. He has his own plant business, specialising in NZ plants, and is an acclaimed town-garden designer for adventurous clients looking for the unusual. His own garden certainly flies the flag for his original ideas. You're greeted by yuccas in window boxes, a snaking path to the front door and strikingly different plants in the small front garden. Step out of the wooden-floored kitchen/breakfast room at the back to follow his wooden paths and push your way, explorer-like, through head-high grasses and a forest of antipodean plants and tall fans of Manuka poles reaching heavenwards. Everything you pass is exotic – spiky phormiums and cordylines sit with many rarities which are a perfect expression of James's passion for the plants of his native country. All the wooden structures – the fans, the pond fashioned from chunky railway sleepers, the decks and sculptures – are made of wood collected from stretches of London's empty docklands. Local wildlife is drawn to the garden's sense of sanctuary, while gardeners delight in the shock of the new.

rooms	1 twin with shower room.
price	From £60.
meals	Good meals available locally.
closed	Rarely.
directions	From Brockley station, cross Brockley Rd & up Cranfield Rd. Cross Wickham Way at church & along Cranfield Rd. Breakspears Rd meets almost opposite. Free on-street parking. Trains: Brockley–London Bridge, 10 mins. Best buses: 171, 36 to central London.

This is fun! A house-cum-gallery in a conservation area where each room exhibits original, modern art. Bedrooms have all the useful things that you don't want to lug around town with you - radio, hairdryer and alarm clock. Bold colours, wooden floors, huge curtain-less windows and indoor trees give an exotic feel. Breakfasts are cooked on the Aga and eaten in the vast and stylish kitchen with deck views over the subtropical garden (breezy days are a bonus as tall grasses ripple and sway). Beatrice, kind and easy-going, has brought a breath of fresh air to the world of B&B.

Sue Haigh
24 Fox Hill,
Crystal Palace, London SE19 2XE

tel	020 8768 0059
fax	020 8768 0063
e-mail	suehaigh@foxhill-bandb.co.uk
web	www.foxhill-bandb.co.uk

This part of London is full of sky, trees and wildlife; Pissarro captured on canvas the view up the hill in 1870 and the original painting can be seen in the National Gallery. There's good stuff everywhere - things hang off walls and peep over the tops of dressers; bedrooms are stunning, with antiques, textiles, paintings and big, firm beds. Sue, a graduate from Chelsea Art College, employs humour and intelligence to put guests at ease and has created a very special garden, too. Sue will cook supper (sea bass, maybe, stuffed with herbs); Tim often helps with breakfasts.

rooms	3: 1 twin/double with bath; 1 double, 1 twin, sharing shower room.
price	From £80. Single occ. £50.
meals	Lunch £15. Dinner, 2 courses, £20; 3 courses, £30.
closed	Rarely.
directions	Trains from Victoria or London Bridge, 20 mins to Crystal Palace, then 7 mins walk. Sue will give you directions or collect you. Good buses to West End & Westminster.

Sue has moved since she appeared in the fourth edition of our Special Places to Stay. Her new home is in the sweet seclusion of Fox Hill. The small gravelled front garden has bobbles of box and a recently planted crab apple – an eye-catching frontage for the pretty Victorian house – but there's much, much more to come. The long rectangular back garden has been completely re-designed and now bursts with colour and interest in every direction. Sue, who once worked at the Chelsea Physic Garden and is a true plant-lover, has cleared and re-planted paved areas by the house and built a raised pond for her beloved fish. The delicate water plants are guarded by tall, spiky agaves which thrust skywards from their containers. Climbers snake up walls, trellises and an arch, while water bubbles soothingly from a water feature. Sue has nurtured a few of the plants that were there when she arrived, a thriving ceanothus and a weeping pear tree among them, but otherwise started with a clean slate. To add a final flourish and to mark her pleasure at having her first-ever garden shed to play with, she has planted a 'Liquid Amber' sweet gum outside its door. This is a young garden packed with promise.

MILL COMMON HOUSE

John & Wendy Pugh
Mill Common House,
Ridlington, North Walsham, Norfolk NR28 9TY

tel   01692 650792
fax   01692 651480
e-mail johnpugh@millcommon.freeserve.co.uk
web   www.broadland.com/millcommon

The house is an elegant Georgian conversion and expansion of an older cottage. There are gorgeous chintzes throughout, and the bedrooms have a luxurious feel with *toile de Jouy* patchwork bedspreads and masses of cushions. Bathrooms have easy chairs, and the one overlooking the walled garden, a sumptuous freestanding bath. Aga-cooked breakfasts taken in the pretty conservatory are a treat - Wendy is a *Cordon Bleu* cook. Flowers everywhere, log fires, French windows that lead onto the terrace: this is a cossetting place to stay in undiscovered Norfolk. There are plenty of inspirational gardens and historic churches nearby.

rooms	3: 1 double with private bath; 1 twin with bath; 1 single/twin available.
price	From £54. Single occ. £37.
meals	Dinner from £20.
closed	Christmas.
directions	A1151 Norwich to Walcott & Happisburgh; left to Walcott. Left opposite The Lighthouse pub. At Y-junction house on left-hand side behind pond.

John and Wendy moved here only a few years ago and have always treated their guests like friends; not surprisingly, their walled garden receives a similar level of tender loving care. The garden is protected from the salty north-east wind by a thick 30-foot-high conifer hedge; this allows a wide variety of flowering shrubs to flourish – hydrangeas do particularly well here – interspersed with Wendy's favourite annuals such as *Nicotiana silvestris* and *Verbena bonariensis*. Roses scramble through trees, over walls, and up the extensive 200-year-old brick and flint barns. 'New Dawn' frames the front door. To the front of the house the old farm pond is surrounded by grasses, camassias, phormiums and valerian; to the rear, a new *Viburnum tinus* hedge has been planted for the planned extension to the garden. In the large Victorian-style conservatory, plumbago and passion flowers weave their way through the wall trellis, and the many geraniums and orchids add colour to the sills. Wendy is a talented flower arranger and loves to grow herbs, lavender, agapanthus and lilies in artistically arranged pots around the terrace. *RHS, The Royal National Rose Society, NT, The Norwich Cathedral Flower Guild.*

LITCHAM HALL

John & Hermione Birkbeck
Litcham Hall,
Litcham, Nr Kings Lynn, Norfolk PE32 2QQ

tel   01328 701389
fax   01328 701164
e-mail j.birkbeck@amserve.com

For the whole of the 19th century this was Litcham's doctor's house and today, over 200 years after it was built, the red-brick Hall remains at the centre of the community, with church fêtes held in the three-acre garden. This is a thoroughly English home with elegant proportions. The hall, drawing room and dining room are gracious and beautifully furnished. There are good reading lights and books by the beds and the big-windowed guest rooms look onto the lovely garden. John and Hermione are friendly and most helpful. *Children and dogs by arrangement; use of pool similarly.*

rooms	2 twins both with private bathroom. Sitting room available. 3rd twin available occasionally.
price	£50-£65.
meals	Dinner £20.
closed	Christmas.
directions	From Swaffham A1065; right to Litcham after 5 miles. House on left on entering village, with stone balls on gatepost.

The Birkbecks' garden has given the family a lot of pleasure over the 35 years since they came to Litcham Hall. The swimming pool has provided fun for children and visitors alike, but John and Hermione have found the design and planting of their garden from scratch the most satisfying project. Yew hedges make a dramatic backdrop for herbaceous borders and the framework for a sunken area with a little lily pond and fountain. Strolling along mown paths through their wild garden is a delight in spring when the snowdrops, azaleas and bluebells are out: in summer you emerge from this spinney through a pergola covered in climbing roses. Behind the house the swimming pool is sheltered in part of a double-walled garden, with a brick-arched veranda-cum-loggia down one side. A vigorous wisteria runs its full length, spreading out over a shady paved corner, a wonderful spot for relaxing in Mediterranean weather. The walled Italian garden is the Birkbecks' most recent creation, inspired by the desire to put to best use some beautiful stone urns they have inherited. Now artfully positioned in a parterre of lavender-filled, box-edged beds, the urns make an elegant finishing touch to a formal composition entirely suited to the period of the house. *Open occasionally for the Red Cross.*

SALLOWFIELD COTTAGE

Caroline Musker
Sallowfield Cottage,
Wattlefield, Wymondham, Norfolk NR18 9PA

tel   01953 605086
e-mail caroline.musker@tesco.net

So many interesting objects it takes time to absorb the splendour;
in the drawing room, gorgeous prints and paintings, unusual
furniture, decorative lamps... Caroline has a fine eye for detail.
The guest room has a Regency-style canopied king-size bed and
decoration to suit the era of the house (1850). The large garden
is just as fascinating, with rooms and a very large, jungly pond
that slinks between the trees. You can eat in the courtyard or
the conservatory; Caroline prepares lovely dinners using much
local produce. *Children over nine welcome.*

rooms	2: 1 double with private bath; 1 single, for members of same party.
price	£50. Single occ. £35. Single £25.
meals	Lunch £10. Dinner £15.
closed	Christmas & New Year.
directions	A11 Attleborough-Wymondham. Take Spooner Row sign. Over crossroads by Three Bears pub, at T-junction left to Wymondham. 1 mile on look for rusty barrel on left, left into farm track.

A deceptive one acre, but the beautiful large pond in front of the house acts as a huge mirror and reflects tall trees, island beds and the building itself, giving a Norwegian 'lake impression' of space and green. When Caroline arrived eight years ago it was swamped and overgrown; hacking her way through, thinning and cutting, she only left what she decided was interesting. These included an impressive swamp cypress, a weeping ash, lots of viburnums, magnolias, a chimonanthus and an as yet unidentified acer she calls the "firework tree" because of its cascading habit and fiery autumn colour. There are also some very old trees: an enormous willow and a vast ash. Caroline adores plants and has a real knack for positioning – they all thrive where they're placed and look good together; there's lilac and pink, shades of green from shrubs and the odd splash of dark red or yellow against the perfect backdrop. An old ditch has been turned into a sunken path with a trimmed hedge on one side and a colourful herbaceous bank on the other. Clematis and honeysuckle wind through trees and shrubs, shade and water-loving plants are deeply content, and all the shapes and colours are soft – there's no ugly rigidity. A tiny, enclosed courtyard has been constructed against one wall of the house and a very pretty pink *Clematis texensis* shoots up it; another wall is capped by curly tiles and there are pots filled with hostas. The pale terracotta-floored conservatory is canopied with vine leaves.

CONIFER HILL

Mrs Patricia Lombe Taylor
Conifer Hill,
Low Road, Starston, Harleston, Norfolk IP20 9NT

tel   01379 852393
fax   01379 852393
e-mail richard.taylor55@virgin.net

A house on a hill - unusual for East Anglia; the lawns fall away
and views stretch out over farmland. Richard and Patricia are
utterly charming and easy to talk to with a passion for fishing and
gardening. Play croquet on the lawn, swim in the pool or explore
the county from this red-brick Victorian house. Light and space,
family photographs, agricultural prints, fresh flowers to spoil you,
a comfy sitting room with a roaring fire for chilly nights. All the
bedrooms have thick carpets and a quiet Victorian elegance.

rooms	3: 1 twin/double with bath; 1 twin, 1 double, sharing bathroom.
price	£60. Single occ. £30.
meals	Good pubs and restaurants nearby.
closed	Occasionally.
directions	A143 Diss/Yarmouth for 9 miles. At r'bout left for Harleston, then immed. left to Starston. Over x-roads, into village, over bridge, immed. right. After 0.5 miles, drive on left by white railing.

Built by Richard's grandfather in 1880, Conifer Hill's garden was laid out at the same time. When the 1987 hurricane destroyed 40 mature trees, the Lombe Taylors decided to give the three acres a complete overhaul, and in the process discovered the original layout of beds and shrub borders. Horticultural taste has changed since Victorian times, so you won't find the mass of bedding plants you'd have seen here a century ago; and being practical, Patricia says she is in any case less interested in labour-intensive plants these days. This is nevertheless a much loved garden and it celebrates family rites-of-passage as well. It wasn't only the Queen who celebrated her Golden Jubilee in 2002: the golden wedding anniversary at Conifer Hill was marked by a new border of golden shrubs underplanted with grey. The Lombe Taylors' silver wedding anniversary bed of roses is flourishing too. A recent project brings the garden right up to date: a modern sculpture created by a local craftsman displayed in a roundel of yew hedge; children find the five-foot-tall copper resin sculpture with its abstract verdigris curves irresistible to touch. This is a family garden with much to interest the plantsman. *RHS, The Norfolk & Norwich Horticultural Society.*

GUILSBOROUGH LODGE

Mrs Tricia Hastings
Guilsborough Lodge,
Guilsborough, Northamptonshire NN6 8RB

tel   01604 740450

There are always fresh flowers in Tricia's house: her style is a
mixture of the fresh and chintzy as well as the horsey, with an
eclectic mix of sporting prints on the walls. Stripped pine
windows, and both sitting and drawing rooms opening onto the
terrace. A roaring log fire in the dining room in winter, and you'll
notice the unusual kilim or Chinese tapestry covered fireside
stools that Tricia and a friend trade in. The bedrooms still have
their original little Victorian fireplaces, and both rooms have
lovely views towards the church.

rooms	2: 1 twin with private shower; 1 twin with private bath & wc.
price	£60. Single occ £40.
meals	Available locally.
closed	Christmas & Easter.
directions	A14 junc. 1 (A5199); 2.5 miles to Northampton; right to Guilsborough.

Built in the 1890s as a hunting box for the Pytchley Hunt, Guilsborough Lodge makes a handsome focal point for the garden with its mellow brick and tall chimneys. In a commanding position 600 feet up, it has lovely views to the church and over a reservoir that attracts abundant wildlife. Tricia was for many years a professional flower arranger, so the flowers in her herbaceous border are chosen for their suitability for cutting: she loves phlox, stocks and pinks, and anything that has good structure or a wonderful scent is brought into the house. She's particularly fond of a wide variety of viburnums – there's always at least one flowering at most times of the year. The border leads down to a hidden sunken garden by the tennis court, planted with her favourite soft pastel colours. When the weather's lovely, breakfast can be served on the terrace; you can even have a game of croquet on the lawn at the front, where there's a growing collection of old-fashioned roses. A peaceful and tranquil spot to stay in an area rich in well-known gardens to visit: Coton Manor Gardens and Cottesbrooke Hall to mention but two.

THE OLD COACH HOUSE

Clive & Eileen Wood
The Old Coach House,
Lower Catesby, Daventry, Northamptonshire NN11 6LF

tel   01327 310390
fax   01327 312220
e-mail coachhouse@lowercatesby.co.uk
web   www.lowercatesby.co.uk

A Victorian former coach house in open countryside, elegantly
converted into a large-roomed family house: the four huge
windows along the 40-foot drawing room were once the
carriage entrance doors. Lovely westerly views across country
from the dining room, where French windows open out onto a
terrace massed with container plants. Large bedrooms are light
and freshly decorated, with comfy beds and cushions, family
pictures and plenty of interesting books - why are the physiology
textbooks so well thumbed? The twin room overlooks a
monastic pool and has a big bathroom; both bathrooms
have excellent showers.

rooms	2: 1 double, 1 twin, both with bath.
price	£70. Single occ. £45.
meals	Excellent pub food 1 mile.
closed	Very occasionally.
directions	A425 Daventry to Leaminton Spa. Left at Staverton Garage, to Catesby/Hellion; 2 miles on right, for Lower Catesby. House left of clock.

Standing on the terrace, gazing down, you are immediately aware that Eileen loves to create circles in her garden. "Circles flow, and contrast with the square and rectangular shapes of the house and garden perimeter," she explains. Thus the santolina-edged circle with a bird bath in the middle of the potager... and, over there, the deep red 'Roseraie de l'Hay' circle with a maroon 'Minnehaha' weeping standard as its central focal point. Down the terrace steps and along the grass path bordered by soft trusses of 'Ballerina' you come to another circle with a central statue. Eileen has always loved gardening, but this is the first garden she has created entirely from scratch. Clive helps with the heavy work, and is also in charge of a productive vegetable garden. Ultra-white-barked silver birch (*Betula jaquemontii*) back the croquet lawn, and a large pond is another source of delight: wild ducks breed, dragonflies swarm, carp and perch abound, and the heron hovers beadily. Pass the autumn border with its rose pergola and return to the wide variety of plants in containers up the steps and on the terrace – lavender, phormium, agapanthus, roses, and alpines. There's always a splash of colour here – in circles of course.

ARCHWAY HOUSE

Erica McGarrigle
Archway House,
Kirklington, Newark, Nottinghamshire NG22 8NX

tel   01636 812070
fax   01636 812200
e-mail mcgarrigle@archway-house.co.uk

It's a special spring time treat to turn into the drive at Archway House. In the spinney, up the curving drive, is a sensational display of bulbs from February right through until May – first snowdrops, then *Anemone blanda* and daffodils, and finally, a magnificent flourish of bluebells. With Hodsock Priory's Snowdrop Spectacular not far away, early spring is a good time to visit: look from the lawn behind the house right across the fields to a distant manor house framed by trees – a fine view. Erica's lush herbaceous border leads down the sunny side of the lawn from an archway, on the other side of which she has planted hostas and shade-loving foliage plants under the trees. Follow your nose down the box-edged path to her most recent achievement: the sight and scent of a mass of old-fashioned shrub roses – a sensualist's delight. Hundreds of shrubs and trees in the grassed area beyond – chosen for their variety of shapes and shades – merrily melt into the surrounding countryside. A variegated maple stands out against clipped yew, and autumn colours glow right through to the end of the season. *RHS.*

rooms	3: 1 double with shower; 1 double with private bathroom; 1 twin with bath.
price	£56. Single occ. £33.
meals	Dinner, for 4 or more, £22 p.p.; light supper £12 p.p.
closed	Christmas & New Year.
directions	From A617 Newark-on-Trent to Mansfield; 0.25 miles west of Kirklington, right at two small white bollards, just before turn to Eakring.

When owners love their home and enjoy sharing it with guests you can't fail to have a good time. Colin and Erica are such people and have nurtured the well-proportioned house, built in 1917, into its present happy state. Numerous rooms lead off a big, open hall filled with flowers, guests have two sitting rooms with deep sofas and log fires, and there's so much to do in the 13 surrounding acres: golf (six holes), snooker, darts, croquet, tennis, swimming... if the weather's dreary, there are more games to play by the fire. Bedrooms have ample lounging-around space and fireplaces; bathrooms are big and one has black and cream Edwardian tiles.

ASHDENE

David Herbert
Ashdene,
Halam, Nr Southwell, Nottinghamshire NG22 8AH

tel   01636 812335
e-mail david@herbert.newsurf.net

Just a mile west of bustling Southwell and its lovely Minster, this
stunning rosy-bricked house was once the old manor house of
Halam and dates from 1520. Much travelled, David and Glenys
have packed their house with wonderful paintings, samplers,
embroidery, books on history and travel, lovely old rugs and
comfortable furniture. Guests have their own drawing room with
open fire and the bedrooms are gorgeous: pretty white bed linen,
spotless bathrooms with fluffy towels and relaxing, neutral
colours. Don't creep around on egg shells, come and go as you
like – but do ask about the area, they know it well.

rooms	2: 1 double with shower; 1 single with bath & shower.
price	£45. Single £25.
meals	Available locally.
closed	Occasionally.
directions	A1, then A617/A612 to Southwell. Take sign to Farnsfield. In Halam left at crossroads, past church, house 200 yds on left.

An imaginative, really special garden – how many others have had Alan Titchmarsh rushing to view their special paulownia tree because it flowered? Both David and Glenys have done the hard work: a gravel and boulder garden tucked around the front of the house has scented plants for spring and autumn, two huge yews have been cut to tall stumps, then their later sproutings coaxed and designed by David, one into a spiral, the other into a witty Rastafarian topknot. There's a white spring garden and a woodland walk along serpentine brick paths with precisely coppiced hazels. A long grass walk up a slope takes you away from the house and is edged with hornbeam – rest at the top, a favourite quiet spot. There are over 50 species of damask roses, paths through brick-raised beds of mixed planting and a central circle of five pillars around an Ali Baba urn. Trellises, covered in scented roses, create hidden corners and add height. The vegetable garden is fecund but neat, the sunken garden and the terrace by the house have good seating areas. David's topiary is artistic and fun – he's creating a Cheshire cat out of an unusual muehlenbeckia, nicked a juniper into a table (his Chinese libation cup) and is training ivy along a tunnel of wire like a long roll of carpet – so this is what retired surgeons do! Their use of chemical help with all this? None. An organic garden which attracts many birds (38 nests at the last count) and a centuries-old colony of bees. *NGS, RHS.*

GOWERS CLOSE

Judith Hitching
Gowers Close ,
Sibford Gower, Nr Banbury , Oxfordshire OX15 5RW

tel   01295 780348
e-mail jhitching@virgin.net

So how does a popular English garden writer like Judith Hitching actually garden herself? With great originality and a witty eclecticism that has created a cleverly sophisticated sheltered cottage garden. Eight years ago, this was an unappetising, bramble-choked half-acre graveyard of dead conifers and heathers. But she inherited an ancient wisteria which covers the back of her thatched home and some tumbledown pig-sties from which she rescued old stone to make paths, walls and steps. There's a touch of formality in the box-edged parterre filled with herbs, surrounding blue wooden obelisks which support old-fashioned sweet peas and clematis. The two lawns are divided by a clipped hedge and two statues of musical cherubs guard the steps down. The first lawn is edged by three borders – a shady one for hostas, lilies and hellebores, and two that are stuffed with shrub roses, penstemons, pelargoniums, alliums and campanulas, in soft shades of pink, mauve and purple. The long pergola is swagged with roses, clematis and wisteria and frothed at path level with *Alchemilla mollis*. This leads down to the second lawn, shaded by silver birches and with two more borders backed by clipped yew hedges. Scent is very important – so prepare to be carried away by the powerful fragrance of lilies, auriculas and pineapple-scented salvias. The wide terrace is a perfect place to sit and glimpse the rolling Cotswold Hills. Judith has created something memorable for all the senses.

rooms	2: 1 double with private bath; 1 twin with bath.
price	£70. Single occ. £45.
meals	Dinner £25.
closed	Christmas.
directions	Sibford Gower 0.5 miles south off B4035 between Banbury & Chipping Campden. House on main street, same side as church & school.

Be soothed by music, the scent of fresh coffee, dried flowers hung from beams, restful, pastel bedrooms and a deep sense of history. Gowers Close was built in about 1580 and adjoins what was once the Court House. Three tiny rooms, now Judith's larder, broom cupboard and a loo, are thought to have been the village lock-up. Nothing is level here - the many beams and flagstones are all angled by age. This is very much a home and Judith is an amusing, easy hostess who is delighted to chat about plants and garden plans.

PARTWAY HOUSE

Erica & Malcolm Brown
Partway House,
Swalcliffe, Banbury, Oxfordshire OX15 5HA

tel   01295 780246
fax   01295 780988
e-mail ericabrown@ukonline.co.uk

An ex-nurse, Erica is particularly thoughtful about taking good care of her visitors. Everything is spotlessly clean, and all needs are catered for, with eye pads, medical kit, spare razors. There are garden and plant books and fresh flowers everywhere, and a fish tank in the dining room; double doors lead to the rose garden and the sitting room has sliding doors to the terrace. There's a double bed with a half-tester canopy and a quilted and bowed counterpane in peach and sage green, and elegant French windows into the shower room overlooking the garden. The blue and yellow twin room has coronets over the beds, and a huge shower in the private bathroom.

rooms	2: 1 double with shower; 1 twin with private bath.
price	£59–£69. Single occ. £39.50–£44.50.
meals	Dinner £18.
closed	Christmas & New Year.
directions	B4035 to Shipstone-on-Stour; left to Sibford Ferris at top of hill. House on left.

What luck to have a son who owns a renowned local nursery! Malcolm and Erica often lend a hand at Compton Lane Nurseries: in return, some interesting, or even rare plants have found their way to Partway House. It's only a few years since the garden was started in earnest, yet it's already remarkably mature. A broad herbaceous walk between clipped beech hedges cuts across the centre, with arches in the hedge leading on one side to the vegetable garden and shrub borders, and on the other to the lawn behind the house. The lawn curves beyond Malcolm's rock feature towards a glorious spring array of rhododendrons and azaleas, fronted later in the year by bold hostas. Blue *Columnar chamaecyparis* screen a conifer bed and a variegated oak, *Quercus cerris variegata*. Treasures in the shrub borders include *Lespedieyia thunbergii* with its plumes of pink flowers in late summer, *Enkianthus campanulata*, and the rare *Dipelta floribunda*, all of which flourish in this acid soil (unusual for this generally alkaline area). The south-facing wisteria-clad terrace is planted with many interesting sun-loving plants, and a raised rose garden is prettily edged with lavender: all this is a treat for plantsmen and non-gardeners alike. *NGS*.

SOUTH NEWINGTON HOUSE

Roberta & John Ainley
South Newington House,
South Newington, Banbury, Oxfordshire OX15 4JW

tel   01295 721207
fax   01295 722165
e-mail rojoainley@btinternet.com

A charming, listed, 17th-century hall house surrounded by five acres of gardens and paddocks. Bedrooms have chintz furnishings, good beds, cushioned window seats and garden views. There's a ground-floor cottage annexe - a perfect haven for two - prettily furnished with its own little sitting room and kitchen, and some exposed stone walls. The conservatory is a delightful spot for breakfast - unless it's warm and then you may eat on the terrace. Roberta and John love cooking so you will be spoiled; eggs, fruit and veg are (mostly) home-grown. Inglenook fires in the drawing room and dining room are lit on cooler days.

rooms	3: 1 double, 1 twin both with private bathroom. Cottage: 1 double.
price	From £60.
meals	Dinner £25. Supper £18.
closed	Christmas & New Year.
directions	A361 Banbury to Chipping Norton. In South Newington 3rd left signed 'The Barfords'. 1st left down tree-lined drive.

The Ainleys are a great team. They work well together both as hosts and as organisers for the National Gardens Scheme – and the fruits of their joint efforts are particularly apparent in their garden. The five acres of gardens and paddocks round the old hall house have been established over the last 18 years. A walled garden at the front of the south-facing house is surrounded by weathered honey-coloured Hornton stone – a marvellous backdrop for roses and wisteria. Here they are also creating a parterre and the box hedging dividing the area into four formal beds is already in place. The conservatory is filled with hoya, plumbago, stephanotis and jasmine – their scent fills the house; it's the perfect place to sit and view the garden. The drive curving around the house is a profusion of mixed planting: primroses and spring bulbs brighten a central island bed; herbaceous borders, rose bed and trellis look gorgeous in high summer. Hellebores and snowdrops, winter-flowering honeysuckle, evergreen shrubs and cornus stems brighten dull winter days. The orchard is carpeted with daffodils in spring, and by summer its pond is almost covered with water lilies. An impressive kitchen garden provides a comprehensive range of organic vegetables and soft fruit. Roberta's "gardeners" are her bantams: eggs don't come fresher or more free-range. *NGS, RHS.*

MANOR FARMHOUSE

Helen Stevenson
Manor Farmhouse,
Manor Road, Bladon, Nr Woodstock, Oxfordshire OX20 1RU

tel	01993 812168
fax	01993 812168
e-mail	helstevenson@hotmail.com
web	www.oxlink.co.uk/woodstock/manor-farmhouse

Many are the plants in this garden which encourage and feed birds and other wildlife – including the deer which regularly chew the 'Kiftsgate' rose climbing the old apple tree. This charmingly informal garden was created from scratch after the Stevensons arrived in the mid-70s. Helen planted interesting shrubs and trees right at the start but further plans had to be shelved for years as children romped and rode bikes in their garden playground. Now the children have grown up, Helen has found more time to focus on gardening and developing this third of an acre surrounded by fields. In spring, the grounds sparkle with generously planted snowdrops, crocus, pulmonaria, sweeps of aconite and drifts of daffodils. Her beloved bluebells are allowed to do their own thing. Those first plantings of trees and shrubs – presided over by an eye-catching golden *Acer platanoides drummondii* – have now come into their own and create areas of dappled light and a fresh, natural feel. Her chemical-free, curved borders and raised beds behind low stone walls are packed with colour – she's a great bargain hunter and eagerly swoops on the plant stalls at her local gardening club. When we visited she was gleefully ripping out a leylandii hedge to replace it with a handsome stone wall... yet another pleasing touch for her colourful, informal English country garden.

rooms	2: 1 double, 1 twin, sharing shower room.
price	£50–£60.
meals	Available locally.
closed	Christmas.
directions	From Oxford's ring-road A44 north. At r'bout, 1 mile before Woodstock, left onto A4095 into Bladon. Last left in village. House on 2nd bend in road, with iron railings.

Hand-painted Portuguese pottery sits on the dresser in the bright dining room and over breakfast you'll be watched by an amusing collection of wooden birds including an inquisitive lapwing and avocet. The main double guestroom has had a make-over from a Laura Ashley catalogue and is as pretty as you'd expect. Guests share a large shower room, so Manor Farmhouse is ideal for families or friends travelling together; the spiral staircase to the twin is steep, but the room feels very private. The family's pet sheepdog Chloe is spoiled by guests - she even receives an annual Valentine's card from one American fan.

LAKESIDE TOWN FARM

Theresa & Jim Clark
Lakeside Town Farm ,
Brook Street, Kingston Blount, Oxfordshire OX9 4RZ

tel   01844 352152
fax   01844 352152
e-mail townfarmcottage@oxfree.com
web   www.townfarmcottage.co.uk

A dream setting - and a picture-perfect traditional farmhouse hidden at the bottom of a quiet lane, but built 14 years ago from reclaimed materials, so everything is spick and span. The drawing room for guests is large and light with plenty of sofas and chairs for lounging. Bedrooms are not huge but colourful and filled with lovely fabrics, ornaments and fresh flowers. A thoughtful touch is a little decanter of sherry in the room and a fridge outside for your own bottles of wine. Wake up to the smell of freshly baked bread, and fill up on Jim's hearty farmhouse breakfast.

rooms	2: 1 double with shower; 1 twin with bath.
price	From £55. Single occ. from £45.
meals	Available locally
closed	Very occasionally.
directions	M40, junc. 6, B4009 for Princes Risborough. First left in Kingston Blount. After 300 yds right into Brook St; immed. left down drive to last house.

With luck you'll see a red kite – successfully re-introduced on a nearby estate. Theresa started taking gardening seriously in the late 1980s when she and James built a new home on their working farm. It all began with a rockery and the garden fence has been moving further and further back into the adjoining fields ever since… Today what was once sheep pasture is 1.5 acres of superbly planted, well-designed areas which range from the formal to the completely wild. Theresa has created rockeries, scree beds and herbaceous borders which are being extended all the time, as well as a restful waterfall and two lakes. The garden is divided into a series of well-defined areas, each with a mood of its own and with witty decorations including an old telephone kiosk and street lamp. You'll find a rose-smothered pergola, an ornamental grass border, decorative arches, manicured lawns and a glorious vegetable garden. Theresa is a self-confessed plantaholic and avidly collects new treasures; the garden has been featured in *Gardener's World*, among other programmes. 'Albertine' roses climb through apple trees, a vigorous 'American Pillar' decorates an arch. Best of all is Theresa's supreme wildflower garden surrounding one of the ponds: a snowy mass of ox-eye daisies studded with corn cockle, corn marigolds and other wild beauties. A gem. *NGS, RHS.*

LARCHDOWN FARM

David & Cally Horton
Larchdown Farm,
Whitehall Lane, Checkendon, Reading, Oxfordshire RG8 OTT

tel   01491 682282
fax   01491 682282
e-mail larchdown@onetel.net.uk

"10/10 on the wow scale," wrote one visitor, and indeed the sight of honey-coloured rafters to the ceiling and the polished ash floor and balusters along the gallery in the entrance hall is breathtakingly unexpected. This open space connects the two ends of the house: visitors have the right-hand end to themselves, with their own drawing room where breakfast is also served. An extremely comfortable family home with lovely pictures and books: the dining table is beautifully laid in preparation for the Horton mega-breakfast. The large ground floor bedroom leads out to a wild area of the garden that attracts many birds.

rooms	4: 1 double with bath; 1 double with shower; 2 singles sharing bath.
price	From £70. Single occ. £55.
meals	Good food available locally.
closed	Christmas & New Year.
directions	A4074 to Oxford; right to Checkendon. In village pass pub, church & cricket pitch; right after red phone box. Whitehall Lane out of Checkendon Larchdown on right.

Capability Brown is alive and well and living in Oxfordshire! When the Hortons had finished extending and remodelling the house they bought eight years ago, David's attention turned to the surrounding three acres. JCBs were brought in to dig ponds and landscape the levels, and with the help of copious amounts of manure, the different areas responded quickly with profuse colour. Cally produces the plants in large quantities, David builds and also looks after the enormous kitchen garden and polytunnel which extends the produce season; jointly they maintain the borders. Delighted that Chelsea 2002 favoured the 'back to nature' look, they felt that Larchdown could be considered the height of fashion. Planting around the bog garden, the three ponds and the little stream that connects them is abundant, and in the Mediterranean area and along all the gravel paths, flowers self-seed freely. You'll find greater formality in the sunken garden and parterre, and also in the clipped box beneath the roofed pergola that David built around the dovecot. Recently they have planted over 70 trees in the first stage of creating an arboretum. This enthusiastic garden reflects the personality of its owners to the delight of the many visitors.

HERNES

Richard & Gillian Ovey
Hernes,
Henley-on-Thames, Oxfordshire RG9 4NT

tel   01491 573245
fax   01491 574645
e-mail oveyhernes@aol.com

In 1968 Gillian and Richard took over the family estate with two full-time gardeners to look after the huge Victorian garden. When one of them died unexpectedly the then somewhat unhorticultural Gillian, with three children under four, knew something had to change. Thirty years on the garden is mercifully a little smaller but it is in extremely capable hands. Some elements of the original Victorian layout remain: the wisteria arbour, the nut walk, the croquet lawn and the wild garden – Gillian's favourite spot. The garden has many family associations and memories: majestic Wellingtonias that mark the 21st birthdays of elder sons, the holly 'house' and the giant toadstool on which children love to perch like pixies, the ha-ha looking out to the old cricket meadow, the carpets of bulbs under the trees. New since the Sixties are the pool garden, the rose arbour (planted to celebrate Gillian's retirement as a school governor) and the hornbeam walk. The vegetable garden continues to supply delicious produce, and while Gillian plans new projects for the future (ask her about her philosophical "labyrinth of life"), she remains realistic about all that maintenance. This garden is essentially a gentle place in which to enjoy peaceful contemplation.

rooms	3: 1 four-poster with bath; 1 double with private bathroom; 1 twin with shower. Self-catering available in lodge.
price	From £80. Single occ. from £60.
meals	Good pub & restaurants within a mile.
closed	December–mid-January.
directions	At traffic lights in Henley centre turn into Duke St. At next lights right into Greys Rd. After 2 miles (on leaving 30mph zone) 2nd drive on right, 'Hernes Estate. Private Drive. Main House Only'.

Ramble through the ages in this home, much loved by five generations of Oveys. A stately yet comfortable place to stay: a panelled hall with open fire and grand piano, a drawing room with original inglenook fireplace, a billiard room with easy chairs by a log stove. Large bedrooms overlook the garden; one has a fine four-poster, another a large sleigh bed. Long soaks in the Victorian blue claw-foot bath are a treat. On Sundays tuck into the traditional Ovey breakfast of porridge (in winter), kedgeree and boiled eggs - served in the dining room hung with family portraits. A super place.

THE WILDERNESS

Peter & Tarn Dearden
The Wilderness,
Empingham, Nr Oakham, Rutland LE15 8PS

tel   01780 460180
fax   01780 460121
e-mail dearden@empingham.fsnet.co.uk
web   www.rutnet.co.uk/wilderness

The Wilderness awaits you in a quiet and elegant way. The pretty, creeper-clad stone house dates from 1690 (although with some Georgian tampering) and in a quiet village close to Rutland Water. The entrance hall is stone-flagged, the pale blue drawing room (with honesty bar) is large and inviting with plenty of books and games and the dining room is grand with a high ceiling and huge windows. You're spoiled in the bedrooms – one is pink and flouncy with Colefax & Fowler fabrics, the other is bright lemon – and the bathrooms, with power showers and fluffy robes. Tarn is glamorous and fun, and Peter is charming.

rooms	2 twin/doubles with private bath.
price	£80.
meals	Dinner £25.
closed	Christmas & New Year.
directions	From A1 to Empingham, into village, 250 yds past 30mph sign, house on right behind stone wall with yew hedge – 50 Main Street.

Peter's grandfather was a great collector of seeds and cuttings from all over the world which encouraged his enthusiasm for growing things and creating beautiful gardens. Two years ago the garden was re-designed by Peter and Tarn; they have added walkways and pergolas to link the different rooms, then planted new beds and – Tarn's great love – lots of old-fashioned roses. They have ended up with what they wanted, a garden that looks both natural and elegant. A huge, bouncy lawn leads to long pergola walkways with borders front and behind – all smothered in roses, and a shrubbery with mounds of hebe, mahonia and climbing hydrangeas. The croquet lawn looks out to an SSSI (with some rare wild orchids) and is bounded by a mixed hedge of beech and copper beech, walnut and horse chestnut trees, a colourful shrub bed and a woodland bed with roses under a line of sycamore trees. An old espaliered pear climbs up the side of the house and there is a peaceful orchard with soft fruit, apples and plums, guarded by larger trees and an ancient folly. Bounded on one whole side by an ancient yew hedge the garden is well protected and a haven for birds: pheasant, partridge and woodpeckers of both varieties potter and swoop with the smaller, wild species. Real enthusiasts, Peter and Tarn have not finished yet. In a few years their planting will mature so it's a treat for those who want to keep coming back to watch developments.

MICKLEY HOUSE

Pauline Williamson
Mickley House ,
Tern Hill, Nr Market Drayton , Shropshire TF9 3QW

tel   01630 638505
fax   01630 638505
e-mail mickleyhouse@hotmail.com

Downstairs, the house retains traces of its Victorian origins. A
large double room on the ground floor is super-comfortable with
its Louis XV-style double bed, sofa and easy chairs; the autumnal-
coloured twin room sports Sanderson fabrics and an extra large
bath. Both have wheelchair access, and three rooms have fridges
- a practical touch. Upstairs has a more modern feel: a cosy, pine-
clad double with a patchwork quilt, and a twin with a little
balcony overlooking the garden. From the central dining room you
can walk onto the patio; there's also a comfortable drawing room.
Guests are free to roam the garden or stay in the house all day.

rooms	4: 2 doubles, 1 twin. all with showers; 1 twin with bath.
price	£50-£70. Single occ. £30-£40.
meals	Excellent pubs & restaurants nearby.
closed	Christmas & New Year.
directions	On A41 at Tern Hill r'bout A53 to Shrewsbury; right to Fauls Green 1 mile. 4th house on right.

Happy is the woman who has a man able and willing to create structures that she can clothe with plants! Keith's most striking achievement is the pond that he constructed with a few friends and a JCB. The deep hole was puddled with clay, huge rocks from the local quarry were manoeuvred into craggy shapes behind, water was invited to cascade from an upper pool. The pond perimeter is planted with lobelia, ferns, lysichitum and cannas, while alpines and ground cover plants sprout from the rockery. The pergola to one side is entwined with Pauline's favourite clematis – they do better than roses here – and everlasting sweet peas. Project number two was a long brick wall to back a south-facing herbaceous border. An arch framed in *Clematis montana* 'Marjorie' leads through the wall to the Millennium Walk – an avenue of silver birches, underplanted with *Alchemilla mollis*, hardy geraniums and dahlias. A hosta bed flourishes in the shade down against the wall, and there is an interesting collection of trees – swamp cypresses, an *Acer brilliantissimum* (the shrimp-leafed tree), and *Cercis canadensis* (the Canadian pansy tree), grown for its purply copper foliage.

THE CITADEL

Sylvia Griffiths
The Citadel,
Weston-under-Redcastle, Nr Shrewsbury, Shropshire SY4 5JY

tel   01630 685204
fax   01630 685204
e-mail   griffiths@thecitadelweston
web   www.thecitadelweston.co.uk

Everything is on the grand scale, as you'd expect from your first glimpse of The Citadel in the distance... lofty ceilings with beautiful plasterwork picked out in white against deep colours, an elegant living room with French windows to the garden, a large billiard room with a full-size snooker table, and an elegant, very large dining room. A great staircase leads up past a ticking longcase clock to the bedrooms where canopies and rich French wallpaper abound. Baths sparkle with gold clawed feet, pale American quilts cover beds. Dreamy.

rooms	3: 2 twins/doubles with bath; 1 double with bath.
price	£90-£96.
meals	Dinner £23.
closed	Christmas & Easter.
directions	From A49, 12 miles north of Shrewsbury, to Weston/Hawkstone Park. House on right, 0.25 miles after taking Hodnet road out of village.

These beautifully tended, skillfully designed three acres perfectly complement the Gothic Revival architecture of The Citadel and the dreamy rural beauty which surrounds it. The house was built for the dowager Lady Jane Hill who lived at nearby Hawkstone Hall and the garden is full of surprises, so take your time. As the enthusiastic Sylvia says – she and husband Beverley are devoted gardeners – it's a garden to explore. You'll find new delights at every turn... sweeping lawns with views to Wales and the Shropshire countryside, great banks of lusciously healthy rhododendrons and camellias on a sandstone outcrop, a secret Victorian woodland folly, a charming rustic thatched summer house gazing across fields, woodland walks, an immaculate potager kitchen garden where flowers bloom among the vegetables, and a walled, manicured croquet lawn. The delights start by the house with its patio edged by burbling water features and a newly-made pergola. You are led past rhododendrons and high hedges to the croquet lawn and kitchen garden and then into woodland, with a hidden folly and an acer glade which glows with colour in autumn. Mature trees everywhere: oaks, Scots pine and, most spectacular of all, the great copper beech which lords it over the bastion-like façade of this architecturally stunning 1820 folly. *NGS*

GREENBANKS

Christopher & Tanda Wilson-Clarke
Greenbanks ,
Coptiviney , Nr Ellesmere , Shropshire SY12 0ND

tel   01691 623420
fax   01691 623420
e-mail wilson.clarke@ukonline.co.uk

All is comfort and elegance in Tanda and Christopher's pretty,
mellow red-brick Victorian home, built in 1865 for a local wine
merchant. Relax in the large, sunny, pale yellow-walled, south-
facing drawing room. Linger over a hearty breakfast at the long
table in the charming dining room. A cheery rocking horse greets
you outside the bright bedrooms and light pours in through floor-
to-ceiling windows. Soft carpets, brass beds, gorgeous views... and
a wonderful shower that American visitors tell Tanda is the best
they've found this side of the Atlantic.

rooms	2: 1 twin/double, 1 twin, both with bath. Separate shower room.
price	£70. Single occ. £45.
meals	Dinner, £20.
closed	Christmas.
directions	From M6, M54, A5 to Shrewsbury. At 1st r'bout, right for Ellesmere. There, A528 for Shrewsbury at r'bout. 10 yds on, left into Swan Hill. 1 mile on, left onto 'No Through Road'. 0.5 mile on, left over cattle grid.

In the mid-1980s this charming, informal country-house garden, carefully worked to blend in with its lovely rural setting, was a jungle surrounding a derelict house. If there had been a garden before, there were no clues, just masses of rampant vegetation. Four years before Christopher and Tanda bought Greenbanks, the two acres had been cleared and sternly disciplined. When they arrived in 1989 they inherited a clear canvas, an open acre with mature trees, a magnolia and just a couple of narrow borders. Both are wildlife-lovers and they have developed the grounds with plants especially attractive to birds, insects and butterflies. "We aimed to create a haven for both wildlife and guests," Tanda says, and they have succeeded brilliantly. The large pond, guarded by an old oak tree, has been cleared and planted with water-lovers (including water lilies), many trees introduced, borders dug and decorated with good shrubs. One of the garden's most charming features is its young woodland planted 10 years ago with mixed native broad-leaved trees, including a grove of silver birch hiding the tennis court. The open, sunny, south-facing main lawn has lovely views across the open countryside, and the small walled patio area is a sun trap in fine weather. Judicious planting of many evergreen berried shrubs, winter-flowering honeysuckle, bulbs, virburnums, roses and very good herbaceous plants ensure all-round interest. Informal, welcoming, full of interest, a delightful garden to explore and enjoy.

WHITTON HALL

Mr & Mrs Christopher Halliday
Whitton Hall,
Westbury, Shrewsbury, Shropshire SY5 9RD

tel   01743 884270
fax   01743 884158
e-mail whittonhall@farmersweekly.net

Elegant, never intimidating - mellow brick, cast-iron baths, fading carpets and honey-coloured panelling - and there's a sense of timelessness. Even the breakfasts reflect another age: kedgeree and soft fruit from the garden are seasonal additions. The Georgian bedroom has long views over the carp-filled lake, the other bedroom has a Chesterfield in its bay window, but do stir yourself to wander through these stunning gardens and the woods beyond. There's a large self-catering cottage, too.
Children over 12 welcome.

rooms	2 + 1 cottage: 2 doubles both with private bath & shower. Cottage sleeps 4.
price	£70. Single occ. £45. Cottage from £300 p.w.; short breaks available.
meals	Packed lunch available.
closed	Christmas & New Year.
directions	From Shrewsbury bypass (A5), B4386 to Westbury. There, right at x-roads opp. The Lion pub. 1st left, 50 yds on, left for Vennington. After 0.5 miles, drive on left; house at end, on right.

Pure poetry, from the rugged, red-brick 17th-century dovecote rising above yew topiary to the charming, beautifully restored, oriental-looking summer house. This is a manorial garden in which grandness and lavish planting have been skillfully combined with natural woodland. The Hall's frontage is a mass of sweet-scented wisteria in season. Gaze across a rising front garden which acts as a ha-ha to give an uninterrupted view of the large, wildfowl-haunted lake edged by pollarded willows. Step around the corner past the dovecote to discover the privacy of what was once a formal rose garden; sheltered by manicured hedges and walls, it has been transformed into a lawned compartment with deep herbaceous borders and old-fashioned shrubs and climbing roses. Walk across the wide, generous lawns behind the house past the summer house into gorgeous woodland. Mature trees blend harmoniously with the many young trees which Christopher and Gill have planted over the years. Walk through woodland to a delightful, restored ornamental canal – its banks are a mass of water-loving plants set among shades of green from the tree canopy above. This is a garden for most seasons. In spring you'll see masses of daffodils, crocuses and other early flowers and in summer, beds and borders alive with the colour and leaf of thriving herbaceous plants and very good shrubs. Autumn is a riot of golds and reds as the trees and shrubs do their stuff in a final display before winter sets in. Ravishing.

LAWLEY HOUSE

Jackie & Jim Scarratt
Lawley House,
Smethcott, Church Stretton, Shrewsbury, Shropshire SY6 6NX

tel   01694 751236
fax   01694 751396
e-mail   lawleyhouse@easicom.com
web   www.lawleyhouse.co.uk

More than 50 types of rose bloom in wild profusion – including a 'Paul's Himalayan Musk' that vigorously scrambles through an acacia. Deep herbaceous borders glow with colour and the secret pond garden sparkles with water lilies. This was a weed-choked three acres of sloping ground when Jim and Jackie came 27 years ago. Since then they have gardened devotedly and imaginatively, creating a richly planted design of lawns, beds, trees and shrubs to draw the eye across the valley to the hill scenery beyond. They began with a massive clearance programme which unearthed stone steps and the now restored pond. Today the mood is sunny, delightfully informal and traditional – they love scent and have carefully planted to provide all-year interest among a sequence of different sections divided by immaculately tended lawns. Acid-lovers, including rhododendrons and camellias, thrive and so do the traditional garden flowers: lupins, sweet peas and delphiniums. A lovely country-house garden with long views – the Wrekin, Lawley and Caradoc hills are all in view – you can even spot distant Clee Hill on a clear day.

rooms	2: 1 double with private bath & shower; 1 twin/double with bath & shower.
price	£50–£60. Single occ. £35–£40.
meals	Excellent pubs and restaurants nearby.
closed	Christmas & New Year.
directions	From Shrewsbury, south on A49; through Dorrington, right to Smethcott; after 2 miles drive on left over cattle grid.

Built on the lower slopes of north Long Mynd to take in the view, this imposing Victorian house is large and comfortable. You can lie in bed in the morning with the sunlight streaming in and gaze over beautiful countryside - or enjoy it all from the proper timber conservatory downstairs. William Morris fabrics and big furniture give a traditional feel. There's a sense of privacy too - you have your own staircase - while bedrooms welcome you with flowers, bathrobes, books, duckdown pillows... Jackie and Jim are delightful hosts and great fun.

ACTON PIGOT

John & Hildegard Owen
Acton Pigot,
Acton Burnell, Shrewsbury, Shropshire SY5 7PH

tel   01694 731209
fax   01694 731399
e-mail   acton@farmline.com
web   www.actonpigot.co.uk

Ferocious fecundity – as if the entire two-acre garden had been magically manured and then left to marinade. John's mother is a great gardener (if you want another treat ask to see her next-door paradise) and she laid out the structure. John and Hildegard have worked hard to bring it into line and the results are magnificent. Dividing the garden into sections the drive up to the house is heaving with huge euphorbias in raised aubretia-clad stone beds, there are thousands of bulbs, an iris bed, large shrubs planted through with ramblers and lovely giant yew balls for structure. The front garden is enclosed with a lawn and a huge late-flowering magnolia leans against the almost green house; the back section is all mixed borders with a walled garden by an old swimming pool where sun-lovers are planted. A vegetable, fruit and herb garden provides goodies for the kitchen. There are many rare shrubs and trees – John has planted 6,000 this year alone – and there is a wood for each of their three children. Scent is important, especially near the terrace – a wonderful spot for *al fresco* meals or simply sitting. The garden gently peters out with no boundary to open fields and a lake where ducks, geese, curlews and other water birds flap happily – go quietly and you will hear that lark rising. Hildegard says "you can't force nature" but she has done a jolly good persuading job.

rooms	3: 1 double, 1 twin/double, both with bath & shower; 1 family with shower room.
price	£55–£65. Single occ. £32.50.
meals	Supper or dinner from £15. Meals also available locally.
closed	Christmas & New Year.
directions	From A5 & Shrewsbury, onto A458 for Bridgnorth. Approx. 200 yds on, right to Acton Burnell. Entering A. Burnell, left to Kenley. 0.5 miles on, left to Acton Pigot. House 1st on left.

From the double room, with hand-printed wallpaper and oak chests, you look to Acton Burnell hill – England's first parliament was held here. The yellow room has lovely views of a lake, the garden and the Welsh hills; sunsets can be spectacular. Wooden doors, floors, carved settle and chests sit well with elegant furniture, lovely prints and photographs. The two-acre garden hugs the house, with a pool for summer and a croquet lawn. Parts of the house were built in 1660; the site is mentioned in the Domesday book. Very special.

UPPER BUCKTON

Hayden & Yvonne Lloyd
Upper Buckton,
Leintwardine, Craven Arms, Shropshire SY7 0JU

tel   01547 540634
fax   01547 530634

Cue Mr Darcy: a gracious Georgian house standing in lush gardens that dip down to a millstream and sweep across meadows to the River Teme - such wonderful views. Good-sized bedrooms with fine furniture, excellent linen, bathrobes and bathroom treats - there's no stinting on generosity here. It's a fascinating place with a millstream and a weir, a motte and bailey castle site, a heronry, a point-to-point course and a ha-ha. Yvonne's reputation for imaginative cooking using local produce is a great attraction for walkers returning from a day in the glorious Welsh Borders, and there's a good wine list, too. *Children by arrangement.*

rooms	3: 2 twin/doubles both with private bath; 1 double with shower.
price	£70. Single occ. £45.
meals	Dinner £20.
closed	Very occasionally.
directions	From Ludlow, A49 to Shrewsbury. At Bromfield A4113. Right in Walford for Buckton, on to 2nd farm on left. Large sign on building.

This site has been inhabited for centuries. A corn mill downstream from the weir was mentioned in the Domesday Book, and the mound in the Lloyds' garden constitutes the motte and bailey remains of a 12th-century castle. Upper Buckton itself dates from Georgian times, and is still a working farm today. Over the last 25 years Yvonne has added beauty to an already handsome house by creating a garden that makes the most of the tranquil setting. Recline on the veranda that runs the full length of the south-facing elevation and look down the lawn, across the millstream at the bottom of the garden, out to the open fields beyond the ha-ha and the rolling woodland beyond that. Along the stream are wonderful mounds of hostas, and in the borders, a mixed planting of peonies and roses, with delphiniums and lilies that Yvonne has grown from seed; there's something of interest for every season. A heather bed looks cheerful in the early spring, and at the height of summer a barn wall is smothered with roses and clematis with captivating names – 'Dentelle de Malines', 'Vyvyan Pennell', 'Bells Jubilee'.

THE OLD PRIORY

Jane Forshaw
The Old Priory,
Dunster, Somerset TA24 6RY

tel   01643 821540

Ancient, rambling, beamed and flagstoned, with sunshine filtering through medieval windows, Jane's 12th-century home is as much a haven for reflection and good company today as it was to the monastic community who once lived here. She has stamped her own style on the priory, with funky Venetian-red walls in the low-ceilinged, time-worn living room with its magnificent stone 14th-century fireplace and, in one bedroom, decoratively painted wardrobe doors. The big bedroom is unforgettable - undulating oaken floor and four-poster - and deeply authentic. A rare place.

rooms	3: 1 twin, 1 four-poster, both with bath; 1 double with private shower.
price	£60-£70. Single occ. by arrangement.
meals	Available locally.
closed	Christmas.
directions	From A39 to Dunster; right at blue sign 'unsuitable for goods vehicles'. Follow until church. House next door.

Jane Forshaw's bewitching walled garden in the beautiful little west Somerset town of Dunster is a wonderfully personal creation. You'll discover a bounteous blend of formal touches with shrubs, small trees and climbers which are allowed to express themselves freely. The garden perfectly complements her ancient priory home... a place of reflection, seclusion and peace. A tall mimosa greets you at the little gate on a lane overlooked by the Castle, mature espaliered fruit trees line the garden path and then comes Jane's most formal touch, the square, knee-high hedged box garden. The shrubs for this were rescued from the Castle's 'Dream Garden' when the National Trust abandoned it because they thought it would be too labour-consuming to maintain. Jane piled as many of the uprooted shrubs as she could into the back of a van, heeled them into some empty land and later arranged them into their present design. Informally planted herbaceous borders and a little lawn in front of the house complete the picture. Through an archway you wander into the church grounds with stunning long beds which Jane helps maintain. When the writer Simon Jenkins drew up his list of the best churches in England, Dunster received star billing and the grounds did even better. He described it as the most delightful church garden in England... see if you agree.

FRIARN COTTAGE

Michael & Penny Taylor-Young
Friarn Cottage,
Over Stowey, Quantock Hills, Bridgwater, Somerset TA5 1HW

tel   01278 732870
fax   01278 732870

Nothing happens by accident here. Classically designed to make the most of a superb setting, this garden was laid out in the 1920s but Penny and Michael have given it a modern twist without interrupting the eye line; the terracing has been cleverly concocted so that the views flow seamlessly in a series of curves and swoops, like the flight paths of the birds which hover above it. The positioning of benches, pots and stone tables is considered carefully, nothing must interrupt, and huge swathes of colour are cleverly used to balance corner vision. Stone paths ensure you walk the garden to maximum effect: large herbaceous borders on both sides are bursting with foxgloves, lupins, daisies, peonies, red hot pokers and aquilegea, the colours as carefully balanced as the sizes and shapes. Look back now and another, perfect, vista assails you, with a long line of towering rhododendrons and a weeping birch as the focal points. At the very bottom is a hidden rectangular lawn, bounded by a neat organic vegetable plot and another border full of roses, artichokes and nepeta – the purple you glimpsed from the house. Michael has relaid a sundial garden with stone flags and wild geraniums peeking through, kept in order by two neatly clipped bushes and two new small box plants. Fruit trees include a crab-apple, walnut, mulberry, pear and fig; wild flowers are encouraged in the meadow and a small pond attracts dragonflies. Glorious Hestercombe is under ten miles away and well worth a visit.

rooms	1 twin/double with bath.
price	£53-£57.
meals	Dinner £12-£15. Light supper £7.
closed	Rarely.
directions	From Bridgwater, A39 through Cannington. Main road forks right (at Cottage Inn); straight on & over x-roads to Over Stowey. Left signed Ramscombe Forestry Trail. Keep to tarmac by turning right up hill. Cottage in front. Left through gates.

The Quantocks are a treat and from here you have at least 38 square miles of great walking. Wildlife bounds, flits and creeps through the garden, woods and heathland: wild deer, hill ponies, badgers and over 50 species of birds. Laze on the terrace or say hello to the two friendly Exmoor ponies and chatty free-range hens. You have your own self-contained wing with sitting room, old and antique furniture, china and flowers. Breakfast *al fresco*, have supper by candlelight or eat at the local pub – the Taylor-Youngs will drive you to and fro.

HARTWOOD HOUSE

David & Rosemary Freemantle
Hartwood House,
Crowcombe Heathfield, Taunton, Somerset TA4 4BS

tel   01984 667202
fax   01984 667508
e-mail hartwoodhouse@hotmail.com

Having run 'Gardens of Somerset' tours, David and Rosemary are experts at both looking after their guests and showing them the Quantocks' most beautiful nooks and crannies. Their bedrooms are light, airy and uncluttered with pretty fabrics; one of the doubles has a sunken bath and separate walk-in shower. Complete privacy (not counting the family of house martins nesting in the eaves outside the Blue Room!) in your own end of the house with sitting room and woodburning stove, a sprawl of easy chairs and stacks of lovely books to read. Immaculately kept and everything works properly – a joy in itself.

rooms	4: 2 twin/doubles, 1 single, all with bath; 1 single with private bath.
price	From £60.
meals	Dinner £25, occasionally.
closed	Occasionally.
directions	A358 from Taunton. After 9 miles left signed Youth Hostel & Lydiard St Lawrence. Over railway bridge, past YHA, right. 400 yds on, house 4th on left.

Quite literally a labour of love; eight 'Dublin Bay' roses – a ruby wedding present – grow up a circle of eight pillars in the centre of a lush formal garden. Bordered by colour-themed beds of yellows (tulips and wallflowers in spring, herbaceous in summer), whites and purples, mauves and pinks and a sunny side bursting with tender plants. In the adjoining potager, which is home to an octagonal greenhouse, more ruby wedding gifts bear suitably coloured fruit and veg – beetroot, red lettuce, chard and loganberries. The woodland garden too, teems with interesting plants – wander among *Cornus kousa* 'Norman Haddon', *Stewartia sinensis*, rhododendron 'Teddy Bear' with pink, felt-backed leaves – and magnolia trees and pittisporum in the glade. The beautifully kept croquet lawn is clearly not just for sport; look closer and you'll see a resin bronze sheep peering at a sculpted white pig (a present from a grateful guest) which lives in a white-scented wisteria. Other occupants include a davidia tree, a halesia, covered in tiny white blooms, and a katsura tree with its characteristic fragrance of burnt sugar. Beside the house a rockery, full of David's beloved grasses and neighbouring borders of pinks and blues and, in spring, a mulberry tree standing on a carpet of fritillaries. In borders there are yellow shrubs planted with blues, apricots and yellows which lead round to a really hot border of oranges and reds. Interesting planting which looks good all year.

MONTYS COURT

Major & Mrs A C W Mitford-Slade
Montys Court,
Norton Fitzwarren, Taunton, Somerset TA4 1BT

tel 01823 432255
fax 01823 433623
e-mail tonymitfordslade@montyscourt.freeserve.co.uk

A mansion in the grand manner, its history evident throughout
the house. The dining room's great windows look out over the
rose garden and ancestral portraits gaze down from the walls.
The big, light, double drawing room has tall windows, family
photographs and a baby grand piano. There are always lovely
flowers in the large entrance hall, and here the main feature is
the magnificent staircase – a hint of Manderley? There are views
of roses from every bedroom, pictures vary from military to
landscape, and the double bedroom has an unusual beamed
barrel ceiling.

rooms	3: 1 double with bath/shower; 2 twins with private bath & shower.
price	£60. Single occ. £35.
meals	Dinner £15, October-March.
closed	Christmas.
directions	M5 exit 25, A358 towards Minehead. B3227 at Cross Keys Roundabout through Norton Fitzwarran. House 1 mile further on left.

The stately mature trees give an indication of the atmosphere and origins of Montys Court (the name derived from a Saxon word 'muntior', meaning a house in a glade). The lovely house was built by one of Tony's forebears in 1838 after a successful military campaign, and the collection of specimen trees was planted at the same time to create a park-like environment. With far-reaching views over to the Quantock and Blackdown Hills, the garden looks its best in spring and in summer. Standard roses welcome you up the drive – but Montys Court's main glory is its elaborate formal rose garden, consisting of 16 beds laid out in the Victorian era in the shape of a Maltese cross around a sundial. It's a splendid sight not only in summer but also in spring when the 1,600 underplanted tulips give a massed display. Two tennis courts and a swimming pool are tucked in a secluded area sheltered by shrubs and roses, and a patio under a magnificent oak tree provides a pleasant sitting area with views over the garden and park. This is also an ideal stage for open-air performances: plays are performed here in aid of charity, the ample lawns accommodating audiences of over 200 quite comfortably. Winter walking is excellent on the Exmoor and the Quantock Hills. *NGS*

GATCHELLS

Mandy Selhurst
Gatchells,
Angersleigh, Taunton, Somerset TA3 7SY

tel   01823 421580
e-mail info@gatchells.org.uk
web   www.gatchells.org.uk

Built in 1420 and later lived in by Thomas Gatchell, this is one
of the oldest houses in the area. The rooms are immaculate and
dramatic. A huge inglenook fireplace with a vast beam houses
a woodburning stove and dominates the guest sitting room.
Breakfast is served in the large kitchen or in the sunny
conservatory overlooking a swimming pool where you can enjoy
a summer splash. Sloping ceilings, soaring beams and pale walls
in the bedrooms, and, if you have the main bedroom, don't miss
the rings on the beams etched in the 17th century – they ward
off evil spirits, so you should sleep soundly.

rooms	3: 1 double/family, 1 twin/double, both with bath & shower; 1 double with private bathroom.
price	£46–£60. Single occ. £35–£40. Family occ. £70.
meals	Dinner £14–£16.
closed	Occasionally.
directions	From Trull, just south of Taunton, right for Angersleigh into Dipford Road. Follow for 2 miles. House signed on right. Take country track to cottage at end.

Trundle down the long farm track past rich fields and, at the final twist of the drive, a secluded, sturdy thatched home comes into view, wrapped in the leaf and colour of the beautifully tended cottage garden. It has panoramic views across fields and hills, and was already in good shape when Mandy and Mike arrived in 1991; they have only made minor changes, enhancing the basic layout they inherited. The one-acre garden has strong bones with low stone walls, rockery beds, a paved terrace with *Alchemilla mollis* peeping through the cracks, a meticulously cared-for, near-formal vegetable and fruit garden and a dappled orchard which has recently been re-planted. 'Albertine' roses bring subtle scent and colour to the front of the house and Mandy adores traditional favourites including iris, showy oriental poppies, fine old roses and, a speciality of hers, stately lupins, all of which she weaves into colourful displays. But she also takes a keen interest in finding new and unusual plants, and there's nothing she enjoys more than chatting about gardens with visitors. One of her recent projects is the turfed spring garden in the little spinney opposite the front of the house.

Mike & Christabel Cumberlege
Carpenters,
Norton-sub-Hamdon, Somerset TA14 6SN

tel 01935 881255
fax 01935 881255
e-mail mikecumbo@hotmail.com
web www.carpentersbb.co.uk

Down a sleepy lane in a hamstone village lies a house heavy
with local history. A purple wisteria embraces the front door
of Carpenters which dates from the 1700s and, until the 1930s,
was a carpenter's home; the sunny sitting room where guests
are welcomed was the workshop. Christabel places posies from
the garden in every room and, in the hall on the day we visited,
deliciously scented daphne cuttings. The house, with soft-coloured
walls and carpets, is immaculately cared for with pretty
wallpapers in bright bedrooms. Traditional breakfasts with
local produce are served in the large kitchen, once used by
the village baker.

rooms	3: 1 twin, 1 single, 1 child's room, sharing bathroom.
price	£20–£55. Single occ. by arrangement.
meals	Dinner £20. Packed lunch available. BYO red; Carpenters white on the house.
closed	24 December–2 January.
directions	From A303, A356 for Crewkerne. Ignore turn to Stoke-sub-Hamdon; on for 1 mile to x-roads. Left into Norton-sub H, 1st right into Higher St. Up to bend, straight through gate by small greenhouse.

Christabel once worked at the plant centre at nearby Montacute House and took a City & Guilds gardening course at Cannington. She and lawnsman/pruner Mike are an excellent team. When they came to Carpenters 14 years ago they inherited a highly-managed, sloping garden enclosed by local hamstone walls with views to Ham and the Chiselborough hills. Over the years they have added unusual trees and shrubs to create height and structure; the catalpa they planted at the start is now large enough to sit under on a summer's evening – a perfect place to enjoy a glass of Mike's delicious home-made wine. (His half-acre vineyard lies just beyond the garden.) Formally shaped borders have been planted in a loose, informal manner with hardy geraniums, shrub roses and as many violas and other favourites as Christabel can pack in, while striking architectural plants, like acanthus and phormiums, tower above.
A climbing frame is festooned with 'Sander's White Rambler', clematis and honeysuckle. Mike keeps the lawns in pristine condition, prunes trees and shrubs and has carved a straggling yew hedge into dramatic, sentinel-like shapes beyond the double borders. From the first spring flowers to the late autumn blaze of acer, this garden holds your interest. The sole exception to Mike and Christabel's strict organic rule is the occasional anti-slug defence of their vegetable garden. *RHS, HPS.*

BROOKE HOUSE

Jane & Iain Galloway
Brooke House,
Thorne Coffin, Yeovil, Somerset BA21 3PZ

tel   01935 433396
e-mail jane@logspt.demon.co.uk

Brooke House was built in 1690 of local hamstone, one of four farms in this conservation hamlet. With mullioned windows, it's furnished traditionally and comfortably: a big open fire in the drawing room is lit on cooler days, and some of the pictures are watercolours painted by talented friends. The large south-facing double bedroom is decorated in peach and blue with views over the rose garden, while the rose and green twin overlooks the sunken garden. Both rooms have attractive American-style patchwork quilted bedspreads.

rooms	2: 1 double with shower; 1 twin with private bath.
price	£62. Single occ. £72.
meals	Dinner £17-£20.
closed	Christmas & New Year.
directions	From A303, A37 to Yeovil, up hill to big r'bout, follow signs to Thorne. Right at r'bout, straight across at next 2 x-roads. 1st right to village; house 1st on right.

Brooke House was only a field when the Galloways moved here in 1988, but they saw the potential, and immediately tackled the brambles and nettles, starting near the house and clearing and planting outwards. They've been here long enough now to be developing and altering some of their original creations: in 2001 they changed their sunken parterre into a paved area with a central pond. In spring the perimeter is a dramatic mass of black, burgundy and white tulips; as summer wears on the colours soften with the advent of peonies, perovskia and artemisia and arum lilies. A large rose garden is spread across the slope up from the house, with 70 old-fashioned and repeat flowering roses underplanted with hardy geraniums and penstemons: the effect is a sea of fresh pinks, blues and whites through the summer. The wild garden above is a carpet of cowslips, bluebells and camassias in springtime. Wisteria and ceanothus are trained over the front of the house, but there are quirkier touches too: Jane's eye lit recently on shrubs flanking a *Garrya elliptica*, she took up her shears, and behold – two topiary snails with box bodies and antennae and lonicera shells. Infinitely preferable to the real thing.

KING INA'S PALACE

Mrs Shirley Brown
King Ina's Palace,
Silver Street, South Petherton, Somerset TA13 5BY

tel   01460 240603

Shirley and Trevor have done an amazing restoration job on their garden. When they arrived twelve years ago there was much out-of-control yew; now clipped hedges and twelve topiary goblet shapes give a superb framework for Shirley's talented and artistic plantsmanship. Her passion for plants, originally inspired by her father, is evident, and she loves colour co-ordinating borders; blue flowers are her favourite. Hence the recent gold/yellow/blue bed of anchusa, corydalis, iris and tradescantia mixed with golden elder, the unusual yellow magnolia 'Butterflies', yellow cotinus, and yellow and gold heuchera. A blue and white garden features a wedding cake tree (*Cornus controversa variegata*), and, from an old sundial, a yew arch frames the entire length of the garden. A 30-foot rose arbour smothered in 'Paul's Himalayan Musk', 'Veilchenblau' and 'Cecile Brunner' leads to a pond, destined to become a shady bog garden with candelabra primulas, hardy orchids, ferns and rodgersia. This immaculate garden opens to the public and to horticultural societies several times a year, finally opening in September for the massed display of cyclamen. *NGS.*

rooms	1 twin with shower.
price	£58. Single occ. £40.
meals	Good pubs nearby.
closed	Christmas.
directions	A303 roundabout at eastern end of Illminster bypass, follow signs to South Petherton Village. Through village; right to 'East Lambrook'. House down hill on left.

In case you're wondering, Ina was a Saxon king of Wessex, but this heavenly house, Grade II*-listed, wasn't started until the late 14th century. It was given its romantic name in the 16th century, and underwent major renovation in Victorian times. The medieval banqueting hall, with Victorian carved fireplace, is now the sitting room. Tall windows and a medieval fireplace in the dining room; a half-panelled oak staircase leads to the bedrooms, which are fittingly furnished with Victorian-style pieces. Shirley and Trevor are warm hosts, and justifiably proud of their loving restoration.

BEER FARM

Philip & Susan Morlock
Beer Farm,
Bere Aller, Nr Langport, Somerset TA10 0QX

tel   01458 250285
fax   01458 250285
e-mail philipmorlock@aol.com

You know you've arrived when you turn into the definitely 'ex-farmyard': no tractors or chickens, but pot plants, creepers and rose-smothered barns. Step inside the Grade II-listed farmhouse and gaze right through the hall to the French window opposite and the lovely terrace, full of colour in summer; sit out and take tea, or enjoy breakfast on a fine morning. The bedrooms are chintzy and pretty; the sunny, low-ceilinged twin is rose-pink and cream, with a garden view; the yellow and blue double overlooks the courtyard. Candlelit meals are wonderfully atmospheric, as befits this romantic place.

rooms	2: 1 double, 1 twin, both with private bathroom.
price	£64.
meals	Dinner £18.
closed	Christmas & New Year.
directions	North from Langport, A372 through Aller & after 1 mile right at left-hand bend for Beer. Ignore Bere Farm on right; 1st left at stone barn to Beer Farm. Approx. 4 miles from Langport.

The ancient, wild woodlands of Beer and Aller hang down the edge of their escarpment forming a stately backdrop to Beer Farm below. The house sits with its back to the ridge, looking out over Sedgemoor to the Quantock and Blackdown hills beyond. This is no longer a working farm, so Sue has seized the opportunity to cover every available wall with a profusion of climbing plants. Honeysuckle, vines, solanum and roses smother barns; wisteria and a banksia rose weave up the south elevation; more roses tumble over the old potting shed, and the rambling rose 'Seagull' looks like blossom in an old pear tree. Sue and Philip have created the garden since they moved here in 1993. Sue's favourite soft pinks, mauves and blues in peonies, campanulas and hardy geraniums give a cottage-garden feel to the south side of the house; gradually the garden has expanded and crept around to the west side, where there's now a wildlife pond and a hornbeam-enclosed potager (a fecund source of fruit and vegetables for the table). Sit still for long enough and you too will blend into the rural landscape – just like the garden.

PENNARD HILL FARM

Phoebe Judah
Pennard Hill Farm,
Stickleball Hill, East Pennard, Shepton Mallet, Somerset BA4 6UG

tel   01749 890221
fax   01749 890665
e-mail phebejudah@aol.com
web   www.pennardhillfarm.co.uk

The estate is perched on a hilltop so the views are magnificent:
the Mendip hills to the north and Glastonbury Tor and the Vale
of Avalon to the west. Utterly tranquil and private, the estate has
been meticulously renovated: the Main House, the Victorian Barn
and two lovely cottages are luxurious and individually designed
with a keen eye for detail and a flair for the unusual. All have
their own drawing rooms and kitchen/dining rooms, the barn
has an indoor swimming pool with a vast Gothic window. All
is private and there is no invasion of noise. Perfect. *Children
welcome in cottage only.*

rooms	10: House: 1 double, 3 single. Barn: 1 double. Cottages: 3 double, 1 single, 1 double.
price	£100-£200.
meals	Lunch from £17.50. Dinner from £25.
closed	Rarely.
directions	From Wells, A39 to Glastonbury. Left at North Wootton sign. Follow signs for West Pennard. At T-junc. right onto A361. After 400 yds, 1st left. Through tunnel of trees, drive on left.

Over the last fifteen years Phoebe has created a gloriously open, natural garden around her stunning house on a Somerset hillside. The main garden is about an acre but it spills over into several more acres of home paddocks beyond. All the planting – the hundreds of trees and miles of hedge – is native: the ash, oak, beech and lime of ancient parkland. There's a pond too, attractive to many birds, first recorded before Domesday; the farm is on the ancient pilgrim route from Ditcheat to Glastonbury. The natural and native theme continues in the gardens around the house: Phoebe doesn't like fussy borders but encourages masses of foliage and skilfully plants potted lilies among perennial herbaceous plants to give added colour. The cobbled courtyard is edged with free-growing euphorbias, Jerusalem sage, jasmine and mimosa with a glorious collection of plants in large pots juggled around delightfully to ring the changes. Closed on three sides by the house and two barns, the courtyard is watched over by nine classical sculptured heads and has wonderful views of the surrounding land. The cottages have gardens of their own, just re-landscaped using most unusual plant and shrub combinations and with round views. In the summer swallows and house martins swoop in their hundreds, wild duck babble on the pond which is planted round with more native species; bullrushes, flag irises and water lilies. A blissful place and a garden which makes the most of its greatest asset – those views.

PENNARD HOUSE

Martin & Susie Dearden
Pennard House,
East Pennard, Shepton Mallet, Somerset BA4 6TP

tel   01749 860266
fax   01749 860266
e-mail susie.d@ukonline.co.uk

One of the grandest houses in this book, Pennard has been in
Susie's family since the 17th century – the cellars date from then.
The superstructure is stately, lofty Georgian, but the Deardens are
delightfully unstuffy and welcoming. Guests have the run of the
library, formal drawing room, billiard room and six acres of garden
with a freshwater Victorian swimming pool. Or walk in 300 acres
of cider orchards, meadows and woods. Martin runs his antique
business from the house; Susie was born and brought up here and
is familiar with all there is to do and see in the area. It is warm
and civilised here with plain, properly unhotelly bedrooms.

rooms	4: 1 double, 1 twin, both with shower/bath; 1 twin/double, 1 single, both with private bathroom.
price	From £60. Single £30. Single occ. by arrangement.
meals	Available locally.
closed	Christmas.
directions	From Shepton Mallet south on A37, through Pylle; next right to East Pennard. Pass church to T-junc. at very top. House on left.

Sweeping lawns, mature trees, a 14th-century church below, a south-facing suntrap terrace, a formal rose garden, pools and curious topiary... Pennard House is one of those dreamy landscape gardens straight from the pages of P G Wodehouse. All seems serene, free and easy – and on a grand scale – yet a huge amount of time and hard work has gone into developing and restoring the grounds of Susie's family's house. Shady laurels and yews were the dominant feature until the couple launched a clearance and restoration campaign after taking advice from expert friends. Pennard House has, in fact, two gardens within a garden, divided by a little lane. There are the open, sunny lawns of the house garden and, across the road, a second garden with clipped hedges, a formal rose garden and an inviting spring-fed Victorian swimming pool which in turn feeds a series of ponds below. Don't miss the wacky topiary cottage, rabbit and other creatures which the gardener has created over the years. Susie always has some new project afoot – a recent success was ripping out cotoneaster below the terrace and replacing it with a pretty, formally-planted combination of rosemary, roses and lavender. Drag chairs onto the lawn and curl up with a book, swim in the crystal clear water of the pool, or simply stroll among the colour, the scents and the blooms.

GANTS MILL AND GARDEN

Alison & Brian Shingler
Gants Mill and Garden,
Bruton, Somerset BA10 0DB

tel   01749 812393
e-mail shingler@gantsmill.co.uk
web   www.gantsmill.co.uk

In Victorian times the resident miller brought up his family of 13 children here - the place had to be extended for the task. Brian has a fine photograph of the bearded patriarch and brood. Today you can breakfast at their original table or, on sunnier days, enjoy the wisteria-clad conservatory with the present-day family's pet dogs and cats. Bedrooms are large and comfortable, with brass bedheads and dark wood furniture, flower prints and displays of old plates. Do ask Brian for a tour of the adjoining watermill where he grinds grain for his sheep and keeps a small museum.

rooms	3: 1 family with shower; 1 double, 1 single both with private bathroom.
price	£50.
meals	Available locally.
closed	21 December-2 January.
directions	Signed off A359, 0.5 miles south-west of Bruton.

An exciting young garden packed with detail and much photographed for magazine articles and television programmes – a star! This is an intricately planted 30mx60m area created over the past seven years and now open to admiring NGS visitors. The complex plan was drawn by a professional and Alison and Brian successfully turned drawings into reality in this new garden bounded by farmhouse, little river and fields. Successions of small seating areas are linked by walks with different aspects, visual surprises and the sound of running water from the stream that Brian made with old stones found on the farm. It rises in a swirl pool and gurgles under bridges, over miniature waterfalls and through a lily pond and bog garden where water-lovers like *Primula candelabra* flourish. Alison loves traditional plant favourites like iris, her 25 varieties of delphinium, rose, clematis, penstemon and 80 varieties of dahlia which she lifts and stores each winter in the adjoining mill. Arches glow with climbing roses and there are eye-catching details such as a horseshoe of 'Iceberg' roses. Colour is themed subtly with red/yellow/blue/white, pink/mauve/purple and blue/gold. This is a garden where you can admire colour and detail on any day, from the early flush of iris to autumn's golden leaf displays. *NGS.*

BERYL

Eddie & Holly Nowell
Beryl,
Wells, Somerset BA5 3JP

tel   01749 678738
fax   01749 670508
e-mail stay@beryl-wells.co.uk
web   www.beryl-wells.co.uk

A lofty, mullioned, low-windowed home - light and bright, devoid of Victorian gloom. The Nowells have filled it with a fine collection of antiques and every bedroom has a talking point... a four-poster here, a time-worn baby's cot there. The flowery top-floor rooms in the attic have a 'Gothic revival' feel with arched doorways; one first-floor room has a stunning old bath, sumptuously clad in mahogany and with its very own tiny staircase. Candelit dinners carefully prepared by Holly, breakfasts in the sunny dining room, tea in the richly elegant drawing room. All this and the wonders of Wells just below.

rooms	8: 2 four-posters, 3 doubles, 3 twins, all with bath/shower.
price	£70-£105. Single occ. £55-£75.
meals	Dinner £22.50.
closed	Christmas.
directions	Leave Wells on Radstock road B3139, follow sign 'H' for hospital & The Horringtons. Left into Hawkers Lane opp. garage. Follow lane to top & sign Beryl.

Holly says 'Beryl' means a meeting of hills; Eddie has his own description: "a precious gem in a perfect setting". Beryl is a small, early-Victorian mansion with south-facing grounds gazing down to dreamy Wells Cathedral. Eddie, one of the city's most colourful characters, runs an antique shop at Beryl and, in season, wears a buttonhole of his favourite rambling rose, 'American Pillar'. He is a devoted gardener who has put in countless hours to restore the grounds from an overgrown shambles to their original Victorian splendour. A broad terrace leads to open lawns, a formal staircase and a wildlife pool, while avenues draw the eye towards the views. The striking steel armillary sphere is a memorial to their son Julius, who loved this large garden. Beyond lies well-tended woodland – Eddie has planted more than 4,000 trees and strewn wild daffodils among them – and Beryl's most ravishing feature, the very large walled garden. There are garden rooms and deep, generously planted borders intersected by paths edged by catmint and low box hedges. A cutting bed provides a rich supply of flowers for the house and the vegetable beds will furnish your plate. Eddie collects hollies as a tribute to his wife's name and he celebrated her 50th birthday by planting 50 white hydrangeas. Victorian garden elegance, flowers in profusion, magical woodland walks… no wonder Beryl's charity open days are such a celebration.

MELTON HALL

Mrs Lucinda de la Rue
Melton Hall,
Woodbridge, Suffolk IP12 1PF

tel   01394 388138
fax   01394 388982

A beautifully proportioned house in seven-and-a-half acres of
gardens, meadows and woodland. Cindy is energetic, with enough
enthusiasm for her young family and her guests. Flagstoned hall,
a large oak table in a striking burgundy dining room and a fine
sitting room with French windows. The bedrooms are well
furnished and have maps, books, radio, fresh flowers and garden
views; one has a wrought-iron four-poster with beautiful
embroidered linen.

rooms	3: 1 double with bath: 1 double, 1 single sharing bathroom.
price	£62-£78. Single from £24.
meals	Dinner £16-£24. BYO wine. Lunch & packed lunch available.
closed	Rarely.
directions	From A12 Woodbridge bypass, exit at r'bout for Orford & Melton. On for 1 mile to lights; there, right & house immed. on right.

A curving drive past mature trees leads to rural peace in a town setting. Passers-by peep through the tall gates in spring to admire snowdrops, aconites and crocuses and later, thousands of daffodils. In summer, roses scramble up the porticoed façade of the de la Rue's elegant home set among lawns with an imposing flagpole, walled gardens and borders. A dozen box balls add a formal flourish to the sunny terrace. Within the Georgian walled area you'll find a formal paved rose garden with roses growing between flagstones. Walk through a rose-covered arch past a fruiting fig to the large kitchen garden with its immaculate little box hedges leading you along the paths. A complete change of mood comes at the far end of the main lawn, with a superb meadow on a gentle slope and woodland. This is a Country Wildlife Site with southern marsh orchids and a profusion of other wild flowers. More than 100 species have been recorded, from spring's meadow saxifrage and cuckoo flowers to summer's carpets of ladies' bedstraw and the purples and whites of knapweed and yarrow. A grass path follows the meadow's perimeter and goes through the adjoining woodland with two ponds. Bird-lovers will be in their element: spotted flycatchers, mistle thrush, song thrush, both great spotted and green woodpeckers. A garden that perfectly combines the formal and informal with the natural beauty of an all-too-rare plot of uncultivated, flower-filled grassland.

THE ISLAND HOUSE

Heather & Brian Massey
The Island House,
Lower Road, Lavenham, Suffolk CO10 9QJ

tel   01787 248181
e-mail islandhouse@dial.pipex.com
web www.lavenham.co.uk/islandhouse

A neat, attractive, award-winning modern house in a quiet
setting. Views of interesting Lavenham village with its half-
timbered houses to the front, and at the back, the garden and
open countryside. Bedrooms are compact, furnished with old pine
and pretty fabrics, and painted in cool, neutral colours. Beds have
good mattresses, white cotton sheets, and there are plenty of
cushions for sprawling. Bathrooms sparkle. A private sitting room
with games and books also has a veranda overlooking the garden.
Breakfast is a feast – as much fresh, local produce as possible and
home-made marmalades and jams. *Minimum two night stay.*

rooms	2: 1 double with bath, 1 twin with shower.
price	£60.
meals	Good food locally.
closed	Very occasionally.
directions	From Market Place to bottom of Prentice Street, right into Lower Road. House immed. on left.

Heather is a passionate plantswoman – as Secretary of The East Anglian Garden Group she knows her patch inside out and can arrange private visits to other gardens. Every plant – when it flowered, when it was pruned or divided – is recorded on a database and used to increase knowledge. This is not a huge garden – just under an acre – but Heather and Brian understand form and shape so have created a little mystery to delight and inspire. There is a woodland walk along the old mill race round the back of the garden, hedged on both sides and filled with many shade-loving woodland plants. A damp area is the perfect ground for moisture-loving perennials like ligularias, hostas, *Peltiphyllum peltatum* and glorious primulas and irises. Several large beds display interesting herbaceous plants – nearly all grown here – and some areas are for spring plants only: pulmonarias, dicentra, hellebores and fritillaries. There's a rose walk in delicate shades of yellow and a wild garden where the grass is only cut twice a year allowing hundreds of bluebells to flourish. The vegetable and soft fruit garden (Brian's domain) is pristine, neatly laid out in four-foot-wide formal beds. In summer there are displays of hostas, lilies, lamium and hydrangea, the newly planted culinary herb garden dazzles on a south facing slope and all those roses scent the air. The River Brett runs right through the garden and its natural banks encourage wildlife. *NGS, RHS, East Anglian Garden Group.*

THE HATCH

Bridget & Robin Oaten
The Hatch,
Pilgrims Lane, Cross Green, Hartest, Suffolk IP29 4ED

tel   01284 830226
fax   01284 830226
e-mail theoaten@tiscali.co.uk

Immaculate – gleaming antique furniture, fine fabrics, fresh
flowers and sherry on the oak dresser (17th century, no less).
The house is 15th century, timber-framed and thatched and one
bedroom has its own sitting room with books and an open fire.
Home-laid eggs for breakfast, local bacon and home-made bread.
A measure of the Oatens' generosity, the bedrooms have goose
down duvets, fresh fruit and Penhaligon's smellies, along with co-
ordinated furnishings and comfortable pocket-sprung beds.
Delightful people who really enjoy having guests. *The Oatens
might be moving house! Within the village and with the same
telephone number.*

rooms	2: 1 twin/double with bath & shower; 1 double with small sitting-room & bathroom.
price	£65-£70. Single occ. £40.
meals	Excellent local pubs & restaurants.
closed	Occasionally.
directions	From Bury St Edmunds, A413 for Haverhill; B1066 for Glemsford for 6 miles to Hartest. After 30mph signs, on for approx. 0.25 miles, lane on left (signed Cross Green) on sharp double bend.

The Hatch is a deeply pretty thatched house that makes the perfect backdrop to its half-acre garden. The Oatens have a happy knack; everything they grow in the garden looks glorious and pretty as a picture – especially in summer when all the roses are out. The box-hedged bed that guards the drive is planted with a jolly mixture of old-fashioned and new English roses. The underplanting of chionodoxa in the spring is succeeded by violets, and later by 'Pink Panther' ornamental strawberries so there is always something new popping up. A second bed of roses – all yellow – is edged with perennial geraniums, and the climber 'Graham Thomas' scrambles over a trellis behind. The ground-floor room has its own south-facing patio with blossoming fruit trees in the spring: most of the trees in the garden have roses or clematis climbing up through them, from 'Rambling Rector' to the repeat-flowering 'Gardinia' – the scent is intoxicating. The mixed herbaceous planting around the house, and the new 'red hot' bed, extend the season of colour from spring through to autumn. From seats on the raised terrace look out over rolling High Suffolk grazing land and the village to Hartest Hill, or take yourself off to the Oatens' meadow over the road.

GARDEN HOUSE FARM

Hans & Elizabeth Seiffer
Garden House Farm,
Rattlesden Road, Drinkstone, Bury St Edmunds, Suffolk IP30 9TN

tel   01449 736434
fax   01449 736560
e-mail gardenhousefarm@dial.pipex.com

The original 16th-century house has been sympathetically
extended using reclaimed bricks - a successful blend of historic-
picturesque and modern. Lovely large rooms, a long oak-beamed
sitting room with a log-burning stove for chilly days and a
gleaming breakfast/dining table at one end. Downstairs, a bright,
stone-flagged hall; upstairs, pale carpets and walls and white bed
linen and towels give the bedrooms a luxuriously light and airy
feel; one has a beamed ceiling, the other a 'loo with a view' over
the lake. Flowers from the cutting garden, and home-produced
eggs and honey for breakfast are further treats.

rooms	2: 1 double with bath; 1 double with shower.
price	£70.
meals	Available locally.
closed	Very occasionally.
directions	A14 exit 47 for A1088 to Woolpit; right at Skoda garage; left at village centre; right at Bear pub. At T-junc. right; left at Drinkstone Green. Left into Rattlesden Road; 2nd lane on left.

What luck that this house, surrounded by the former display gardens of Barcocks Nursery, should have been bought by the Seiffers. Elizabeth is a keen and knowledgeable plantswoman, and has seized every opportunity to use the interesting plants and trees she found here to form the basis for extending her 11 acres. Hedges divide the garden into sections representing the seasons. The well-established spring woodland garden is a showcase for magnolias and camellias strewn about with bulbs, while in early summer the old-fashioned rose garden comes into its own, its beauty enhanced with campanulas and aquilegias – a carefully colour-themed garden rather than a fully rambling cottage garden. The hot garden is at its best in high summer, when the tropical foliage of the bananas and tender cannas, along with the billowing grasses, provide a luxuriant backdrop to vivid, late-summer dahlias. A newer, more formal area, with stone paths and a central pond, is named the Gold Garden after its planting: it glows even in dull weather. Colour and interest are sustained in the winter garden with its witch hazels, birch barks, *Prunus serrula*, rainbow stems of cornus and willows, heathers and grasses. The whole place is a honeypot for the plantaholic. *NGS, Good Gardens Guide.*

BRAMBLES

Genny & Tony Jakobson
Brambles,
Worlington, Bury St Edmunds, Suffolk 1P28 8RY

tel   01638 713121
fax   01638 713121
e-mail genny@trjakobson.freenetname.co.uk

A striking 1920s house that could soon look different. The Jakobsons are considering painting the half-timbering a soft blue-green and the plasterwork cream - a fantastic backdrop for their three-acre garden. Pale colours inside enhance an already bright and airy house; Genny's decorative style is feminine, fresh and unfussy. In the hall a large mirror reflects the light, and she fills the house with flowers. Tony is a racing journalist and can take you to the Newmarket gallops if you're up for an early start. In any event, you've picked a winner if you stay here!

rooms	3: 1 double with bath & shower; 1 double with shower; 1 twin with private bath & shower.
price	£68. Single occ. £44.
meals	Good pub in village.
closed	Christmas & New Year.
directions	From A11 for Thetford/Norwich, B1085 to Red Lodge & Worlington. Right at T-junc. through village; house 200 yds on right.

Some gardeners design gardens in rooms, and some prefer to remain unrestrained. Genny falls into the latter category – she loves space. And space she has: the lawn sweeps down to a stream, framed by copses of trees to right and left. The garden at Brambles had already been landscaped when the Jakobsons moved in ten years ago, and Genny has worked along similar lines since, adding her own touches gradually. To give height to the rose garden she and Tony introduced a four-pillared gazebo, clothed it in summer jasmine and clematis, and underplanted it with delphiniums to add depth of colour. The dark hedge of yew round the rose garden makes the perfect backdrop to three colourful herbaceous beds. In the sunken garden, with its lily pond, Genny allows verbena, evening primroses and pale Californian poppies to self-seed in the gravel. Her relaxed touch has also allowed the drive to reinvent itself as a gravel garden: pretty cross-bred poppies, campanulas and sisyrinchium seed themselves here and there from surrounding borders. Snowdrops, aconites and hellebores carpet the one-acre dell garden, so even early in the season you can expect a floral welcome.

THE ELMS

Richard & Teena Freeland
The Elms,
Toft Monks, Beccles, Suffolk NR34 0EJ

tel   01502 677380
fax   01502 677362
e-mail richardfreeland@btconnect.com

Flemish flax weavers used to wash the flax in the moat and dry
it in the magnificent barn. Grade II*-listed, red-brick and mellow,
the house has a grand scale: soaring ceilings, handsome
fireplaces, huge sash windows, cast-iron baths, good, large beds.
It's full of light, and parquet floors; chandeliers, balustrades and
frescos add grandeur. Guests have their own sitting room.
Evenings here are heavenly - a drink on the terrace, dinner,
then a wander through the garden or even a game of tennis.

rooms	2: 1 double with private bath; 1 twin with bath.
price	£80. Single occ. £50.
meals	Dinner from £27.50.
closed	Occasionally.
directions	A143 Yarmouth & Beccles road. In Toft Monks take Post Office Rd (opp. Toft Lion pub) for 0.4 miles to T-junc. Right down Aldeby Rd for 0.1 mile, fork right & house on right, 0.2 miles on.

Drive down the sleepy lane through waving crop fields to find this secluded garden redeveloped over the past 20 years. The house has been in the family for 150 years; once there were three full-time gardeners, today Teena and Richard manage with the help of one part-timer. The bones of the grounds are glorious: fine walls, a backdrop of lofty, mature trees, views to Suffolk farmland, a moat where water lilies prosper, a large pond overhung with flowering shrubs. And Teena has embellished with great style; planting, weaving a tapestry of new features and always keeping labour-saving in mind. Where once there were time-consuming displays of annuals there are now shrubs and perennials. Hyacinths and daffodils bloom in happy profusion by the moat in spring-time, and the little copse is a mass of snowdrops. In summer the arched rose walk neatly underplanted with box balls comes into its own; Teena loves topiary. Relax on the lavender-scented patio with an evening drink, gaze down from the little bridge over the moat and watch the fish play, and walk among the many specimen trees Richard has planted in the dappled grassy area between lane and moat. Throughout, the Freelands have introduced the colours of maturing shrubs, trees and winding borders in golds, coppers and every shade of green.

HEASLEIGH

Derek & Dawn St Romaine
Heasleigh,
239 Hook Road, Chessington, KT9 1EQ, Surrey

tel   020 8397 4187
fax   020 8397 4187
e-mail   dawn@gardenphotolibrary.com
web   www.gardenphotolibrary.com

Privacy and independence here with your own keys to the separate ground floor entrance. At the rear of the house both bedrooms have sitting areas and doors into the garden: the double room has original parquet flooring, fresh *toile de Jouy* fabrics, soft blue colour-washed furniture and an old conservatory where visitors love to relax. The twin in calming pale green and cream has bamboo print duvets and cane furniture, and a chic black and white shower room. An ex-airline stewardess, Dawn makes you feel really welcome, and serves a delicious breakfast in your dining room using fresh herbs and edible flowers.

rooms	2: 1 double with shower; 1 twin with shower.
price	From £70. Single occ. from £45.
meals	Good local restaurants and pubs.
closed	Very occasionally.
directions	M25 junc. 9, A243 to junc. with A3 (Hook r'bout). Drive completely round r'bout & back up A243. Heasleigh approx. 300yds on left; pelican crossing outside.

To stay here is a real treat, particularly for anyone artistic or interested in plants or garden design. As a leading horticultural photographer, Derek has an artist's eye for colours and colour combinations, a passion for different types of greens and textures of foliage, and a disciplined sense of form and structure. Half the garden's design is based on circles: a round gravel garden planted with grasses, herbaceous borders around a circular lawn mown in concentric circles and formally edged with standard variegated hollies and low box balls, and a round pond edged with large-leafed plants. The potager through the yew hedge is a study in intensive planting. Within an 80'x45' area there are 30 fruit trees (bush, fan, espallier and cordon), an octagonal arbour of eight laburnums, rose swags that become pumpkin swags in autumn, living willow wigwams, and up to 60 different vegetables and herbs, most grown from seed each year. The garden is Derek's outdoor studio: using it as a set design for his photographic work, he enjoys trying out the rare, strange or unusual, and experiments with carefully colour co-ordinated combinations in the different borders. Alive with variety and extremely labour-intensive, Derek and Dawn's garden is a triumphant accolade to their dedication and imagination. *NGS, Good Gardens Guide, Garden Writers Guild, NCCPG.*

THE OLD BOTHY

Mr & Mrs Tom Heesom
The Old Bothy,
Collendean Lane, Norwood Hill, Nr Horley, Surrey RH6 0HP

tel   01293 862622
fax   01293 863185
e-mail willo@heesom.fsnet.co.uk

An ultra-modern house in a fabulous setting with far-reaching
views across fields to the North Downs and interesting, much
travelled people. Willo is a potter – her studio is in the garden –
and there are collections of art and sculpture from all over the
world in the huge upstairs drawing room. The guest bedroom
is downstairs, chic and compact; pale blue walls with uplighting,
an Art Deco bedhead painted with moon and stars, slender angle-
poise lamps, a natty smoked glass wall and curtains of maroon
shot silk. The bathroom has a basin like a white salad bowl
on a black granite stand and Italian hand-made tiles in
mottled aquamarine.

rooms	1 double with bath.
price	£70. Single occ. £50.
meals	Available locally.
closed	Christmas, New Year & occasionally.
directions	From M23, junction 9 follow A23. At The Longbridge r'bout A217 towards Reigate, fork left for Norwood Hill. After 1 mile left into Collendean Lane; house on right after 0.75 miles.

A foliage fiesta! Green rather than flowery and fascinting for plantsmen, the garden was designed by Anthony Paul who lives locally and is renowned for his fondness for big-leafed plants and the creation of a Mediterranean look. Tom is as keen as Willo (a love inherited from his great aunt who had a nursery) and has labelled everything. As you turn into the drive there are great stands of interesting shrubs and mature trees underplanted with shrub roses and carex and it is lined with black walnut, amelanchier and *Viburnum Rhytidophyllum*. By the house there's a dry bed with a wisteria, and a *Sophora microphylla* leans close to the guest bedroom window. The house is well climbed over by a Canadian concord vine, a *Magnolia grandiflora* and a jasmine – and around the side is the shady garden. Here, ground cover plants include euphorbias, *Asarum europaeum*, *Ophiopogon japonica*, many ferns and tightly packed Japanese anemones. A little path leads to a white bench with a sculptured back in the shape of a reclining, bikini-clad lady – she and the rest of the shady area are low lit at night so that they glow orange. As you emerge through to the back of the garden there are staggering views, a lawn with a night-lit weeping willow underplanted with snowdrops and aconites, and a colourfully clashing corner of mixed perennials. The decking is of diagonal wood planks and there's a shady clump of prolific fig trees beside a pebble garden which sports a Jane Norbury sculptured head. *RHS*

HAZELS

Mrs Susie Floud
Hazels,
Walliswood, Nr Ockley, Surrey RH5 5PL

tel 01306 627228
e-mail susie.floud@ukgateway.net

A deeply posh crunch up a gravelled drive to your own cottagey annexe of this Arts and Crafts style house. Walk straight in to a cosy criss-cross beamed sitting-room with white walls and patterned rug; plump chairs and sofa-bed for extra people, crammed book shelves, solid furniture and a little table in the window. Steep stairs to a pale terracotta bedroom with two easy chairs, floral curtains, tiny sparkling bathroom and a sloping ceiling - not for giants. Enjoy being outside too: this is the leafiest and remotest bit of the county - the South Downs Way can be reached on foot and the Surrey cycle path is a mile away.

rooms	1 double with shower.
price	£55. Single occ. £35.
meals	Packed lunch £5. Good pubs nearby.
closed	Rarely.
directions	From M25 junc. 9, A24 south. Turn onto A29 to Ockley. Right on B2126 to Forest Green. Left fork at Parrot Inn. House 1.5 miles on left with 5-bar gate.

Jekyll style informality and fun. Tumbling from arches, little walls, beds, pergolas and pots are hundreds of old roses – not a hybrid tea in sight – mixed tightly with geraniums, clematis and hot coloured shizostylis. Everything grows strong and tall in these two and a half acres; lawns, border for deepest reds and purples, white border, wildflower meadow with rare orchids, specimen rhododendrons – the result of 24 years of expert planting with not an inch of bare soil anywhere – all connected by the most attractive original paths in herringbone brick design. Huge, mature trees guard the garden and house: gum and silver birch, a handkerchief tree, a tulip tree and many beeches oaks and maples. Susie has brought cuttings of roses and maples back from her native Australia and they are flourishing here under her expert care. There are hidden areas here too – with seats for resting and thinking, a new pond, a rhododendron lawn and a secret garden – all interlaced with many more species of old roses and clematis. The greenhouse groans with cuttings, some of which you can buy – but only if there is no space for it here! Thousands of bulbs bedazzle in spring – this is packed planting at its very best. *Garden open once a year for local charities.*

EASTON HOUSE

Mary Hartley
Easton House,
Chidham Lane, Chidham, Chichester, Sussex PO18 8TF

tel   01243 572514
fax   01243 573084
e-mail eastonhouse@chidham-fsnet.co.uk

Lots of beams, charming bedrooms, a cosily cluttered drawing room with a Bechstein piano and comfortable armchairs... this is a haven for musicians - and cat-lovers. It has the feel of a well-loved and lived-in family home; Mary has lived here for 30 years. The house looks out over Chidham harbour, is "five minutes walk from the water's edge" and is surrounded by great walking and bird-watching country. A lovely setting for a delightful house.

rooms	3: 1 twin, 1 double sharing bathroom; 1 double with private bathroom.
price	From £46.
meals	Excellent pub in village.
closed	Christmas.
directions	From Chichester for Portsmouth. Pass Tesco. Exit off r'bout to Bosham & Fishbourne. Follow A259 for 4 miles, pass Saab garage on right. Next left into Chidham Lane. Last on left, 1 mile down.

Mary's garden is as laid-back as its owner and her home. All is informal and cottagey and in perfect harmony with this old Sussex farmhouse on the Chidham peninsula. Half an acre set in farmland, it has evolved over the past 30 years. Its dominating feature, on the main lawn behind the house, is the catalpa tree which Mary planted 25 years ago and which now stretches its loose-limbed branches in a handsome umbrella of pale green leaves. Around the house, borders are piled high with shrubs and herbaceous plants, including blue agapanthus and stately acanthus, while climbers reach up the façade. Herringbone brick paths lead you past banks of roses and vigorous shrubs from one area to the next. In one corner there is a circular mini-garden edged with grass, shrubs, a surround of brick and stone and, above, the shady embrace of a walnut tree. Mary's latest project is an elaborate knot garden, with a pattern of curves made from low-cut box hedges. Her cats laze in the little grove of silver birch with its dappled shade, the sound of birdsong is everywhere and the sea breezes are soft. Perfect peace.

73 SHEEPDOWN DRIVE

Mrs Angela Azis
73 Sheepdown Drive,
Petworth, Sussex GU28 0BX

tel   01798 342269
fax   01798 342269

A short walk from the centre of the historic town of Petworth,
No. 73 lies in a quiet, 70s cul-de-sac and has glorious garden
views. Once chairman of the National Gardens Scheme, now a
vice-president, Angela has a background that will fascinate
anyone who loves gardens and, of course, she has a particular
insight into the gardens and nurseries of Sussex. Her conservatory
overflows with plants (so no room for breakfast!) but it's a real
pleasure to enjoy a coffee - and a gardening book - here in the
sun, and soak up that blissful view.

rooms	2 twins sharing bath & shower.
price	£45. Single occ. from £25.
meals	Restaurants in Petworth & nearby villages.
closed	Christmas & New Year.
directions	From Petworth on A283; Sheepdown Drive east of village centre.

From the back of the house the view across the small valley to the South Downs is outstanding. Since taking on this sloping, 60-foot garden two years ago, Angela has transformed a tricky plot. Visible in its entirety from the windows above, the planting has been cleverly designed with many hidden corners. The area has been divided across the middle, with the view from the top end framed by the herbaceous borders that curve down either side. A central oval bed conceals an entrance through to the lower part of the garden and from here plants frame the view without obscuring it: a prunus gives height and shade to one side; azaleas, rhododendrons and weigela will be pruned as they grow to maintain a particular size. Owners of small gardens will delight to find one here with which they can comfortably identify. A gate at the bottom leads to a network of footpaths that lead you around much of the area without having to resort to the car. Walk round to the town – heaven for antiques-lovers – or down through the fields to the pub in Byworth for supper. *NGS Assistant County Organiser.*

COPYHOLD HOLLOW

Frances Druce
Copyhold Hollow,
Copyhold Lane, Borde Hill, Haywards Heath, Sussex RH16 1XU

tel   01444 413265
e-mail bbgl@copyholdhollow.freeserve.co.uk
web   www.copyholdhollow.freeserve.co.uk

As pretty as a picture. Protected on one side by an ancient box hedge and fed by a natural spring, the garden is literally 'in' the hollow with the house. Frances has developed the whole thing herself over the last nine years creating an acre of joy. Water-lovers paddle happily around the stream's edge including flag irises, astilbes, unusual and prettily marked red and yellow mimulus, hostas and *Crocosmia lucifer*. Corkscrew willows flank an innovative green Giverny-type bridge, over which is fixed an arched tunnel of natural hazel stems now covered in wisteria, clematis, roses and jasmine. There's another of these delicate hazel arbour tunnels further up the brick path, smothered in *Trachelospermum asiaticum*, roses and clematis. Over a little lawn is a small brick patio – eating out here is fun – and there is so much protection from the weather, tucked in beneath the natural hanger of mature beech and oak trees and a giant redwood. Behind the house there is a bank up to the tree line which Frances is now tackling: mowing or strimming paths and planting lots of camellias, rhododendrons and azaleas. The soil is acid and very heavy clay so not an easy job all on your own, but it all looks perfect. Come at any time of year for something special and in the spring the garden is especially merry with wild daffodils, snowdrops, bluebells and wild orchids. The High Beeches and Arthur Hellyer's Orchards are near.

rooms	3: 1 double, 1 twin, both with shower; 1 single with bath.
price	From £60. Single occ. £40.
meals	Available locally.
closed	Never.
directions	South on M/A23 to Cuckfield, B2114/B2115. There, by Esso garage, right at 1st mini-r'bout, left at 2nd, right at 3rd. Left at T-junction. Copyhold Lane 1st on right, after entrance to Borde Hill Gardens.

First a farm, then an ale house, the 16th-century building seems small from the outside, but opens into a quirky interior with attractive exposed timbers. Frances did the renovation herself and landscaped the gardens; nightingales and owls enjoy the woodland parts. The guests' dining room and inglenook sitting room are oak-beamed, uncluttered and cheerful; bedrooms are also beamed, and neat, with views over meadow and woodland. Your lively, independent-minded hostess will happily find time to chat by the fire.

ELM GROVE FARM

Ann & Bryan Nicholls
Elm Grove Farm,
Streat Lane, Streat, Nr Plumpton, Hassocks, Sussex BN6 8RY

tel   01273 890368
fax   01273 890368

Surrounded by its own meadows and a quarter mile off a country lane, this is a fine, listed Tudor farm. Ancient yes, but with its two modern extensions you are not short of comforts. There are cosy inglenook fireplaces in both the central dining hall, with big oak table, and in the sitting room, with its electric organ - ask Bryan to play you a tune. The staircase leads up from the hall; two of the bedrooms have both a double (one queen-size) and a single bed, giving you generous and flexible sleeping arrangements. The third bedroom is painted a glorious pink. Model aeroplane enthusiasts may like to view Bryan's remote-controlled creations in action!

rooms	3: 2 twin/doubles, 1 double, all with bath & shower.
price	£55–£70. Single occ. £35–£42.50.
meals	Good food available locally.
closed	Christmas & New Year.
directions	From M23, A23, B2116 to Streat Lane. 1.9 miles down narrow lane.

Gardening is a special pleasure when both partners work together – and it's particularly useful when one is a builder by trade. This garden is full of quirky surprises, many constructed out of recycled materials by Bryan – and adorned by Ann. Their energy is prodigious; new ideas don't just occur, they are carried out and completed annually. The potting shed was recently converted into a summer house with a bench along its pretty covered veranda, and the barbecue is unique: Bryan has created a mock ruin, with a genuine Tudor brick chimney to house it. The timbered indoor garden is a mini-jungle with its koi pool and waterfall, rampant jasmine and self-seeded ferns; the peach tree is happily productive in this humid atmosphere. There are several ponds, and a long winding stream with a waterfall; two walled gardens, two terraces, a gravel garden and numerous flowering shrubs; and a 120-foot-long arched rose walk that includes several varieties of clematis and wisteria. A woodland garden is currently being developed and underplanted with bucketsful of daffodils and bluebells. The Nicholls open frequently for an enthusiastic public. *NGS.*

SHORTGATE MANOR FARM

Ethel Walters
Shortgate Manor Farm,
Halland, Lewes, Sussex BN8 6JP

tel   01825 840320
fax   01825 840320
e-mail david@shortgate.co.uk
web   www.shortgate.co.uk

The house is almost more flower-stocked than the garden - not only with the fresh variety, but painted on porcelain (Ethel's expertise is astonishing), hand-crafted in sugar, and dried and hung in arrangements from the beams. All the rooms in this lovely old house are a generous size, one bedroom in particular. Now fully tile-hung, the house was originally built in 1790 as a shepherd's cottage for the Earl of Chichester, and subsequently extended. Delicious breakfasts are served in the bright dining hall. An excellent and comfortably relaxed place from which to explore some wonderful countryside.

rooms	3: 2 doubles with shower; 1 twin with bath.
price	From £60. Single occ. from £35.
meals	Available locally.
closed	Very occasionally.
directions	North on A22 to Uckfield; left at Halland Forge roundabout; Shortgate 0.5 miles on left.

It's roses, roses, all the way up the poplar-lined drive to Shortgate Manor Farm. More than 50 different varieties of white, pink and deep-red ramblers festoon an avenue of poplars – and the Sussex barn at the end is simply smothered in white 'Bobby James', 'Rambling Rector' and 'Seagull'. The Walters started with the roses when they first began to create the garden, but gradually became so moved by the gardening bug that they have widened the scope of plants and increased the number of beds over the years. Several pergolas frame rampant clematis and honeysuckle – and yet more roses. Recent additions include a new hot bed, and a wonderful collection of grasses which gives structure to the garden during bare winter months. These exciting new schemes are fuelled by Graham Gough's nursery of unusual plants close by in the village. Shortgate can now rightly be called a plantsman's garden, and marks a radical change of direction in the Walters' lives: pre-bed-and-breakfast days they used to breed thoroughbreds for flat racing – although David does still travel in his capacity as an internationally renowned judge of show horses. *NGS, HPS.*

BATES GREEN

Mrs Carolyn McCutchan
Bates Green,
Arlington , Nr Polegate, Sussex BN26 6SH

tel   01323 482039
fax   01323 485151
e-mail batesgreen@nlconnect.co.uk
web   www.batesgreen.co.uk

Once a gamekeeper's cottage, now a tile-hung farmhouse on a working sheep farm. Each pretty bedroom overlooks a part of the two-acre garden; keen birdwatchers might catch sight of nuthatches, greater spotted woodpeckers and song thrushes; spotted flycatchers may nest outside your window. There's tea to welcome you in the oak-panelled sitting room with its open fire, and you get the full farmhouse breakfast - not only local bangers, bacon and free-range eggs, but kippers on the bone, and hot oak-smoked salmon with scrambled eggs.

rooms	3: 1 double, 2 twin/doubles, each with private bathroom.
price	From £65.
meals	Choice of restaurants nearby.
closed	Christmas.
directions	Between A22 & A27 to Arlington. Bates Green in village between Yew Tree Inn & Old Oak Inn.

You'll find a real plantswoman's choice of plants at Bates Green – something for every aspect and season. Rotate slowly in Carolyn's circular garden, and allow your eye to take in the full, subtly blended spectrum of herbaceous colours. Wander beneath the huge oak underplanted with shade-loving geraniums, cyclamen and hostas, and take a look at the rockery behind the house, wonderful in the spring with its dwarf species tulips. The meadow is managed by cutting the hay in late summer, then grazing it lightly until New Year when it is left alone to encourage a diversity of flora; two decades on, orchids are finally beginning to re-emerge. Newts inhabit the natural pond; beyond lie 23 acres of woodland for walks. You might have thought that all this was plenty to keep Carolyn and John busy, but like all compulsive gardeners they just couldn't resist another project: 2002 has seen them carve into a slope a whole new vegetable area of raised beds, which they have surrounded with York stone and brick paving. Dwarf espaliers are trained up the sandstone retaining wall at the back, and the whole scheme is crowned with a state-of-the-art glasshouse in green. *NGS, Good Gardens Guide, HPS.*

KING JOHN'S LODGE

Jill & Richard Cunningham
King John's Lodge,
Sheepstreet Lane, Etchingham, Sussex TN19 7AZ

tel   01580 819232
fax   01580 819562
e-mail kingjohnslodge@talk21.com

A listed, Jacobean house surrounded by exquisite gardens - it is a privilege to stay here. The house dates back to the 14th century (legend has it King John was kept prisoner here) with 'add-ons' every couple of hundred years. Start the day with a delicious breakfast in the Tudor room and round it off with a sumptuous dinner in the Jacobean dining room - this is a place where the antique and the contemporary rub happy shoulders. Crisp white bed linen, heated pool, tennis, croquet, and delightful hosts who welcome you into their captivating home.

rooms	4: 1 double, 1 family both with bath; 1 double, 1 twin both with private bath.
price	£35-£40.
meals	Dinner available. Pubs & restaurants nearby.
closed	Christmas & New Year.
directions	From M25 junc. 5 south on A21 to Flimwell. Right to Ticehurst (B2087). There, left, pass church; 1st left into Sheepstreet Lane. House 1 mile on, on right.

Fantail doves coo in the dovecote, sheep graze in the fields, shining lawns are the brightest green. The fine old King John's Lodge stands serenely in its romantic gardens in deepest rural Sussex... a delight. Jill is a serious, gifted gardener, a lover of the best plants, the right colour combinations, a skilful designer who has combined the formal, the informal and the natural with huge flair. She and Richard inherited a good garden with strong bones when they came in 1987 but almost immediately had to contend with the Great Gale as it ripped its devastating path across the region. All is tranquil once again in Jill's eight acres, which she has been designing and re-designing over the years; her ambition was to create a romantic English country-house garden and she has succeeded. The many linked areas start with a formal flourish: a lily pond and fountain with yew hedging and herbaceous borders. Then, a wild garden orchard and wildlife pond, filled with espaliered apple trees and arches scented and coloured by rambling roses. Spring heralds a sea of snowdrops, wild orchids, narcissi and tulips in succession. There's a shady white garden too, and, for wildlife lovers, a secret garden. A waterfall splashes into a pool surrounded by candelabra primulas and other water-loving plants. Jill sells plants and garden statuary, urns, troughs and fountains – so you can, if you wish, carry home a memento of this lovely place. *NGS, Good Gardens Guide, Historic Houses Association.*

HAYES FARMHOUSE

Julia & Thierry Sebline
Hayes Farmhouse,
Hayes Lane, Peasmarsh, TN31 6XR, Sussex

tel   01424 882345
fax   01424 882876
e-mail   julia.sebline@virgin.net
web   www.hayesfarmhouse.co.uk

A gorgeous, oak-doored, 15th-century farmhouse with a hipped roof and asymmetric beams. Julia has considerable flair and style, and the place is looking immaculate having been redecorated recently. Sweet bedrooms, softly carpeted and gently lit, share a wonderfully cosy sitting room with big log fire. All the rooms are large, with south-facing leaded windows letting the light stream in. Dip into the big collection of garden books in the drawing room, and do stay for dinner; Julia is a super cook. The central hall at the hub of the house serves as the dining room, a manorial setting for meals.

rooms	3: 2 twins both with private bath; 1 double with shower.
price	From £76. Single occ. £45.
meals	Dinner available.
closed	Christmas.
directions	A21 to B2089 for Rye. Leaving Broad Oak, left for Peasmarsh. Down hill; right into Hayes Lane. Past Oast House is Hayes Farm House.

What a relief to discover that the densely populated south east still has pockets of rural calm. A handy 10 minutes from Rye, Hayes Farmhouse lies in the sleepy and tranquil Tillingham valley. Roses are Julia's greatest passion – she's always able to sneak in another new, unresisted purchase somewhere. The orchard is full of them, growing as shrubs in the grass, or scrambling up through the trees. The house itself is a commanding presence in the middle of its four-and-a-half acres: a most striking building with towering Tudor chimneys and diamond-paned mullioned windows. It's a handsome foil for a very lovely English country garden with its backdrop of mature trees, good show of spring bulbs and burgeoning herbaceous border. Although the garden is well-established, Julia often experiments with new plants, or creates new areas of interest. Two ponds are being developed, and the latest project is the gravel garden. Somehow Julia also finds time to work for the Gardening for Disabled Trust, a charity that awards small grants to people suffering from illness or disability, to enable them to continue gardening. Gardeners are usually perceived as a generous bunch: you'll certainly find that here.

LITTLE ORCHARD HOUSE

Sara Brinkhurst
Little Orchard House ,
West Street, Rye , Sussex TN31 7ES

tel   01797 223831
fax   01797 223831
web   www.littleorchardhouse.com

Not a hint of the feast to come as you climb the steep, narrow, richly atmospheric cobbled street which leads to Sara's magical home in hauntingly beautiful Rye. But just step outside the back door and you're in another, totally unexpected world. Wind bells chime, paths duck, dive and snake around hidden corners, a few steps lead from one enclosed area to the next. A little sea monster 'swims' across a lawn, its coils rising and falling in the grass. It has taken Sara 10 years to weave this secret garden tapestry from a large, somewhat unprepossessing back garden and transform it into a half acre of romantically informal areas, each with a character of its own and each hidden from the next. Everything here speaks of a passion for gardening and nature. Her pond and herb garden has colour-themed planting, with low, manicured box hedges and thriving espaliered pears. A trellis groans with clematis and for utter peace and contemplation, seek out the little arbour and rest on the seat, leaning back against an old, carved wooden panel beneath the shelter of a golden hop. Nearby a cobbled water feature tinkles while seagulls wheel and cry overhead. Gaze up at the all-seeing watchtower with its weather vane, admire the colour and interest of the well-planted beds and borders and note those little details and personal touches Sara has added, like the cartwheel cleverly placed behind the rockery. No wonder guests love this garden.

rooms	2: 1 four-poster with shower; 1 four-poster with bath/shower.
price	£64-£90. Single occ. £45-£65.
meals	Available locally.
closed	Rarely.
directions	From A268 or A259, follow one-way system to centre, through Landgate Arch, into High St. West St 3rd on left. House half-way up on left. Parking available.

A guest wrote: "Teddy bears inside, hedgehogs outside and a really excellent cat". This most welcoming, rule-free townhouse in history-laden Rye also has fine antiques, masses of books and paintings, occasional groups of amateur dramatists in the big and otherwise quiet garden, a Smugglers' Watchtower and a small library for rainy days. Sara is lively, attentive and fun and will give you big organic/free-range breakfasts. *Children over 12 welcome.*

BLACKWELL GRANGE

Liz Vernon Miller
Blackwell Grange,
Blackwell, Shipston-on-Stour, Warwickshire CV36 4PF

tel   01608 682357
fax   01608 682856
e-mail staying@blackwellgrange.co.uk
web   www.blackwellgrange.co.uk

A former rickyard for the farm has been worked into a quarter acre of pretty English garden around the farmhouse. Old York stones with curved raised beds form grand steps up to the lawn; uninvited visitors between the stones – like tiny wild strawberries – have been allowed to stay where they pop up. There's a soft, relaxed feel to all the planting – no strict colour schemes or design-led rigidity – so that the rhythm from garden to countryside is fluent and delightful. Perfectly clipped hedges, neat lawns and careful planting around arches and pergolas show a more restrained side to the garden but somehow it all looks effortless anyway – a clever ploy. Ancient barns have been used as scaffolding for the old roses, hops, jasmine and clematis which give colour on different levels, and a dear little summer house has splendid views over hills and woods. A circular stone seat hides behind a narrow walkway between the barns with more roses and clematis growing over it and hostas sit contentedly contained in old pots. A productive fruit and vegetable garden is neatly hidden behind the house; Liz's colourful show bantams roam here, checking for insects and laying delicious breakfast eggs. Lamb is reared too and if you want to take a whole one back for your freezer just say the word.

rooms	3: 1 double, 1 twin, both with bath & shower; 1 single with shower. Ground-floor room has wheel-in shower.
price	From £65. Single occ. from £35.
meals	Supper, 2 courses, £15. BYO wine.
closed	Very occasionally.
directions	From Stratford, A3400 for Oxford. After 5 miles, right by church in Newbold-on-Stour for Blackwell. Fork right on entering Blackwell. Entrance just beyond thatched barn.

Admire the Wyandotte bantams strutting across the lawns – they are prize-winners; Liz also keeps quail and you can buy their eggs to take home with you. There are flagstoned floors, beamed ceilings, huge fireplaces and deep-set mullioned windows. The sitting room has old books and polished furniture and the bedrooms, with low ceilings, are peaceful; two have excellent views. One ground-floor bedroom is ideal for wheelchair users. Home-made marmalade for breakfast and home-grown food at supper.

THE OLD MANOR HOUSE

Jane & William Pusey
The Old Manor House,
Halford, Shipston-on-Stour, Warwickshire CV36 5BT

tel   01789 740264
fax   01789 740609
e-mail wpusey@st-philips.co.uk

All garden lovers, but rosarians in particular, will adore the garden Jane and William have created over the past five years. With a background of high mature trees and a sloping three acres, they have built a series of loosely, rather than formally, linked areas. They have added new beech and yew hedges, planted vigorously and sympathetically and made a garden that sits beautifully with their lovely old home. Old roses rule above all, climbing up walls, rambling over pergolas and arches, softening hard corners and, in a final flourish, scenting and colouring a delightful rose avenue. There is a blend of the stiffer hybrid teas, which Jane inherited and can't find the heart to remove, and a riot of treasures from sources including Peter Beales. Jane is sending vigorous climbers like 'Kiftsgate' rocketing up the trees in the orchard. It will be gorgeous, but there is much, much more: cleverly planted borders, a delicious herb garden where sage, fennel, thyme and others rub shoulders, delightful colour-theming in flower beds bursting with good plants and so many details as well as a glorious overall feel to enjoy. William has strong ideas about design, Jane has strong ideas about plants and planting. Between them, they have made the very best of the lay of their three acres and their love of plants and garden design is infectious.

rooms	3: 1 double, 1 twin, both with private bathroom; 1 single (let only to same party as twin), with private bathroom.
price	From £60. Single occ. £32.50.
meals	Dinner available.
closed	Occasionally.
directions	From Stratford, A422 for 4 miles for Banbury. Right at r'bout onto A429 for Halford. There, 1st right. House with black & white timbers ahead.

You'll be in your element if you fish or play tennis, for you can do both from the beautiful gardens that slope gently down to the River Stour. Jane, a *Cordon Bleu* cook, runs her 16th- and 17th-century house with huge energy and friendliness. A pretty blue twin bedroom and a single room are in a self-contained wing with its own large, elegant drawing and dining room; it's seductively easy to relax here. The A-shaped double, with ancient beams and oak furniture, is in the main part of the house; it has a lovely bathroom and shares the drawing and dining rooms.

THE CROFTS FARM

Mrs Stella Davies
The Crofts Farm,
Banbury Road, Stratford-upon-Avon, Warwickshire CV37 7NF

tel   01789 292159
e-mail edstell@croftsfarm.freeserve.co.uk

There's a sense of escape as you leave behind roads and people and set off down the farm's track. The 1750s gentleman farmer's house is red-brick Georgian, so typical of this area - rooms are beautifully proportioned, as you'd expect, and floor-to-ceiling windows add sunny elegance. The bright hall has a particularly delicate staircase teetering above it and at the top you find magnificent oak floors. One of the bedrooms is pale yellow with bold printed curtains and another has a perfect view of the rose garden below. Stella and Eddie are smashing and have a lively sense of humour. *Children over 12 welcome.*

rooms	4: 1 double, 1 family, both with bath; 1 double with private bathroom.
price	From £56. Single occ. £35.
meals	Available locally.
closed	November-February.
directions	2 miles south of Stratford on A422 Banbury road, left at sign to Croft Farm.

Stella does flowers and design and Eddie is the landscaping man; between them they have transformed the grounds around their working 280-acre farm. Stella is a born colourist, cleverly theming areas in shades of pink and white, blue and white and, in one tiny corner, purple; the vibrant *Knautia macedonia* sets off the wonderfully hazy beauty of a Smoke Plant (cotinus). A carefully thought-out rose garden fronts the house and has four box-edged formal beds crammed with good roses – some stiff and upright, others blowsy and floppy. It's hard to believe that until recently this was the old grass tennis court. Elsewhere, Stella has made a series of gardens-within-a garden; a hot, orange-painted corner here, a woodland there where wild flowers grow in profusion. Eddie has moved entire hedges of beech and box to complement the drama of her planting. Yew hedges lead to an elegant white-painted iron fence and gate which gives onto the fields beyond, so you have interest within and without. One of the more recent features is a patio paved with reclaimed bricks, a lily pond and a hefty pergola for climbers. A delightful young garden with all-year interest.

MARSTON HOUSE

Kim & John Mahon
Marston House,
Priors Marston, Southam, Warwickshire CV47 7RP

tel   01327 260297
fax   01327 262846
e-mail kim@mahonand.co.uk
web   www.ivabestbandb.co.uk

Three quarters of an acre laid to lawn with terraces, curved herbaceous borders, beech hedging and a field with an ancient carp pond. Kim claims to be a cheat who doesn't know the Latin names for anything but she inherited this garden 15 years ago and it had nothing except a scratchy old lawn. Since then she has "begged and borrowed" plants and transformed it into a gorgeous space for people and wildlife. Kim is conservation conscious, nothing is sprayed and she hates garish colours so all is soft and gentle, from the south-facing old stone terrace to the open countryside ahead. Many old trees festooned with rambling roses give height and the autumn favourites of maples and acer add vibrant colour. A second big herbacous border lies at the bottom of the garden brimming with gentle colour and backed by a curved beech hedge. Then there is just rolling countryside – a great place for doggie people. There is a relaxed, humorous atmosphere around Kim and her garden – you just know that if your child bounded around boisterously she wouldn't mind and if you didn't know the name of a plant she wouldn't think less of you. A gorgeous place to stay.

rooms	2: 1 twin, 1 double, both with private bath.
price	£54–£60. Single occ. from £35.
meals	Dinner, for four only, £22 p.p.
closed	Rarely.
directions	From Banbury, A361 north. At Byfield village sign, left into Twistle Lane, straight on to Priors Marston. White house, 5th on left with cattle grid, after S-bend.

Kim has the sort of kitchen that city dwellers dream of: big and welcoming and it really is the hub of the house. She and John fizz with good humour and energy and take pride in those times when family and guests feel easy together. You will be offered tea on arrival, home-made jams for breakfast and perhaps even a guided walk round the fascinating, historic village. The house is large with a wonderful garden, tennis court, terrace and croquet lawn. The rooms are big, soft and supremely comfortable with lovely pieces of furniture. A special place and genuine people.

SHREWLEY POOLS FARM

Cathy Dodd
Shrewley Pools Farm,
Haseley, Warwick, Warwickshire CV35 7HB

tel   01926 484315

Everything is exuberant and down-to-earth about Cathy – and so is her garden. Originally planted by her mother-in-law in the 70s, the specimen trees and shrubs remain the same, with climbers and herbaceous perennials allowed to romp freely through the season. Cathy describes it as a fragrant, romantic garden: roses ramble through trees, scented wisteria and honeysuckle weave over the porch, and old-fashioned shrub roses perfume the borders. Great masses of hellebores herald the spring, and 30 different varieties of hostas are protected by the bantams who potter around gobbling up slugs. She enthusiastically reels off names, affectionately describing colours and habits ("There's this lovely little iris in the rockery called 'Mourning Widow' with almost-black flowers and fine leaves…"). Her busy bed-and-breakfast business makes her practical about maintenance: they work hard in the garden at the beginning and end of the season, but leave everything to perform by itself during the summer. And that it surely does. Shrewley Pools is a working farm smothered with flora; you'll see 'New Dawn' roses in the yard and clematis 'Perle d'Azur' romping over the stables. Bring your fishing rod; the newly-cleared four-and-a-half acre lake is stocked with 10,000 carp.

rooms	2: 1 twin; 1 family with double, single & cot.
price	£45–£60. Single occ. £30–£45.
meals	Children's teas, supper or dinner. Good pub 1 mile.
closed	Christmas.
directions	A4177 to Solihull; through Hatton; 1st left at roundabout. Farm 0.75 miles down FiveWays Road opp. Farm Gate Poultry.

An early-17th-century beamed farmhouse on a mixed, arable-animal farm... breakfast couldn't be more farmhouse if it tried. There are Shrewley Pools' own bacon and bangers and organic eggs from next door. Log fires in the dining room, sitting room and hall, beams all over, charmingly irregular quarry-tiled floors, old family furniture and chintz. The twin is beamy, oak-floored and rugged. The family room has a generous king-size bed and single beds, as well as a cot, and fat sheepskin rugs on a mahogany floor. This is a super place for families, with children's teas and babysitting easily arranged.

BULLOCKS HORN COTTAGE

Colin & Liz Legge
Bullocks Horn Cottage,
Charlton, Malmesbury, Wiltshire SN16 9DZ

tel   01666 577600
fax   01666 577905
e-mail legge@bullockshorn.clara.co.uk

An artistic eye for structure, plant associations and colour combinations makes this acre of garden a joy. Mature trees such as cedar, chestnut and magnolia, along with yew, box, unusual hollies and osmanthus, provide the structure; two skyrockets flank the little pond, a reminder of an Italian holiday. An iron millennium arch covered in honeysuckle 'Graham Thomas', wisteria, clematis and pinky-gold rambler 'Phyllis Bide' frames the way to Colin's studio. Underplanted with box balls and allium, this arch looks equally gorgeous in May. 'Albertine' and clematis 'Prince Charles' entwine over the entrance picket gate; the massed pots on the conservatory terrace bloom all season long. The unusual, bright-yellow-centred rose 'Hellenii' climbs an apple tree, 'Paul's Himalayan Musk' shoots through a 30-foot-high holly. Between the start of the season with its spring bulbs and hellebores, and the later colours of autumn, Liz orchestrates an explosion of penstemon, eremus, poppies, alstroemeria, irises and foxgloves. The kitchen garden yields a steady supply of herbs, salads and vegetables for the dinner table. And there is no shortage of seats: take tea on the terrace, or – on a warm summer morning – breakfast in the sun. Liz will lay the table for you in the south-facing rose arbour – what bliss.

rooms	2: 1 twin with bath; 1 twin with private bathroom.
price	£60-£70. Single occ. £35-£40.
meals	Dinner, 3 courses, £18; 2 courses, £14.
closed	Christmas & Easter.
directions	From A429, B4040 through Charlton, past Horse & Groom pub. 0.5 miles on, left signed 'Bullocks Horn – No Through Road'. On to end of lane. Right. House first on left.

A pretty 200-year-old cottage on the peaceful southern fringes of the Cotswolds - and, thanks to the combined talents of an artist and a wife with a flair for interior design, a stylish home. Dine by candlelight in the conservatory, where limestone flags are spread with Persian rugs. More flagstones in the hall, Colin's paintings on the walls, and a large, comfortable, sitting room. Bedrooms are light and comfortable with a cottagey feel; one with pale yellow walls and chintz curtains. Bathrooms are pristine. No duvets here, just proper blankets and cotton or - joy of joys - starched linen sheets.

THE OLD RECTORY

John & Maril Eldred
The Old Rectory ,
Luckington, Nr Chippenham, SN14 6PH, Wiltshire

tel   01666 840556
fax   01666 840989
e-mail   b&b@the-eldreds.co.uk

An architectural oddity - the house has an 1830s façade, yet parts are 14th century. Burning log fires, the smell of coffee wafting from the kitchen and the bustle of family life make you feel immediately at home. Maril has made some bold choices of colour - the strong blue of the dining room has real impact. Bedrooms are big with pretty fabrics and softer colours; the double has a truly huge bathroom. You can play tennis on the all-weather court, try your hand at croquet, swim in the heated pool. Do visit the church; it's a step away, through the gate in the 12th-century wall.

rooms	4: 1 double, 1 twin, both with bath. 2 bedroom cottage annexe.
price	£76. Single occ. £45.
meals	Dinner available.
closed	Occasionally.
directions	From M4 junc. 17, north for Malmesbury. 2nd left, follow road for approx. 5 miles. At Sherston, left onto B4040 for Luckington. 1.5 miles on, leaving Brook End on left, house on left 0.25 miles before Luckington centre.

Pure undiluted Cotswolds' charm in a village so perfect that scenes for *Pride and Prejudice* were filmed at the church. You sweep up the curving drive and immediately see myriad leaf colour in the vibrant borders. John and Maril are hugely modest about what they've achieved in their young garden. They shouldn't be: the two acres around the house sing of the hard work and devotion that they have poured into them. Wisteria drips over the façade and traditional favourites such as sweet peas, delphiniums, tulips and old roses fill the beds opposite. Structural details are interesting, too. The Eldreds have planted a copper and green beech hedge - two coppers, two green, two coppers, etc - which gives impressive contrast and lasting colour; fashionable in the 20s and 30s, this sort of planting is enjoying a revival. Over 100 other trees have been planted, too, mostly around the tennis court, and lawns have been nurtured with impressive results. An interesting feature is the recently added fan-shaped pergola, home to climbing roses and other sweet-scented sun seekers. Maril's successes include the kitchen garden, which has a cutting bed for flowers for the house, and John's the planting of a new orchard and the hiding of unsightly power and telephone lines underground.

IDOVER HOUSE

Christopher & Caroline Jerram
Idover House,
Dauntsey , Nr Malmesbury, Wiltshire SN15 4HW

tel   01249 720340

A large, mature country-house garden which Christopher and Caroline have carefully restored to complement their long, elegant house (18th century and originally the Home Farm for nearby Dauntsey Park). The stables are a reminder of its days as a hunting box for the Duke of Beaufort's hunt. There are glorious lawns, rose-covered dry stone walls and an open, sunny atmosphere. The mature trees are very handsome and include a perfectly shaped decorative sycamore and two lofty Wellingtonia. Rose-lovers will be delighted with the newly restored, formal, 1920s rose garden with its symmetrically shaped beds planted in delicate shades of pink and white; the design was drawn for them by the noted rosarian Peter Beales. The grounds are a mix of the formal, informal and wild, with plenty of colour from a series of borders, including the deep herbaceous border which has recently been replanted. Hedges of yew, beech and lime give structure and form, and a copse of decorative trees gives shade, good leaf form and colour. Kitchen garden enthusiasts will be envious of the Jerrams' productive and beautifully tended plot, reached via the duck pond – surrounded by masses of flag iris – and the yew hedge walk. On sunny days, linger by the pool garden with its summer house. In spring, enjoy the bulbs in the woodland. A charming family garden. *NGS, RHS.*

rooms	3 twins, each with bath/shower.
price	£75. Single occ. £47.50.
meals	Dinner £22.50; not Saturday.
closed	Christmas & New Year.
directions	From Malmesbury, B4042 for Wotton Bassett. 2.5 miles on, fork right to Little Somerford. At bottom of hill, right for Gt Somerford. At x-roads, left to Dauntsey. House 1.25 miles on left at bend.

Grand and friendly, all at once. You can settle down by the huge fireplace in the handsome panelled drawing room with its log fires in winter, and breakfast or dine in the pink, low-ceilinged dining room with its lovely views of the garden. Caroline's a *Cordon Bleu* cook and naturally the scrumptious food includes produce from their wonderful vegetable garden. The guest rooms are light and elegant, the bathrooms pristine. Very much a lived-in family home, with no shortage of horsey pictures and a 'rogues' gallery' of family portraits upstairs. *Children over eight welcome.*

RIDLEYS CHEER

Sue & Antony Young
Ridleys Cheer,
Mountain Bower, Chipppenham, Wiltshire SN14 7AJ

tel   01225 891204
fax   01225 891139
e-mail sueyoung@ridleyscheer.co.uk

Ridleys Cheer, in a hamlet approached down meandering lanes
populated by suicidal pheasants, was originally a small 18th-
century cottage but enlarged in 1989 by the architect, William
Bertram, who restored Highgrove. One addition was the large
conservatory where summer guests can breakfast amid plumbago
and jasmine. The bedrooms, reached by a separate staircase, are
bright, simple and cosy, with pale walls, pretty curtains and
antique furniture and the eye is ceaselessly drawn through the
small windows to the glories below. Sue, a *Cordon Bleu* chef,
cooks delicious meals served at a mahogany table in the low-
ceilinged dining room.

rooms	3: 1 double with bath; 1 double, 1 twin, sharing bathroom.
price	From £70. Single occ. by arrangement.
meals	Packed lunch £8. Lunch £15. Dinner £27.50, inc wine.
closed	Occasionally.
directions	M4 junc 17. At Chippenham, A420 towards Bristol. After 9 miles, right at x-roads in hamlet, The Shoe. Then 2nd left, then 1st right. This is Mountain Bower (no sign). Last house on left; park on gravel drive opposite.

What a name – what a garden! Plantsmen traditionally sacrifice design on the altar of collecting, but Antony and Sue combine both in a breathtaking, informal, 14-acre plantsman's garden packed with rare shrubs and trees. Born gardeners, the Youngs began here modestly 30 years ago. A defining moment came when Antony abandoned industry for garden design. He now works on commissions, including stately homes in this country and châteaux in France. In the lower and upper gardens, lawns sweep through displays including 120 different shrub and species roses, daphnes, a dozen different magnolias and a collection of 25 acers in their own glade. A young arboretum has been planted over the past 12 years with radiating avenues of trees including Serbian spruce planted to attract goldcrests. Beyond is a three-acre wildflower meadow with 36 species of native limestone flora. By the house are witty touches of formality with a potager and box garden, but the overall mood is of profuse informality with glorious details and a ravishing collection of plants. Antony wears his knowledge with engaging lightness and thoroughly enjoys leading guests through the many charms of this horticultural masterpiece. Ridleys Cheer opens for the NGS and guests and visitors should leave some room in the car boot – you can buy plants propagated from the garden. *NGS, Good Gardens Guide.*

THE COACH HOUSE

Helga & David Venables
The Coach House,
Upper Wraxall, Nr Bath, Wiltshire SN14 7AG

tel   01225 891026
fax   01225 892355
e-mail   venables@compuserve.com
web   upperwraxallcoachhouse.co.uk

The elegant two-acre landscaped garden was created from pastureland 17 years ago. The grounds are 600 feet above sea level, where winter winds whip across the surrounding landscape. Shelter is all-important to protect the more tender plants and the solution has been to design a garden which is a splendid blend of open lawns, well-planted borders and masses of well-placed young trees which create large areas of dappled green. Closely-planted shaped banks and a natural rockery give further protection and winter interest. The overall mood is one of a private park with both open and intimate areas and plenty of colour. The main lawn is beautifully tended and becomes an excellent croquet lawn in milder weather. Helga is the flower person, David the tree and lawn specialist; they make an excellent team, having brought together a good collection of unusual herbaceous plants and many varieties of shrubs. Helga loves colour theming, and her planting includes a clever mixture of yellows and bronzes in one herbaceous border. Favourite plants include her groups of euphorbias and hostas. There's a delightful ornamental kitchen garden to one side of the house; like the rest of the garden, it has been carefully planned for low maintenance but maximum interest.

rooms	3: 1 double, 1 twin, 1 single, with private or shared bathroom.
price	£60; single £30.
meals	Dinner £12.50–£15. Excellent local pubs.
closed	Rarely.
directions	From M4 junc. 17, A429 for Chippenham. A420 to Bristol (East) & Castle Combe. After 6.3 miles right into Upper Wraxall. Sharp left opp. village green; house at end of drive.

Big, generous beds and sweeping views across the garden, in an ancient hamlet. This is the sort of impeccably managed house that appeals particularly to American visitors and to those who love their comforts. The huge drawing room with elegant furniture opens onto a paved area where guests can sit and admire the beautiful gardens created by Helga and David over the years. Bedrooms, too, are interesting with sloping beamed ceilings. Helga can tempt you with croquet, tennis and meals on the lawn in summer. Close to Bath and many other gardens of interest.

THE GARDEN LODGE

Mrs Juliet Wilmot
The Garden Lodge,
Chittoe, Chippenham, Wiltshire SN15 2EW

tel   01380 850314
fax   01380 850314
e-mail juliet.wilmot@zeronet.co.uk

An amphitheatre of lovely deciduous woodland surrounds the
hamlet of Chittoe and the Garden Lodge. Originally a head
gardener's cottage dating from 1864, it was cleverly extended by
Juliet to face south over the garden. This extension is where you
stay, and the traditionally furnished bedrooms have large modern
sash windows that make the most of the garden views. A
generously-proportioned and elegant conservatory juts into
the garden ensuring a breathtaking outlook to accompany your
meals. Juliet is an intelligent and amusing hostess; the Garden
Lodge experience is one not to be missed.

rooms	2: 1 twin with bath; 1 twin with basin & private wc, sharing bathroom.
price	£65-£70.
meals	Supper, £20.
closed	November-March.
directions	A342 between Chippenham & Devizes. 0.5 miles south of Sandy Lane Village, turn for Chittoe & Spye Park. Follow lane for 1 mile, past dead end sign; lodge on right.

Until 1990 only horses and an old oak inhabited what was once a two-acre Victorian walled garden. When Juliet moved in, a year's worth of terracing by bulldozers and JCBs set the stage for transformation. Bricks from collapsed parts of the outer wall were hijacked to create retaining walls and edge the many raised beds. The remarkable thing is that the bricklayer is none other than Juliet who – like Churchill – finds bricklaying deeply therapeutic. As the plans became more ambitious she took a course in brick building, and, as she warmed to her task, quirky brick features began to appear: a sun clock, a maze, a game of snakes and ladders, a brick man. In the process of enhancing her constructions by soft planting Juliet has created many and unexpected vistas: to the yew-buttressed borders, down the serpentine yew hedges, along the rose walk with its timber and chain pergola, across to the pond, whose overflow trickles down a little rill. Her recent summer house is the crowning glory: she lettered a poem by Pope into the still-moist plaster around the inside, whose last line encapsulates her achievements: "Paint as you plant and as you work, design." *Good Gardens Guide, RHS, HPS, Wiltshire Gardens Trust (Council Member).*

GREAT CHALFIELD MANOR

Patsy Floyd
Great Chalfield Manor,
Melksham, Wiltshire SN12 8NJ

tel   01225 782239
fax   01225 783379
e-mail patsy@greatchalfield.co.uk

A National Trust house - a rare example of the English medieval manor complete with 14th-century church - but a family home where you will be treated as a guest, rather than a visitor. Flagstones, a Great Hall with Flemish tapestries, a dining room with perfect panelling, fine oak furniture and an atmosphere of ancient elegance inspire awe - but Patsy dispels all formality with a gorgeous smile. Proper four-posters in the stone-walled bedrooms are swathed in the softest greens and pinks, the bathrooms are deeply old-fashioned and the only sound is bird ballad. Unstuffy kitchen suppers follow large drinks in the prettiest panelled sitting room.

rooms	2 four-posters with private bath.
price	£100. Single occ. £80.
meals	Kitchen supper £25 inc. wine.
closed	Occasionally.
directions	From Melksham B3107 to Bradford on Avon. 1st right to Broughton Gifford, through village. 1 mile on sign left to Gt Chalfield.

Stand in the middle of the lawn, close your eyes and imagine that Titania and Oberon have just fluttered past – open your eyes and they have. A structure of neatly clipped yew houses, upper and lower moats, herbaceous borders, huge lawns and an orchard have been immaculately tended and then enchanced by Patsy's love of soft colour and roses. The south-facing rose terrace brims over with scented pink roses that bloom all summer long, ramblers scrabble over anything with height, including old stone walls and the fruit trees in the orchard – and they are not alone; there is honeysuckle in abundance too, rambling hither and thither to waft its gorgeous English smell. Lavender and nepeta – the gentlest of hues – even the "red border" is soft with smudgy colour, never garish. Water weaves through the grass in little streams which feed the serene, lily-laden moats and there is a magical woodland walk. Patsy learned about gardening by "doing it" and gains ideas and inspiration from the tours she organises for 'The Garden Party' – but she has very firm ideas of her own especially when it comes to design and colour. There is a hazy, bloom-filled dreaminess about Great Chalfield. Perhaps Puck really does sprinkle something into your eyes as you go up the long, grassy drive…*NGS, Good Gardens Guide.*

BURGHOPE MANOR

John & Elizabeth Denning
Burghope Manor,
Winsley, Bradford-on-Avon, Wiltshire BA15 2LA

tel   01225 723557
fax   01225 723113
e-mail enquiry@burghope.co.uk
web   www.burghope.co.uk

A historic manor house and all that goes with it, plus modern touches where they matter. It looks imposing outside - arched, mullioned windows, jutting gables, tall chimneys - while the interior is, quite breathtakingly, manorial. The vast Tudor fireplace (complete with Elizabethan graffiti), a whole gallery of ancestral oil paintings and the most fascinating historic furniture and artefacts - it's all intriguing. Bedrooms are sunny, luxurious and charming with big beds and views over the grounds.

rooms	3 twins/doubles, all with bath/shower.
price	£90-£100. Single occ. £40.
meals	For groups only.
closed	Christmas & New Year.
directions	A36 Warminster road out of Bath for 5 miles, left onto B3108, under r'way bridge & up hill. 1st right, turn off Winsley bypass into old village, then 1st left, into lane marked 'except for access'.

The setting and the wonderful medieval architecture of Burghope Manor are everything. It's a historic corner of ancient England hidden by tall walls and steeped in a sense of timelessness. John and Elizabeth have chosen, wisely, to keep garden decoration to a bare minimum and instead have developed an elegant parkland which perfectly complements their stunning home; the emphasis is on beautifully maintained lawns set among stands of handsome mature trees. Elizabeth makes one exception to the overall theme of tall hedges, open lawns and canopies of leaves: a splash of colour by the house itself. This is her narrow, bright much-loved border which blossoms with herbaceous perennials like peonies, carpets of annuals and cheery roses. It is deliberately designed to give newcomers a bright and cheerful welcome before they experience the stunning interior of their family home. Sweet-scented honeysuckle clambers over the low entrance and wisteria flowers elegantly on the gabled main frontage with its diamond-like leaded windows. After a day spent visiting some of the many magnificent gardens in the area, like Stourhead, Iford Manor, Corsham Court and The Courts, relax in the natural beauty of this restful park. Or simply sit in the little summer house and absorb the grandness of the setting.

STURFORD MEAD

Joan & Robbie Bradshaw
Sturford Mead,
Corsley, Warminster, Wiltshire BA12 7QT

tel   01373 832039
fax   01373 832104
e-mail bradshaw@sturford.co.uk
web   www.sturford.co.uk

A fine example of restrained Regency elegance - a large, very original, very beautiful, 1820 Bath stone house. Floor-to-ceiling windows pour light into lofty rooms; a remarkable cantilevered stone stairway fills the central hall, complete with imitation ashlar stone wall finish. Joan and Robbie enjoy telling guests how they brought the house back from the brink; in doing so they have lost none of that country-house feel. Stately bedrooms have private bathrooms with huge cast-iron baths, and breakfast is served in a pastiche print-room overlooking the lake. A fabulous place.

rooms	4: 2 doubles, 1 twin, 1 single, all with private bath or shower.
price	£70. Single occ. £40.
meals	Good food available locally.
closed	Rarely.
directions	A36 Warminster bypass A362 for Frome; over roundabout; 50 yards after old bus shelter on left, left; 50 yds bear right into drive.

Expect to be surprised by this seven-acre garden. As old as the house, and screened by enormous trees, it is almost invisible to the outside world. Behind a dramatic canopy of leaves, lawns curve down to the lake, and beyond that, mown paths wind among specimen trees and channelled rills. The lovely house stands centre-stage, like something from a Rex Whistler backcloth. To the right is the walled garden; to the left, a formal tall-yew-hedged garden designed by Russell Page. And then, beyond the house and huge lawn, with Longleat woods rising to the left, a breathtaking view down the valley that sweeps into Somerset and beyond to the Mendip hills. Such English perfection that one suspects contrivance. This is a garden for strolling in, for the naming of plants down long winding beds; for the watching of sunsets; and for sitting in, on a seat by the lake, watching huge lazy carp meander and counting new moorhen chicks floating like black feathers on the water. *RHS, Wiltshire Gardens Trust, Garden History Society.*

LANDSBROOK FARM

David & Penelope O'Brien
Landsbrook Farm,
Landford Wood, Nr Salisbury, Wiltshire SP5 2ES

tel   01794 390220
fax   01794 390220
e-mail obriendm@freenet.co.uk

Approach the mellow brick house with its distinctive A-line gabled roof through a woodland setting, and Penny will greet you with a cup of tea in the cosy, pretty guest sitting room. All three bedrooms have views over the garden at front and back. The lovely, lemon-yellow Hat Room gives guests something to write home about: its walls are dotted with a fascinating collection of millinery that David and Penny have collected from around the globe. David is a bee-keeper, so Landsbrook honey is on the breakfast menu, as is Penny's delicious home-made bread.

rooms	3: 1 twin with shower; 2 doubles with bath & shower, either private or shared.
price	£55–£65. Single occ. £35 (July & August).
meals	Very occasionally.
closed	Christmas & Easter, occasionally other times.
directions	Off A36 between Salisbury & Southampton; turn east into Landford Wood, down Stock Lane; pass between 2 lodge houses; 400 yds on left is white sign in grass.

Penny's love affair with clematis is most evident during the first week of July. It is during that week that 40 of her 157 different species are at their peak, and it is then that her garden is open to garden clubs. However, the clematis season runs from February through to September, so there is much to interest the connoisseur during these months. And plantaholics in general will find more than clematis to command their attention. Hellebores, azaleas and camellias herald the spring, alongside magnolias and a blazing Chilean firebush. Summer brings a large collection of geraniums, and the three pergolas are dizzy with roses and clematis in June. Autumn produces a mass of colour from acers, azaleas and cornus. Penny's briskly practical approach to gardening avoids the necessity of such dreary activities as weeding and staking: "I just cram plants in and they all prop themselves up". There are lovely walks through the surrounding woods, bluebell-carpeted in spring, and a multitude of birds are to be spotted in every season sharing the peace of this glorious acre of plantsman's garden.

BROOMSGROVE LODGE

Mr & Mrs Peter Robertson
Broomsgrove Lodge,
New Mill, Nr Pewsey, Wiltshire SN9 5LE

tel   01672 810515
fax   01672 810286
e-mail didyrob@hotmail.com

It is a pleasure to stay here, in a pretty thatched house with an owner who has a talent both for gardening and interior design. The sitting room, decorated in terracotta and pale green, leads to a lovely, big conservatory - from which there are fine views of garden and hills. Diana serves breakfast here - eggs from the chickens that strut in the field, and freshly-squeezed orange juice. Fresh, pretty bedrooms, polished bathrooms, plates from Sicily and Portugal on the walls and pictures bought during their time in Hong Kong. Walks along the lush Avon & Kennet Canal are a step away.

rooms	3: 1 twin with bath; 1 twin with private bath; 1 extra single available.
price	From £55. Single £25.
meals	Good food available locally.
closed	Christmas & New Year.
directions	From Hungerford A338 Burbage r'bout B3087 to Pewsey. Right in Milton Lilbourne at sign to New Mill; under bridge, through village, over canal; on left at entrance to farm is lodge.

Some people just seem to have the knack for creating exciting surroundings outside as well as in. Diana moved to Broomsgrove Lodge in 1996 after six months in Hong Kong, and is extremely happy tending home, guests and garden. She and Peter found themselves with a picture book setting: the thatched house gazes over serene and open countryside, with a pretty conservatory that has wonderful long views. From the slope by the conservatory Diana and Peter created a sunken terrace: a mass of pots planted with calendula, hostas, dahlias and the striking schizanthus, all grown from seed. And the pots continue up the steps leading onto the lawn. Their grandchildren love the camomile seat cut into the terrace retaining wall; a lovers' seat encircles the trunk of the oak tree up on the lawn, the perfect spot from which to view the herbaceous border and the gravel garden. Diana's pride and joy is her flourishing vegetable garden that supplies a wide variety of vegetables for family and friends, and, as a disciple of Sarah Raven, she has a cutting garden too, where she grows poppies, foliage plants such as euphorbias, and the puce-pink annual mallow, Malope.

LUGGERS HALL

Mrs K G Haslam
Luggers Hall,
Springfield Lane, Broadway, Worcestershire WR12 7BT

tel   01386 852040
fax   01386 859103
e-mail luggershall@hotmail.com
web   www.luggershall.com

This handsome home was built by the Victorian Royal Academy garden artist, Sir Alfred Parsons. Red and Kay have renovated and remodelled both house - Grade II-listed - and garden. You are given a key to your own wing; staying here is a luxurious experience with swagged curtains and cushions piled high on beds. The sound of gently cascading water drifts up through the window of one room; others look over the garden to the hills beyond. Edwardian origins are enhanced by William Morris-style materials, richly coloured décor and old prints and photographs of Broadway. *Minimimum 2 night stay at weekends. Self-catering available.*

rooms	2: 1 double with small dressing room and bathroom; 1 double with bathroom.
price	From £65.
meals	Many restaurants in village.
closed	Very occasionally.
directions	Off Broadway High Street. Turn off at Swan Inn. Luggers Hall is on Springfield Lane.

Not many glamorous career air hostesses are prepared to seize a knapsack-sprayer to tackle the first stage of reclaiming a garden. This is how Kay began at Luggers Hall, and reinvented herself as a passionate gardener and knowledgeable plantswoman. With husband Red's help, Alfred Parsons' two-and-a-half-acre Edwardian garden has been recreated, using old aerial photographs, prints and Parsons' own paintings as guides to his original layout. Kay, also a trained artist, has an eye for shape, colour and texture, her personal stamp fusing with that of the original owner. Garden rooms surround the central lawn, and clever use of architectural plants with big leaves such as rheums and *Paulownia tomentosa* disguise the flatness of the site. In the walled garden with its central fountain, the richly planted borders lead the eye round carefully blended colours of the spectrum. There are two stunningly planted rose gardens, one with mounds of white roses and white lavender with pale blue salvia, the other with pink roses edged with lavender and in-filled with nepeta and penstemon. Through the castellated yew hedge is a secluded koi pool garden, where it's bliss to curl up by the summer house with a book. The pretty potager below the guest bedrooms leads into Kay's mini-nursery — she has a passion for propagating. Red's newly decked-out tea room caters for visitors on charity open days. B&B guests, of course, can enjoy the delights of the garden at any time. *NGS.*

SALFORD FARM HOUSE

Jane Gibson & Richard Beach
Salford Farm House,
Salford Priors, Nr Evesham, Worcestershire WR11 8XN

tel   01386 870000
fax   01386 870300
e-mail   salfordfarmhouse@aol.com
web   www.salfordfarmhouse.co.uk

An unusual garden as it is divided by a wing of the house – you pass under an open-sided brick and timber barn to cross from one side to the other – making a wonderful shaded area for seating. It has been planted over the last four years but has matured well thanks to the packed planting of roses, shrubs and herbaceous perennials: Jane has a real artist's eye for colour, shapes and groupings, and this is her strength. Lawns as immaculate as bowling greens, groups of plants in pots, a wooden bench under a chestnut tree flanked by stone pots and planted with variegated rhododendrons show off her talent; clever curvy lawns and island beds give the illusion of space. There is always another corner to peek around and plenty of height has been added: a pretty gazebo covered in clematis, weathered deer-fencing screens, and a large pergola the length of one wall. There are fun touches too with natural old log sculptures – one peers out between penstemons looking like the Loch Ness monster. Masses of tulips in spring, amazing interest and colour all summer and chrysanthemums and asters for the autumn make this garden worth visiting at any time. Richard is MD of Hillers, a mile down the road: a fruit farm, farm shop and display garden from which you can buy all the inspiration you might need to take home with you. Have another look at Jane's colour groupings first – one could hardly do better.

rooms	2 twins/doubles, 1 with shower and 1 with bath/shower.
price	£75. Single occ. £47.50.
meals	Dinner £22.50.
closed	Occasionally.
directions	A46 from Evesham or Stratford to Salford Priors. On entering village, right opp. church, for Dunnington. House on right, approx. 1 mile on, after 2nd sign on right for Dunnington.

Undeniably beautiful within, solidly handsome without. Jane is a gifted interior
decorator; the colours are splendid and nothing looks out of place. Jane and Richard are
easy and open: she was a ballet dancer and is refreshingly new to this B&B thing; he has
green fingers and grows the fruit that appears in pretty bowls on your breakfast table.
The kitchen is engagingly beamed and straight out of a smart magazine. There are some
fine pieces of furniture, sofas to sink into and enough comfort to satisfy a pharaoh.

SEDBURY HALL

Sarah Baker Baker
Sedbury Hall,
Richmond, Yorkshire DL10 5LQ

tel   01748 822722
fax   01748 826605
e-mail sarahbakerbaker@hotmail.com

The look is solid, impressive; within, the feel is warm, family,
comfortable, easy. The house was built in 1929 on the site of an
18th-century house, so... masses of architectural history: folly,
ice-house, urns and sundials remain from the original estate. A
stalwart oak staircase and an inner hall are lit by a glass dome
and portraits line the galleried landing. The scale and colour of
the gardens are breathtaking, so are the views; there's croquet
too. Sarah always rustles up a fresh coffee or tea to welcome
you, and is justifiably proud of the house and its history.

rooms	2 twins both with bath.
price	£70–£80. Single occ. from £45.
meals	Restaurants/pubs 5 miles.
closed	Christmas, New Year & occasionally.
directions	A1 to Scotch Corner, then A66 for Penrith. House 0.25 miles after lay-by on left, lodge & white posts; through gates.

What a treat – especially for Sarah, who has loved gardens and gardening since her governess took her on wildflower walks as a child. Now she is not playing but still enjoying looking after a huge concern – four acres of formal gardens set in idyllic parkland. Too much for one person but she has help in the form of Wayne – trained at Durham – and they choose everything together, growing as much as possible from seeds and cuttings. The post war lay-out has been softened and added to including a 54-foot-long laburnum arch, a sculpted curving yew and new copper beech hedge. Nine rose beds edge the lawn, there is a gazebo to sit in and admire the distant folly, a large, old and well-established herbaceous border and a quiet spring garden packed with bulbs and mature azaleas. Through attractive gates is an old walled kitchen garden and a small orchard – and Sarah's cutting beds which really are her passion. A woodland walk is under development for which thousands of primulas are being grown, and trees thinned out to give the bulbs – mainly daffodils and bluebells – a bit of light. The original ice house is interesting to look at and there's an elegant Lady's Walk through the ancient rhododendrons. "A constant battle against rabbits and wind" apparently, but it all looks perfect and set against the backdrop of some really old trees – lime, beech and oaks. Wonderfully English.

MILLGATE HOUSE

Tim Culkin & Austin Lynch
Millgate House,
Richmond , Yorkshire DL10 4JN

tel   01748 823571
fax   01748 850701
e-mail oztim@millgatehouse.demon.co.uk
web   www.millgatehouse.com

Prepare to be amazed. In every room of the house and in every corner of the garden, the marriage of natural beauty and sophistication exists in a state of bliss. The four Doric columns at the entrance draw you through the hall into the dining room and to views of the Swale Valley. Beds from Heals, period furniture, cast-iron baths, myriad prints and paintings and one double bed so high you wonder how to get onto it. Tim and Austin, both ex-English teachers, have created something very special.

rooms	3: 1 double, 1 twin, both with bath/shower; 1 double with private bathroom & private sitting room.
price	£70. Single occ. £45.
meals	Available locally.
closed	Rarely.
directions	Just off Richmond Market Place, house at bottom of square opp. Barclays Bank, next to Halifax. Look for a green door with small brass plaque.

Nothing of the elegant façade of Austin and Tim's home hints at the treasures which lie behind – it makes the shock of discovery even more dramatic. Wandering into the drawing room you are drawn, magnet-like, to the veranda to discover the full impact of the garden below. A stay at Millgate House without exploring it would be an unforgivable omission; no wonder that when Austin and Tim entered the Royal Horticultural Society's 1995 National Garden Competition they romped away with first prize from 3,000-plus entries. This famous walled town garden deserves every last bouquet and adulatory magazine and newspaper article it has received. A narrow shady lane to one side of the house, adorned with immaculate hostas, introduces the main garden. Here the long terraced grounds, sloping steeply down towards the river and overlooked by the great Norman castle, are divided into a rhythmic series of lush compartments. All is green, with cascades of foliage breaking out into small, sunny open areas before you dive beneath yet more foliage to explore further secret areas. Plantsmanship, a passion for old roses, hostas, clematis, ferns and small trees and a love of many different leaf forms come together triumphantly. As William Blake said: "Exuberance is beauty". If you just want to explore the garden you can phone Austin and Tim to arrange a visit. *NGS, Good Gardens Guide, RHS Associate Garden.*

THE OLD VICARAGE

Judi & Steve Smith
The Old Vicarage,
Darley, Harrogate, Yorkshire HG3 2QF

tel   01423 780526
fax   01423 780526
e-mail judi@darley33.freeserve.co.uk
web   www.darley33.freeserve.co.uk

Judi and Steve have lavished care on their sensitive restoration of
this lovely 1849 vicarage set in the heart of a very pretty village.
Balusters and doors have been stripped, old flagstones cleaned,
wooden floors stripped back, National Trust paints used on walls.
The warm, friendly house is full of good china, country furniture,
books, even a teddy bear collection. Immaculate bathrooms, one
with slipper bath; charming bedrooms, one with a stunning Italian
repro brass-and-iron bed. Breakfast in the large dining room
overlooking the front garden, relax on comfy sofas in the
elegant living room.

rooms	2: 1 double with shower; 1 twin with private bathroom.
price	£54. Single occ. £32.
meals	Dinner £17.50.
closed	Very occasionally.
directions	From Harrogate, A59 west. Right for B6451. Right at Wellington pub. House on right, next to Christ Church.

You'll have to take Judi's word for it – this immaculately tended garden was a wilderness when she and Steve enthusiastically took on the restoration of their home in 1995. All is utterly transformed in their three-quarter-acre of front and back garden. The front garden lawn is decorated with pretty topiary beds; the back garden is a delight hidden by beech hedges, entered through a rustic rose arch. Here Judi and Steve have really gone to town, pursuing their passion for the best plants in a setting surrounded by open countryside. To gain as much space as possible for their plants they have removed all grass and made a series of large interlocking herbaceous beds and a tapestry of gravel paths. Steve has created height with sturdy pergolas which now are a mass of old-fashioned rambling roses and a collection of more than 170 different types of clematis. Other favourite plants include iris and peony which make wonderful displays in late spring. The garden has been designed for texture, colour and form and already their grand designs are coming to fruition. A charming feature is the little water garden which sparkles with water lilies. The mood is informal, the air sweetly scented with fragrant plants – the sort of garden that attracts bees, butterflies, dragonflies, birds and, on open days for the National Gardens Scheme, flocks of garden lovers. *NGS, RHS, British Clematis Society.*

THORPE LODGE

Tommy & Juliet Jowitt
Thorpe Lodge,
Ripon, Yorkshire HG4 3LU

tel   01765 602088
fax   01765 602835
e-mail jowitt@btinternet.com

Put together a professional interior designer and a keen gardener, give them a gorgeous Grade II-listed Georgian house in the gateway to the Dales and you have an English idyll. Guests use the South Wing with a separate entrance through the Mediterranean-style courtyard, and dine, deliciously, in the beautiful, green-painted winter dining room with an open fire or, in summer, in the cool white dining room overlooking the courtyard. Bedrooms are sumptuously decorated and truly huge – big enough to lounge in – with long garden views through sash windows. The house has featured in plenty of glossy mags so go home brimming with ideas.

rooms	2 twin/doubles with bath/shower.
price	£80.
meals	Dinner £25. Good pubs and restaurants locally.
closed	Occasionally.
directions	From Southern end of Ripon bypass turn to Bishop Monkton. 0.75 miles left at gateway turning into a wood marked Thorpe Lodge.

Tommy is the gardener, but he had to learn quickly when they arrived here 20 years ago – the garden was in a terrible state. He says he learned "through trial and error, with friends giving advice" but obviously there is natural talent here; almost everything is grown from seeds and cuttings, all is serene and these 12 well-managed acres now open every year. In front of the house is a huge swathe of smooth lawn with curving borders on either side filled with colour – blues, purples, white and silver with black hollyhock as the exception. A ha-ha edges the bottom of the lawn then views of sheep in open countryside complete the bucolic picture. A grassed path leads to the back of the house and a red border: lashings of phlox and elegant day lilies. Through some ornate gates into the walled garden are several more beds and borders, mainly planted with roses and some old varieties: 'Madame Hardy', 'Ferdinand Pichard' and 'Rambling Rector' in pinks, purples and whites. Paths weave between old fruit trees and an avenue of wild cherry leads to a statue of Silenus. A formal series of rectangular pools are interconnected with a contemporary twist in front of a line of 20-foot-high leylandii pillars with life-size Greek god statues. There are plenty of 'views' down walkways – one is of almost pleached hornbeam – down to a Grecian urn surrounded by lilies, purple catmint and nicotiana. Spring is resplendent with snowdrops, daffodils and bluebells. *NGS*.

LAUREL MANOR FARM

Sam & Annie Atcherley-Key
Laurel Manor Farm,
Brafferton-Helperby, YO61 2NZ, Yorkshire

tel	01423 360436
fax	01423 360437
e-mail	laurelmf@aol.com
web	www.laurelmf.co.uk

A superbly solid Georgian house with sweeping views across the Vale of York, yet only three minutes' walk from the heart of the village. In 28 acres that run down to the River Swale (fishing available), it has black sheep, ducks, horses and ponies, a croquet lawn and a tennis court. The house - largely renovated by the good-humoured Sam and Annie - is a treat: the large, stylish rooms are all extremely cosy with quirky touches, and the big beamed bedrooms have books, antiques and window seats. One has a four-poster.

rooms	3: 1 twin/double with shower; 1 double/family with bath; 1 four-poster with private bathroom.
price	From £60.
meals	Dinner £20; good food also available at four pubs a short walk away.
closed	Occasionally in winter.
directions	From A1(M), Boroughbridge exit. At north side of B'bridge follow Easingwold & Helperby sign. In Helperby, right at T-junc., right up Hall Lane. Left in front of school.

All five Keys spent their first year here squeezed into a caravan while building work and landscaping began on a warren of derelict farm buildings. It took two JCBs three weeks to carve out a completely new layout and a further three attempts to achieve the two-and-a-half acres of landscaping we see today. Annie longed for an informal, sprawling country-house garden which would make the most of the views and set off the house; she has succeeded gloriously, adding colour, texture, height and a series of compartments. There were just 15 trees when they began their temporary gypsy lifestyle. Today there are more than 1,500 planted in the garden and their surrounding land where dogs gambol and horses graze. Developed by trial and error over the past 14 years the whole garden has a charmingly organic, natural feel to it, from richly planted herbaceous borders to new, productive orchard. Old brick and stone has been recycled into walls and steps and a small lake created for the family's beloved East Indian ducks. Sam has built a huge paved pergola as a home for climbing roses and the little summer house is a perfect retreat. Annie's greatest joy, she says, is to watch her lovely trees and plants develop year by year and enjoy seeing their huge efforts blossom into a place of beauty. *Winner of the Brafferton-Helperby Gardens Award 2002.*

SHALLOWDALE HOUSE

Anton van der Horst & Phillip Gill
Shallowdale House,
West End, Ampleforth, Yorkshire YO62 4DY

tel   01439 788325
fax   01439 788885
e-mail   stay@shallowdalehouse.demon.co.uk
web   www.shallowdalehouse.demon.co.uk

Each window frames an outstanding view – this spot, on the edge
of the North York Moors National Park, was chosen for its views
and the house arranged to soak up the scenery, from the Pennines
to the Wolds. This is a stylish, elegant and large modern house
with a huge mature hillside garden. The generous bedrooms and
bathrooms are uncluttered and comfortable; the drawing room
has an open fire in winter. Phillip and Anton love what they are
doing, so you will be treated like angels and served freshly cooked
dinners of outstanding quality. *Children over 12 welcome.*

rooms	3: 2 twins/doubles both with bath; 1 double with private bathroom.
price	£70-£84.
meals	Dinner, 4 courses, £24.50.
closed	Christmas & New Year.
directions	From Thirsk, A19 south, then 'caravan route' via Coxwold & Byland Abbey. 1st house on left, just before entering Ampleforth.

Keep climbing and by the time you get to the top of the garden you will feel you've had a hearty country walk; sit on a bench and breathe that Yorkshire air. The many specimen trees planted when the house was built 40 years ago are now grown up: weeping birch, cypress, cherry, maple, acer and copper beech hover over swathes of grass underplanted with thousands of bulbs, a double rockery groans with scented shrubs like viburnum, rosemary and choisya – while cistus, hardy geraniums, ceanothus, fuchsias and potentilla are popped in for colour. A very park-like atmosphere prevails – sadly without the bandstand – but you still feel like just sitting and watching, perhaps nibbling on a sandwich and chatting to a stranger! Nearer the house there are more formal beds, a mini-orchard, a sunny terrace with tinkling water feature and clematis and roses that march over the arches. Mixed planting everywhere but in such good taste. Hard work for just the two of them but Anton never goes up, or down, the hill without an armful of dead-heads and flotsam; their gorgeous dog gambols around while they discuss what to do next.

RIVERSIDE FARM

Bill & Jane Baldwin
Riverside Farm,
Sinnington, York, Yorkshire YO62 6RY

tel   01751 431764
fax   01751 431764
e-mail wnbaldwin@yahoo.co.uk

A charming long, low Georgian farmhouse that overlooks the river and the village green. Gleaming old family furniture, Bill's family photographs up the stairs, and two handsome bedrooms facing south over the scented cottage garden. There's pretty Colefax & Fowler sweet pea wallpaper in the twin, and Osborne & Little topiary trees in its bathroom. Breakfast is deliciously traditional – this is still a working farm – and there's an excellent pub for supper a short walk from the house. Elegant surroundings, excellent value and Jane a practical and generous hostess who will look after you well. Special indeed. *Minimum stay 2 nights.*

rooms	4: 1 double with shower; 1 twin with private bath; 2 singles with private or shared bath.
price	From £50.
meals	Available locally.
closed	November to March.
directions	From Pickering A170; 4 miles to Sinnington. Into village, cross river; right into lane for Riverside Farm.

Not only have Jane and Bill created a two-acre garden over the last 21 years, but Jane is also the National Gardens Scheme organiser for North Yorkshire. Her intimate knowledge of every garden and its owner on her patch means she can arrange private visits – but there is plenty at Riverside Farm, too, to interest the plantsman. As you open the little gate that leads to the front door, two big old stone troughs overflowing with helichrysum and geraniums introduce you to a cottage garden paradise. Jane has drawn inspiration from Rosemary Verey's circular lawn with four beds at Barnsley, keeping a close eye on the colour scheme – she prefers to keep pink plants to a minimum – and a light touch when controlling the self-seeding. The overall effect is beautifully natural and uncontrived – a truly difficult task, as any gardener will tell you. Pretty pink shrub roses have been given special permission to romp in the long, deep herbaceous bed that is, again, artfully natural. This runs parallel to the River Severn which flows down the garden's eastern border. A 'Kiftsgate' rose amply covers a 30-foot barn, and from the garden behind there's a lovely vista through the huge rose arch of 'Félicite et Perpetue' – inviting you to explore the gorgeous wild area, with its pond and meandering paths mown towards young woodland. *NGS*

DOWTHORPE HALL

John & Caroline Holtby
Dowthorpe Hall,
Skirlaugh, Hull, Yorkshire HU11 5AE

tel   01964 562235
fax   01964 563900

Holtbys have lived at Dowthorpe for 108 years, but never can
the house have looked as glamorous as today. Caroline has used
quality materials and swagged curtains generously. Mahogany
furniture, luxuriously soft mattresses, and, in two of the
bedrooms, all-white bed linen – one has four-foot twin beds,
the double a corona canopy. The single room is decorated in
pink and green Jane Churchill fabric, with pink bed linen and
pine furniture. Large coral sofas and a grand piano in the
sumptuous drawing room; the dark navy dining room looks
fabulous by candlelight. Food is beautifully presented using
best china and crystal.

rooms	3: 1 double with private bath, 1 twin/double with bath, 1 single with shared bath.
price	£60-£70. Single from £30.
meals	Dinner £25.
closed	Never.
directions	North on A165 for Bridlington, through Ganstead & Coniston. On right, white railings & drive to Dowthorpe Hall

When Caroline moved into John's family home seven years ago, she expanded her interior design and cooking talents by taking an HND diploma in garden design. Such is her artistic flair that she has not only created a noteworthy garden at Dowthorpe Hall, but is also now much in demand to design other people's. A talented cook too, she uses much of the produce from the traditional kitchen garden, where herbs and salads are grown in a raised border constructed of railway sleepers and telegraph poles. Tomatoes and a vine flourish in the greenhouse, courgettes, pumpkins and squash grow in a hotly mulched bed, and there is abundant fruit from a large orchard. A recently created walled area is formally structured with topiary, box hedging and terracotta pots and tiles, with hostas and ferns providing foliage interest in the shade. In marvellous contrast is the hot border in the secluded Lady Garden, an extravaganza of oranges and reds; more bright colours against a blue-painted fence in the Mediterranean area around the swimming pool. A natural pond looks its best with the primulas and irises out, and is a great attraction for birds. This varied garden's appreciative visitors include gardening clubs on private visits. *NGS*

GRINGLEY HALL

Ian & Dulce Threlfall
Gringley Hall,
Gringley on the Hill, Gringley, Yorkshire DN10 4QT

tel   01777 817262
fax   01777 816824
e-mail dulce@gringleyhall.fsnet.co.uk
web   www.gringleyhall.co.uk

Gringley Hall was once a children's convalescent home and Dulce and Ian took seven years to restore it to its former beauty – a labour of love. The house now feels very much like a family home: big, comfortable bedrooms with armchairs and fresh flowers, and excellent bathrooms with generous towels. Breakfast is an experience not to be missed – delicious fresh fruits, organically produced bacon, sausages and eggs, home-made bread and preserves. Two walled, (dog-happy) acres with a grass tennis court and games room, too.

rooms	4: 2 twins/doubles both with bath/shower; 1 twin with private shower; 1 family suite on request.
price	£60–£70. Single occ. £45–£50.
meals	Dinner, 4 courses, £25.
closed	Very occasionally.
directions	From Bawtry, east on A631. Approaching Gringley, 1st left after school sign. On for 150 yds. House on left with iron gates.

There aren't many hills in this part of the country, but drive up past the Saxon church of historic Gringley-on-the-Hill and turn into the drive at Gringley Hall for rare long views over three counties. There was no garden when the Threlfalls moved here 22 years ago, but Dulce created as the children grew, learning by experience as she went. Bulbs, hellebores and early yellow iris carpet her spring woodland garden, with lots of different viburnums and exochorda. The dry sandy soil and south-facing front of the house suit a pinky/lilac Mediterranean look: wisteria and roses up the wall, banks of cistus and lavender beneath. The hot red, orange and yellow border blooms continuously from March to September, and the summer border flowers right through as well, "including August," emphasises Dulce. Sweeping lawns maintained by Ian incorporate a grass tennis court; a rope-swagged rose pergola encloses a 'secret' garden hiding a pond edged by a pebble beach and a bank. Here is a seat under a rose arbour – a good spot for contemplation. An asparagus bed, and a new potager and fruit cage, are evidence of her passion for growing her own food; she also propagates plants for sale and, now qualified, takes garden designing commissions for the lucky few. *NGS.*

Photography by Hidehara Imai

WALES

"I know a little garden close
set with lily and red rose"

WILLIAM MORRIS

CAPEL DEWI UCHAF COUNTRY HOUSE

Fredena Burns
Capel Dewi Uchaf Country House,
Capel Dewi Road, Capel Dewi, Carmarthen, Carmarthenshire SA32 8AY

tel   01267 290799
fax   01267 290003
e-mail   uchaffarm@aol.com
web   www.walescottageholidays.uk.com

A long, leafy, canopied lane leads to the charmingly informal garden which Freddie has created and cherished in the two acres around her pretty, lime-washed home. It has been hard work. When Freddie moved to Capel Dewi Uchaf from Windsor more than 10 years ago she had to tackle the derelict house first; then came the garden. It was overgrown and overshadowed by many shrubs and apple trees which cast the house into deep shade. On the plus side she inherited a mature woodland backdrop, through which a Roman road runs, and tall, sheltering hawthorn hedges to the east. Trees and undergrowth had to be cleared and clinging roots removed before she could start to garden properly. She planned an informal cottage garden with pretty beds of traditional plants and, very important, a substantial vegetable and soft fruit area to supply the house. Little by little, she has achieved what she hoped for with a relaxed blend of lawns, borders and features including a rose-clad pergola and arch. Her vegetable and fruit patch, edged with recycled railway sleepers, is immaculately tended and very productive. One of the most delightful corners is the front garden with its brightly planted beds which welcome guests to the front door; another, the White Garden, a memorial to members of her family. Sit under the pergola and enjoy the richly-scented roses, walk the woodland in springtime when bluebells, snowdrops and wood anemones flower, or peep into the adjoining field where wild orchids grow.

rooms	3: 1 double with shower; 1 double with bath/shower; 1 twin with private bathroom.
price	£60. Single occ. £40.
meals	Packed lunch £6. Dinner £25.
closed	Christmas.
directions	From Carmarthen B4300 for 5 miles to Capel Dewi. Leaving village follow sign on left & down drive off main road.

For 2 people
August 2003
2 nights b&b   £120
"   " evening meals £80
"   bottles house red £17
Total £217

August 2003.
Lovely place, relaxing country house. Try to get the pink room. Food excellent. Will go again

Freddie has brought new life to what was a neglected, derelict, 14th-century house. She has done a tremendous job by restoring her 'Church of David Higher' in traditional country-house style; the house is higher up the river than its sister house in the village (Capel Dewi Isaf, meaning lower). This is a designated SSSI and you can fish on the private stretch of the water and even have your catch cooked for dinner. You will sink into the comfort of the house, with its brass beds, patchwork, terracotta walls, beams and fascinating memorabilia in utterly peaceful surroundings.

BRONIWAN

Carole & Allen Jacobs
Broniwan,
Rhydlewis, Llandysul, Ceredigion SA44 5PF

tel   01239 851261
fax   01239 851261
e-mail Broniwan@compuserve.com

Carole and Allen's deep committment to the environment and passionate interest in wildlife are what makes this garden special – a Tir Gofal Educational Access farm surrounds it. Carole designed the formal parts around the house, extending and replanting the original beds. There's a small lawned area on the upper level bordered by deep beds of hydrangea, aquilegia, agapanthus and rosemary with a little wrought-iron fence covered in clematis at the front. The narrow pathways, built with bricks from an old pig-sty and original Victorian tiled edging, lead through an archway to a large shrub border… Where, to a marvellous backdrop of mature beech, there are camellias and rhododendrons, bamboo, ceanothus, irises, broom and bright pieris and then more lawns and a rose bed. Further on there is a border of eucalyptus trees and the fruit and vegetable garden. A mown path through the grasses meanders to the meadow; meticulous records are kept of all the animals, birds, wild flowers and trees and the best environment for them is encouraged. Broadleaf woodlands, waterside and wetland areas, hedgerow restoration and maintenance, parkland, pond areas and grassland meadows mean Broniwan is teeming with birds (including the elusive red kite), butterflies, rare wild flowers and even otters. Allen is happy to take guests on farm walks and to talk about his naturally balanced production system. Carole loves the garden and will chat easily about her future plans.

rooms	2: 1 double with shower; 1 double with private bath.
price	From £50. Single occ. £25.
meals	Dinner £18. Light supper £11.50. Packed lunch on request.
closed	Very occasionally.
directions	From Aberaeron A487 for 6 miles for Brynhoffnant. Left at B4334 to Rhydlewis; left at Post Office & shop, 1st lane on right, then 1st track on right.

Carole and Allen, who are devoted to conservation, unfussily draw you into their home, cosy with warm, natural colours in paintings and woollen tapestries; they serve Welsh cakes on your arrival. Their organic farm is Soil Association-registered, so you will eat very well. Plentiful birdlife in their wonderful garden adds an audible welcome to Broniwan: tree-creepers, wrens and redstarts all nest in ivy-covered walls or mature beech trees. Views of the Preseli Hills, and the National Botanic Garden of Wales and Aberglasney to visit.

RHYDLEWIS HOUSE

Judith Russill
Rhydlewis House,
Rhydlewis, Nr Llandysul, Ceredigion SA44 5PE

tel   01239 851748
fax   01239 851748
e-mail judithrussill@aol.com
web   www.rhydlewis-house.co.uk

An 18th-century house in a friendly village with a wealth of nurseries - perfect for gardeners. This ex-drovers' *rendez-vous* houses a stylish mix of traditional and new: modern furniture by students of John Makepeace, exposed stone wall, rugs on polished wooden floors. The dining room has quarry tiles, an inglenook fireplace and traditional Welsh oak cottage-style chairs. A sunny double room with checked fabrics overlooks the garden; warm reds, oranges and creams are the colours of the twin. Judith is a terrific cook who uses mostly local produce (there's an excellent smokery in the village). Single visitors are particularly welcome.

rooms	3: 1 double with bath; 1 twin with shower; 1 double with private bath
price	From £44. Single occ from £22.
meals	Dinner £15.
closed	Christmas.
directions	North on A487. Right at north side of Sarnau, signed 'Rhydlewis'. T-junc. right to B4334. In Rhydlewis at sharp right bend, left. 40 yards on left.

Judith can look out on her acre of garden with pride: the planting, apart from a few mature trees and some crocosmia, is entirely her own. There are several seats from which to admire the fruits of Judith's labours, and the garden, begun in the spring of 2000, has matured well. The upper level of two main areas of lawn has an arbour tucked into an angle of the old workshop building, from where you can gaze back up at the house. On the lower lawn is a *Viburnum mariesii*, and other white-flowering shrubs form a backdrop against a wall to the gravel garden; rest on a bench and admire the hot reds, oranges and yellows of crocosmia in the herbaceous border opposite. Walk through the honeysuckle arch and discover a wide mixture of flowering shrubs: evergreens (protection from the wind), weigela, berberis and hydrangeas for season-long colour, and an under-planting of primroses, violets and *Anemone blanda*. From yet another seat you can watch all the village comings and goings. No modern garden is complete without a deck and Judith's makes an ideal spot for tea or an evening drink; as you sip, admire her pots of hostas, fuchsias and begonias.

COURT ST LAWRENCE

Susan Inkin
Court St Lawrence,
Llangovan, Monmouth , Gwent NP25 4BT

tel   01291 690279

The approach is majestic and the house, deep in countryside between England and Wales, meets all expectations; the lines of the Welsh longhouse blend beautifully with the Georgian and the Victorian. Surrounded by 140 acres of farmland, with gardens sloping down to a small lake and a stream that meanders through the woodland, there's plenty to explore. Lovely wallpapers and curtains, good linen and antique furniture in the large bedrooms, and you breakfast in an upstairs gallery overlooking that lovely garden. The peace and the seclusion are soothing.

rooms	3: 1 double, 1 twin, 1 family, all with private bathrooms.
price	£70. Single occ. £40.
meals	Dinner £17.50-£20.
closed	December.
directions	Please ask for directions when booking.

Everything about Court St Lawrence and its surroundings speaks of grace: the way the long drive slips down through the trees and curves gently up to the house in its serene and stately setting, and Sue's gentle and courteous welcome to the home she loves. Wisteria and *Magnolia grandiflora* spread across the white façade. The garden looks its best in June when arrivals are greeted by the sight of a 'Kiftsgate' rose tumbling out of its acacia tree host, and the herbaceous border is in full and glorious bloom. The big jungly planting suits the proportions of the house behind: tall silvery cardoons, shrub roses, philadelphus filling the air with scent, and, later, the tall white *Nicotiana silvestris*. Round on the west side of the house a pillared veranda with deep wicker chairs is the best spot to catch the late afternoon or evening sun: "My *Out of Africa* experience," says Sue. The wide lawn stretches down to the lake, the stream meanders through woodland. Here are bluebells in spring, and young, recently planted trees. You can use the swimming pool and tennis court, and the gardens of Herefordshire and Gloucestershire are only just over the border.

GREAT HOUSE

Dinah Price
Great House,
Isca Road, Old Village, Caerleon, Monmouthshire NP18 1QG

tel   01633 420216

Caerleon once housed Roman soldiers in barracks by the River Usk and you can still see the baths and amphitheatre. More peaceful now, although Dinah did find a musket ball in one of her walls recently, this 16th-century village house is built for comfort. Exposed stone walls, wooden beams and large fireplaces with woodburning stoves are softened with cool colours and plenty of squashy seating. Dinah's a great bargain hunter so you're surrounded by interesting pictures and old furniture. The bedrooms are immaculately decorated in creams and the single looks over the garden and river. Breakfast royally on Welsh sausages and organic eggs.

rooms	3: 2 twins, 1 single sharing bathroom.
price	From £55. Single £35.
meals	Available locally.
closed	Christmas.
directions	From M4 junc. 25 to Caerleon. Sharp right after 1 mile, just before bridge. Next left & left again; 4th cottage on right.

Dinah has been here for thirty years and copes well with the difficulties of having a fast-running river at the bottom of the garden which can flood at high tide – a gardener's nightmare. Now terraced, the upper level is safe and dry. Clematis is Dinah's great passion and she has hundreds of varieties clambering down one whole border to the right of the upper lawn, mainly in blues, mauves and purples. There is something in flower through all the seasons, and a backdrop of mature trees and shrubs, elegantly laid out, provides the perfect prop for them all. Outside the house is a terrace crowded with clematis and beautiful terracotta pots for annuals; to the left is a huge, curving herbaceous border filled with pink roses, ferns, lavender and yet more clematis. A small hidden pond is crowded with frogs and newts, protected by hordes of water-loving plants and grasses – little brick walls and trellises break up the view and provide structure for more plants – and more clematis! Pots filled with annuals are cunningly moved around the edges of borders to add colour and little gaps in paths have succulents and alpines peeping through: all colourful and pastel, nothing is garish, with blue as the main player. An old wooden table and benches on the lawn are also painted a Mediterranean shade of blue. Dinah's passion for clematis is still unabated, she loves to take cuttings, and to buy cut price bargains – as a challenge! *British Clematis Society.*

GARTHMYL HALL

Tim & Nancy Morrow
Garthmyl Hall,
Garthmyl, Montgomery, SY15 6RS, Powys

tel   01686 640550
fax   01686 640609

This is handsome Georgian on a grand scale with masses
of light and space and not a whiff of cloying cosiness. The
Morrows have brought new life to the old hall with great
decorative flair. The drawing room has Italianate gilded
ceilings and the bedrooms are decked out in a mix of period
and contemporary; every piece of furniture is special.
Duckdown duvets, oak floors, high ceilings, stone staircases,
fruit in the rooms and good fresh food with much garden
produce. Pretty Berriew, Powys Castle and Montgomery
town are all worth a visit and are nearby.

rooms	9: 6 doubles, 2 twin/doubles, 1 single, all with bath.
price	£70–£110. Single occ. £50–£80.
meals	Dinner from £21.50. Hampers also available.
closed	Never.
directions	6 miles south of Welshpool on A483. Drive on right, 50 yds after Nags Head Hotel.

Five acres of formal gardens and over nine acres of parkland and fields - a big job for Nancy. Once a grand Victorian garden and still listed, various parts were grassed over to save on labour. Nancy wants to link it all up again and create interesting walkways which will incorporate the fields and parkland as well as the formal garden. The 'bones' are good: some extremely old and beautiful trees include a marvellous *Magnolia rustica rubra* growing up the side of the house, three ancient cedars of Lebanon, an elegant eucalyptus and a weeping ash. By the house is a large herbaceous border, planted with sweetly scented roses, lavender, eleagnus, *Daphne odora* and mahonias to greet the visitor. A gravelled terrace with old urns surrounded by *Alchemilla mollis* leads out to the sunken lawn (the original Victorian drainage system has been renovated) and an elegant circular stone-walled pond with more urns planted with *Petunia surfina*. Divided lawns sweep down to the pale rosy-bricked walled garden; a grand herbaceous border with mature shrubs and climbers basks against its warmth. The walled garden is now being cultivated; neat rows of vegetables divided by a lonicera hedge and some traditional topiary, soft fruit and old varieties of fruit trees and fig grow up the tall walls. There's an orchard with old varieties of damson, medlar and quince, another herbaceous border bursts with David Austin roses and there's a pretty copse of fir trees.

Photography by Mark Bolton

SCOTLAND

"A sensitive plant in a garden grew.
And the young winds fed it with silver dew."

P.B SHELLEY

ARDSHEAL HOUSE

Neil & Philippa Sutherland
Ardsheal House,
Kentallen of Appin, Argyll & Bute PA38 4BX

tel   01631 740227
fax   01631 740342
e-mail nfo@ardsheal.co.uk
web   www.ardsheal.co.uk

A 600-year-old Stuart mansion blessed with every architectural indulgence you could hope for. The view is staggering - Loch Linnhe shimmers at the end of the fields - and the house is an Aladdin's Cave of beautiful things. A log fire and leather armchairs in the panelled hall, a drawing room in blue and yellow, a grand conservatory for breakfast, and an awesome billiard room where you can pick up a telescope and scan the loch for traffic. Big, country-house bedrooms with maybe a four-poster, loch views or a *chaise longue*. Woodland walks are open to the public. Sensational.

rooms	3 twin/doubles, all with bath & shower
price	From £110.
meals	Several good restaurants nearby.
closed	Christmas & occasionally at other times.
directions	A828 south of Ballachulich Bridge & Fort William. Signed from A828 in village of Kentallen.

It's a long drive up to Ardsheal, winding up through ancient native woodland and huge Scots pines. Broad verges open out, punctuated by shrubs and fine trees, including a 160-foot Wellingtonia, as you approach. The house is poised on an outcrop of pink marble amidst breathtaking scenery, and new woodland walks are being created all around; wonderful views reach to the mountains of Morvern where the garden falls down to Loch Linnhe. Away from the loch, steps lead you down through a large Victorian rockery into a steep wooded valley. It's like a 'lost world' down here, with its own microclimate — eucryphias, fremontodendrons, abutilons and date palms thrive. Where the huge Victorian vegetable garden once stood, Philippa has created a 100-foot herbaceous border all along one side: plants do best here that don't mind damp, like astilbes; Japanese anemones and rudbeckias extend the colour well into autumn. A wide selection of vegetables and soft fruits remain. An enthusiastic bog garden displays groupings of gunnera, ligularia, rodgersia, ranunculus and primulas, and Philippa propagates many of their own plants from cuttings. She and Neil fully deserve the recognition they have earned in restoring this magnificent house and garden. *SGS, Gardens of Scotland, Glorious gardens of Argyll & Bute.*

NETHER UNDERWOOD

Felicity & Austin Thomson
Nether Underwood,
By Symington, Kilmarnock, KA1 5NG, Ayrshire

tel	01563 830666
fax	01563 830777
e-mail	netherund@aol.com
web	www.netherunderwood.co.uk

You'll quickly feel at home in this unusual, elegantly decorated 1930s-style home built by the original owners of the nearby big house. The large yellow drawing room with Adam fireplace has log fires in winter and on chilly summer evenings. Felicity serves delicious food at the refectory table in the dark red dining room - she is a former chef who specialises in Scottish fare and home baking. Antique furniture, rich, thick curtains, lovely cosy bedrooms - the twin has tartan and thistle motifs. Colour everywhere and, in the background, the gentle tick-tock of Austin's collection of longcase clocks.

rooms	4: 2 doubles with bath/shower; 1 twin with private bathroom; 1 double, sometimes available, with bath/shower.
price	£90. Single occ. £55.
meals	Afternoon tea & dinner available. Excellent pubs & restaurants locally.
closed	Occasionally.
directions	From Glasgow, A77 for Ayr. Pass Little Chef, left for Underwood & Ladykirk. Left at T-junc., over bridge, past farm on right, down hill & left. Pass gates to Underwood House, then immed. left. Signed. At end of lane.

Felicity is a very keen gardener and she relished the huge challenge of these grounds when she and Austin moved here 10 years ago. They inherited wonderful 'bones' with an 18th-century, two-acre walled garden and a further 13 acres of woodland and fields with sweeping views. The downside was that the garden, which had once been the kitchen garden for the nearby manor, had been abandoned for years and had reverted to a jungle. Two years of relentless work followed - clearance, weed control and rescue work on hedges and neglected plants. The stranger, most interesting specimens were dug out, fed and re-planted with masses of mulching. The Thomsons called in a landscape gardener for advice on an overall design and began to breathe new life into the grounds: lawns were rejuvenated, new borders laid out and the rose garden nurtured back to colourful splendour. Lots of ornamental planting was introduced to add all-year interest, with good shrubs and trees. An avenue of pleached lime has been planted as well as other formal features including low box hedges as edging. A kitchen garden has been established for soft fruit, vegetables and cut flowers for the house. One of the garden's greatest bonuses is the stream; it runs though the garden and into the woodland beyond, and the banks are home to ducks and water-loving plants. The sleeping beauty has awoken and matured into a charming example of informal gardening in a natural setting.

THE MOUNT

Elizabeth & Robin Black
The Mount,
Newfield, Dundonald, Ayrshire KA2 9BH

tel   01563 851047
fax   01563 850981
e-mail blackmount@mail.com

A neat house where you will be elegantly entertained.
Immaculate and pretty bedrooms (the downstairs twin has a
sitting area of its own), spotless bathrooms, thoughtful extras
such as books and garden magazines to make you feel at home,
and a large drawing room window that beckons you onto the
terrace and into the glorious garden. Elizabeth and Robin bend
over backwards to make you feel comfortable and welcome; they
are also knowledgeable about the many golf courses in the area,
and seem to have memorised the local ferry timetables should you
choose to head off and discover the gardens of Arran, Bute, Argyll
or Northern Ireland.

rooms	2: 1 twin with sitting area, bath & shower; 1 double with shower.
price	From £52. Single occ. from £32.
meals	Dinner £20.
closed	Christmas & New Year.
directions	From Dundonald main street turn east into Kilmarnock Rd at War Memorial. Right after 0.4 miles into farm road for 30 yards; gates on left.

Elizabeth and Robin started to create their garden 12 years ago; as a long-term member of the NCCPG, and erstwhile chairman of the local group, Elizabeth had a fair idea which plants would suit the site. The first consideration was shelter: gales carry salt inland from the sea three miles away and firs or evergreens would have been burnt by wind. So in went indigenous varieties of tree like beech and whitebeam, interspersed with more exotic specimens such as Himalayan sorbus (birds don't fancy the berries of these particular rowans). Shrubs were added to form structure, and – gradually – hellebores, anemones, bulbs and masses of different pulmonarias were popped in underneath to complete the picture. The sunny Japanesey summer house at the top of the lawn is the perfect spot from which to review the display of herbaceous colour; there's so much here to interest the curious plantsman. Step down onto the patio where self-seeded aubretia pop up through the paving cracks; alpines have established themselves in troughs and retaining wall. Through one garden door drought-resistant plants enjoy a dry and sunny east-facing courtyard; in contrast, primulas, irises and astilbes thrive in a damp patch in the corner. Each plant is contented in its carefully chosen spot. *RHS, NCCPG, The Scottish Rock Garden.*

11 WARRISTON CRESCENT

Nicola Lowe
11 Warriston Crescent,
Edinburgh, Edinburgh EH3 5LA

tel   0131 556 0093
fax   0131 558 7278
e-mail nickylowe@totalise.co.uk

Nicola is a talented and sought-after garden designer who has had the unexpected and perhaps doubtful pleasure of designing her own garden twice. She moved here in 1996, and just as her first creation was reaching maturity, four years later, the Water of Leith flooded to a depth of 12 feet and swept all before it, including boundary walls. No faint-heart, Nicola mopped up the house and started again on the garden, and here it is, reaching its best. Wisely she has divided the 100-foot length into three distinct sections. By the conservatory, the predominantly foliage plants — mostly clipped bay and box — give an Italianate feel. In the central area you find a gentle English country-garden planting with the silvers, pinks and blues of old-fashioned roses, clematis and geraniums; here, garden furniture is suitably traditional. And finally, on the deck at the end, Nicola has created a dry garden where drought-resistant plants such as euphorbias, phlomis and grasses pop up through the gravel and paving as if defying the Water of Leith to flood again.

rooms	1 double with private bath; 1 twin with shower.
price	£70. Single occ. £45.
meals	Wide choice of restaurants nearby.
closed	Occasionally.
directions	250 yards from East Gate of Royal Botanical Gardens.

So peaceful is this listed 1820s townhouse in a quiet tree-lined cul-de-sac that you would never know you were so near the city centre. Here is a bright and elegant house with big Georgian windows and strong decorative colours that are a striking foil for the contemporary art that Nicola loves collecting. ("More pictures than sense, Mum," says her daughter.) Guest bedrooms are down the stairs from the front door at garden level; the conservatory is yours to use too. Nicola runs a fruit farm just outside Edinburgh, so for breakfast there is fresh fruit in season with home-made jams and compotes. *Two nights minimum in August.*

CAMBO HOUSE

Mr & Mrs TPN Erskine
Cambo House,
Kingsbarns, St Andrews, Fife KY16 8QD

tel   01333 450054
fax   01333 450987

This is a Victorian mansion in the grand style, with staff help. Magnificent, luxurious bedrooms – the four-poster room was once used for servicing the dining room, which is more of a banqueting hall. You are welcome to view this, and also the first floor billiard room and drawing room (though you may prefer to use the sitting room), and you have breakfast in the smaller dining room downstairs. If you B&B in the studio apartment for two, with a dear little sitting area in a turret, you can come and go as you please during the day.

rooms	3: 1 double, 1 four-poster, 1 twin.
price	£96. Single occ. £48.
meals	Dinner £36.
closed	Christmas & New Year.
directions	A917 to Crail, through Kingsbarns. Follow signs for Cambo Gardens, follow drive to house.

A garden of renown, stunningly romantic all year round. There is a spectacular carpet of snowdrops, snowflakes and aconites in the 70 acres of woodland following the Cambo burn down to the sea; bulbs, including many specialist varieties, are available by mail order. A woodland garden is in a continuing state of development, and, in May, the lilac walk through 26 varieties is a glorious display which also smells delicious. The Cambo burn carves its way across the two-acre walled garden: in here a huge range of herbaceous perennials and masses of roses fill the borders with colour through summer. A willow weeps artfully between a decorative bridge and a Chinese-style summerhouse looks as though it has jumped out of a willow-pattern plate. A new potager in 2001 has matured brilliantly, hot red and yellow annuals amongst the vegetables and herbaceous perennials carrying the colour through August, as does the inventively-planted annual border with its castor oil plants, grasses and *Verbena bonariensis* – no Victorian bedding plants here. In September the colchicum meadow is at its best, and an autumn border is being developed using late herbaceous perennials mixed with grasses. There's always something new at Cambo, and it's on a high with the buzz of success about it. *SGS, Good Gardens Guide.*

BIRKHILL

Countess of Dundee
Birkhill,
Cupar, Fife KY15 4QP

tel   01382 330200
fax   01382 330230
web   www.birkhill.org.uk

L aid out in the 1920s this garden is considered to be one of the finest on the Scottish east coast. This is no mean achievement – there are acres of lawns (four mowing days a week!) and a 2.5 acre walled garden with its original 1780 greenhouses, still producing nectarines, peaches, figs, apricots, blueberries and grapes. A vegetable garden – all organic – includes some of the unusual things that Siobhan likes to use for cooking: borage, nasturtiums, lovage and nettles. A long rose border includes some old-fashioned scented varieties and bursts with colour in May and June. A lovely wild garden is Siobhan's retreat – she says she is "not a digger but a potterer", and one of her favourite things to do is mow paths through the long grass. Leaving overhanging branches she creates tunnels – ancient cathedrals? No wonder she feels so peaceful there. The woodland garden runs down to the Tay and was mainly planted with magnolia and rhododendrons in the 1930s; gushing through it is a stream with skunk cabbages, primulas and white box marigold. A walk along the river – studded with thousands of bluebells in spring – takes you to an ancient abbey through the estate policies which have many mature oak, beech and redwood trees; there is even a rare 200-year-old larch. A private stony beach on the banks of the river is a good spot for a picnic. Take a proper wicker basket, cool the wine in the water and imagine yourself back to a gentler past. *NGS*

rooms	5: 2 doubles with private bath; 3 twins with private bath/shower.
price	£120. Single occ. £80.
meals	Kitchen supper £15. Dinner £27.
closed	Very occasionally.
directions	Ask at time of booking.

In William Wallace's day Lord Dundee may not have given you such a jolly welcome – the present Earl is still the Royal Standard Bearer for Scotland but is happy to have the old enemy come to stay. A grand house but also a family home: the huge guests' drawing room has an open fire, gleaming wooden floors, exquisite furniture; interesting modern paintings jostle with family portraits. The dining room looks out over the gardens and the River Tay. Bedrooms are elegant with pretty fabrics and comfortable chairs, bathrooms have original wallpapers and white enamel baths. Siobahn's dinners are legendary and she is great fun – relax and enjoy it all.

THE FACTOR'S HOUSE

Davina & Robert Howden
The Factor's House,
Berriedale, Caithness, Highland KW7 6HD

tel   01593 751280
fax   01593 751251
e-mail robert@welbeck2.freeserve.co.uk

A Victorian family house on a traditional sporting estate and a hugely comfortable place to stay. Day loves colour, and has had fun in the dining room creating strong terracotta paint effects - using bin liners! Warm yourself over the winter log fire in the drawing room with its huge Victorian bay window neatly framing the jaunty sea views. More seascapes from the double - a lovely room with a handsome brass bed dressed in Indian silk and cotton; there are homely touches on other beds with Day's patchwork quilts. The ground-floor twin has French windows that open onto the garden. Perfect.

rooms	3: 1 double, 1 twin, both with private bath; 1 twin with private shower.
price	£80. Single occ. £50.
meals	Dinner £25.
closed	Christmas & Easter.
directions	A9 north of Helmsdale, before bottom of Berriedale Braes left to Langwell House. Right at mirror, up to white gates; left & left again to house.

There is a particular talent to gardening 300 feet above the North Sea. It involves patience born of an unconquerable love of plants, and persistence that only comes from a deep urge to till the soil. Here by Berriedale you'll find two treats. Robert is the factor to Langwell, a traditional sporting estate vaunting a glorious and immaculate walled garden primed to peak in August and September; meanwhile, up at the Factor's House, Day cares for her own smaller, equally lovely, walled flower garden. Divided by gravel paths and local flagstones, edged with low pergolas, each section is reached through arches of climbing plants. In one bed her favourite soft pinks, mauves and purples, in another, bright reds, yellows and gentian blues. An autumn block with late alstroemeria, cercidiphyllum and acer, underplanted with primulas and meconopsis, gives a dash of spring colour. Day loves unusual plants and can never resist trying out new ones, often propagating from friends' cuttings or from seed: *Hedisarum coronarium* and *Ononis rotundifolia* are doing well. "This isn't a garden, but a collection of plants I like," she says. She should not be so modest: her garden is a triumph of optimism over (almost) insuperable odds. *SGS, Good Gardens Guide, HPS, RHS, Plant Life.*

GLECKNABAE

Ian & Margaret Gimblett
Glecknabae,
Rothesay, Isle of Bute PA20 0QX

tel   01700 505655
fax   01700 505655
e-mail glecknabae@amserve.net

The wonderful view is a fabulous surprise as you walk in through
the front door to the dining hall: the windows opposite look down
over the front garden to a 180° view of the sea and islands.
Tapestries on walls, Aubusson-style rug on polished ash floor, and
a log fire in the sitting room. Everywhere is light and bright:
guests' pretty little bedrooms are at one end of the house, with
comb ceilings and velux windows. The Gimbletts treat guests as
friends, and you are welcome to have your meals in their large
and stylish blue and terracotta kitchen with its warm Aga.

rooms	2: 1 twin, 1 single with privat or shared bathroom.
price	From £50.
meals	Dinner from £12.50.
closed	Very occasionally.
directions	Follow Shore Rd to Port Bannatyne. At T-junc. left at Kames Gate Lodge towards Ettrickbay, bear right, cross bridge, bear left. Follow track road over cattle grid to end of tarmac. Right into parking area.

The usual exclamation from visitors to Glecknabae is "Magic!", but the Gimbletts had the foresight and imagination to realise that when they bought the place derelict in 1993, brambles, nettles, warts and all. Within two years, having reconstructed the house, they won an award for their courtyard garden: since then they have created a series of small gardens all around the house, divided by hedges and trees. Deliberately avoiding the usual Scottish theme of rhododendrons and azaleas, they have planted a garden for all seasons: snowdrops in January, a natural area of trees and shrubs, a bog garden stashed with primulas and irises. Alpine plants take every advantage of the naturally stony environment, popping up through cracks in smooth rock and clustering in raised beds in the gravel garden. From seats in sheltered spots you can gaze at the unsurpassable views down Bute, over to mainland Argyll and across to the islands of Arran and Inchmarnock. It's only three minutes' walk down to the shore and the wildlife is abundant: you can see deer and otters, or basking shark and porpoises if it's warm, and the place is full of birds from buzzards and the occasional golden eagle to tiny goldfinches. Magic indeed. *SGS, HPS.*

KIRKNEWTON HOUSE

Tinkie & Charles Welwood
Kirknewton House,
Kirknewton, Midlothian EH27 8DA

tel   01506 881235
fax   01506 882237

Rooms are lovely and large, having once been part of a more extensive house dating from the 17th century. Since the complete reorganisation of the ground floor in the 80s, modern comforts have been added to compliment the history. A fine, polished oak staircase, fresh flowers in the hall (Tinkie is an accomplished flower arranger), rugs on the floor. The large double bedroom has a four-poster bed with a white canopy and a view over the rose garden and its little fountain. Lots of fruit for breakfast; feast upon it in a stately manner in the dining room, or snug up to the Aga in the kitchen.

rooms	2: 1 double, 1 four-poster, both with private bath.
price	£65-£70. Single occ. £50-£57.50.
meals	Dinner £22-£50.
closed	Christmas-February.
directions	From either A70 or A71 take B7031. 0.25 miles from Kirknewton going South, drive on left opposite small cottage.

You get the best of two worlds at Kirknewton: a large and comfortable house in peaceful landscaped woodland gardens, and Edinburgh, 30 minutes by car or train. The Welwoods have farmed here since they took over the family home in 1981; both are keen gardeners, so they set to maximizing the potential of the garden the moment they arrived. There are azaleas and rhododendrons in brilliant abundance in spring, and primulas and meconopsis scattered throughout; and in order to lengthen the season a long herbaceous border was created in a walled garden – wonderful in summer. A single long wall remains from an old part of the house that was demolished after the war: it faces south, sheltering the garden from the prevailing wind, and is covered in a glorious array of climbing roses such as 'Alchemist', 'Maigold', 'Schoolgirl' and 'New Dawn'. A stream flows down by the spring border into a pond in front of the house, and here rodgersia and the stately gunnera flourish. You are close to Malleny Garden, and as Tinkie is a county organiser for Scotland's Gardens Scheme, she is well acquainted with all the private gardens in the area. *SGS*.

ROSSIE

Mrs David Nichol
Rossie,
Forgandenny, Perthshire PH2 9EH

tel   01738 812265
fax   01738 813314
e-mail judynichol@hotmail.com

Built in 1657 the dazzling white painted front with splashes
of climbing colour and huge archway are more Algarve than
Scotland. Don't expect gloomy ancestral portraits and stags
heads – the interior is stylish and immaculate with deep, pale
carpets and excellent lighting. Bedrooms are filled with fine
furniture, designer wallpapers and fabrics, crisp cotton sheets and
soft woollen blankets. Fresh flowers do as they're told in cut-glass
vases and shining bathrooms are littered with gorgeous goodies
from the fabulous Floris. David and Judy are pretty perfect too –
they exude efficiency and warmth in equal measure.

rooms	3: 1 double with bath; 2 twins both with private bath.
price	£80.
meals	Available locally.
closed	Christmas & New Year.
directions	From Edinburgh M90 for 30 miles. Exit 9 to Bridge of Earn, then Forgandenny. Past Post Office on right then entrance & lodge on right.

Rossie was used as a home for refugees during the war, and the garden – unloved and uncared for – grew wild and lost its figure. David and Judy have been here for 23 years, and have four grown up children so they now have the time to indulge their passion for designing and planting their ten seamlessly linked acres. Their main charm is the trails through the woodland; there are fine examples of shrubs, a canopy of mature trees and splashes of rhododendron colour from March to June. Hellebores, bluebells, trillium, meconopsis, primulas, epimediums and other shade-lovers swiftly chase a carpet of snowdrops and aconites. Trail through the garden over elegant bridges and along a stream ending with a pond – a gorgeous sculptured heron is fixed in take-off – and then a sunken garden. Here an old stone summer house is annually smothered in the deep red heart-shaped leaves of *Vitis coignetiae* and pink roses clamber up its side. The partially restored walled garden is a scented haven of old-fashioned roses, mighty herbaceous borders and the wafted vanilla of *Magnolia lypolenca*. A yew-hedged garden next to the house gives room and board to climbing roses, wisteria, solanum, lilies, yuccas and penstemon – all jostling under the eye of a lazy stone boy looking rather scornful and a 20-foot high *Cornus kousa* var. *chinensis* with its rose-tinted huge bracts. A garden for all seasons, but autumn – with acers abounding – is especially lovely. *SGS*.

GREENACRES

Mrs Hazel Harward-Taylor
Greenacres,
Chapelhill, Logiealmond, Perthshire PH1 3TQ

tel   01738 880302
fax   01738 880416

Across the surrounding countryside you can see the beginning
of the Highland line, and the Ochils, Sidlaw and Lomond -
romantic names for the far hills. Guests' ground-floor bedrooms
have been given names: the double-bedded Harebell looks out
over the azaleas to one of the two summer houses, while from
the twin-bedded Cowslip you may admire Hazel's Victorian
fernery tucked into the lee of the cottage. Home-grown
strawberries and raspberries from the organic vegetable garden
are on the breakfast table during the season; savour your after-
breakfast coffee in the morning sun by the little pond just outside
the garden door.

rooms	2: 1 double, 1 twin with bath/shower, either private or shared.
price	£45-£50. Single occ. £28.50-£31.
meals	Good food available locally.
closed	Occasionally.
directions	A9 to Inverness, 1st exit to Logie Almond & Battleby on B8063. On right 6 miles beyond Battleby, tall conifer hedge on roadside.

Are you an ecological nature-lover, a wannabe Bob Flowerdew? Hazel was the winner of Perthshire's Millennium Environmentally Green Garden Award, and conservationists will nod in appreciation when they see the sheer denseness of the planting in her sheltered half-acre garden. Weeds don't have a chance against the mass of packed shrubs and perennials, though treasures such as aquilegias and other cottage garden favourites are allowed to pop up at will. It's a sanctuary for birds, a haven for birdwatchers. Late in 2000 Hazel cast her thoughtful eye upon her neglected swimming pool: apprehensive lest she might be making a terrible mistake, she screwed her courage to the sticking post, and achieved a cunning conversion using brilliant recycling ideas. With little to spend, unlikely ingredients such as old tyres, rotted turf rolls and plastic bread trays became the key to the triumphant transformation of swimming pool to stunning water garden; straight edges were curved and softened with marginal planting, and the whole project attracted considerable interest. The pool changing-hut underwent a similar makeover: it is now a delightful summer house where guests can sit and catch the last of the day's sun over a glass of wine. *NGS.*

AUCHNAHYLE

Penny & Alastair Howman
Auchnahyle,
Pitlochry, Perthshire PH16 5JA

tel   01796 472318
fax   01796 473657
e-mail howman@aol.com

An 18th-century farmhouse hidden away on the edge of Pitlochry – wonderfully peaceful, yet convenient for the town and its theatre. Arrive for tea in the conservatory overlooking the croquet lawn; a prolific vine yields black grapes for the cheese board at dinner. Take breakfast here too, if it's warm. The dining room has lovely rugs and a picture of roaring stags above the sideboard; the sitting room is cosy with rich colours and a log fire. And note Alastair's tapestry cushions, whose designs are based on oriental rug patterns. Pretty, light bedrooms have views over the garden to hills beyond.

rooms	3: 1 twin, 2 twin/doubles, all with bath.
price	From £70.
meals	Supper £17. Dinner £23.
closed	November–March.
directions	In Pitlochry turn into E Moulin Road. 4th turn on right into Tomcroy Terrace to end. Right up drive.

The Howmans have become experts in gardening with peacocks. There was a bit of garden when they arrived here 22 years ago, but they have since extended it successfully – despite the avian competition. "The birds are curious about new seedlings, but with enough quick-growing herbaceous plants, we generally win," says Penny. She got the idea for her yellow and white border from a Japanese display at the Glasgow Garden Festival: four laburnums underplanted with golden elder and yellow and white flowers lead down to the little white summer house. Rowans and crab apple trees have been planted with hardy shrubs; at least one of them flowers at any given moment during the season. Old-fashioned roses survive the climate well, and climbing plants neatly evade those peacocks – there are lots of ivies, a *Hydrangea petiolaris*, golden hop, an actinidia. Alastair tends two vegetable patches, two polytunnels, a herb garden and a huge soft fruit cage, supplying the family and all their visitors with fresh produce most of the year. An amusing touch: there's an eight-foot-long dragon emerging from a shrubbery, constructed from recycled metals by a local blacksmith sculptress.

EAST LOCHHEAD

Ross & Janet Anderson
East Lochhead,
Largs Road, Lochwinnoch, Renfrewshire PA12 4DX

tel   01505 842610
fax   01505 842610
e-mail   eastlochhead@aol.com
web   www.eastlochhead.co.uk

A substantial farmhouse built in 1886 from the local grey-cream stone. In winter a log-burning stove glows in the huge living room with its big comfy chairs and piano. But the best thing is the view from the picture windows on the far side across the lovely garden to the spectacular lochs beyond. The alcove extension is like a garden room - a delightful spot in which to enjoy Janet's delicious meals. Capacious bedrooms upstairs with modern family paintings; stay in the twin for the 50-mile view of the lochs from the loo. A large downstairs bedsitting room is suitable for wheelchair-users - or a big family.

rooms	3: 1 double, 1 twin, both with bath/shower; 1 double with shower.
price	£60–£80. Single occ. £37.50–£47.50.
meals	Dinner from £22.50
closed	Very occasionally.
directions	M8 westbound junc. 28a; follow A737 for Irvine. Bear right when road divides. Right at r'bout to A760; Under 2 bridges, past bungalow, East Lochhead next house on left (behind trees).

The setting is idyllic. East Lochhead looks onto pastureland – where the Andersons' sheep and Highland cattle graze – to Loch Barr and Castle Semple Loch in the distance. A framework of evergreens characterizes this garden, with rhododendrons and azaleas protecting plants from the cold east winds and providing year-round foliage colour. Maples add extra blaze in autumn. A startling spring carpet of snowdrops and *Crocus tommasinianus* brings many visitors to admire the display. Primulas and marsh marigolds border the small stream that runs through the garden, and the pond is planted with irises and handsome waterside gunneras. Clematis thrive here and wind up through shrubs and evergreens – and there's a good show of delphiniums in herbaceous areas. Pathways meander round borders of hostas and hardy geraniums, and you'll find plenty of seats and secret areas to escape to. The outbuildings bordering the courtyard have been converted to self-catering units, and the courtyard walls overflow with jasmine, wisteria, honeysuckle and clematis, creating a really pretty welcome. The barn has become a hall with a warm kitchen range for special dinner parties and celebrations. *SGS, RHS.*

HOME FARM

Hugh & Georgina Seymour
Home Farm,
Stobo, Peebles, Peeblesshire EH45 8NX

tel   01721 760245
fax   01721 760319
e-mail hugh.seymour@btinternet.com

At the Seymours' home you can explore two utterly contrasting gardens: their own plant and shrub filled garden around the house divided into rooms – orchard, kitchen garden, rose garden; and through a gate in one corner, the famous and magical Stobo Castle Japanese Water Garden. The castle, now a health spa, originally belonged to the family but the Seymours have kept up the connection by maintaining the Water Garden as well as their garden next door. Stobo Water Garden is a rare example of Japanese-influenced design in Scotland, laid out nearly 100 years ago. Imaginative planting is as much a feature here as the visual impact – not to mention the glorious sound of rushing clear water. There is a dramatic waterfall, and lots of rills and mini cascades. The water is forged by frequent stepping stones, inviting visitors to criss-cross from one bank to the other. Azaleas and rhododendrons, and many fine specimen trees, are at their best in May and June, and again in October. The view of the humpback bridge, probably the focal point of the garden, has been much photographed and will be familiar to many who have not been within miles of Stobo. *SGS, Good Gardens Guide.*

rooms	2 + cottage: 1 twin, with dressing room with single bed & bathroom; 1 twin with private bathroom. Self contained twin-bedroomed cottage.
price	£60. Single occ. £40.
meals	Dinner from £20.
closed	Occasionally.
directions	From A72 Peeble/Glasgow, B712. Right down Stobo Castle Health Spa drive then right before small bridge, over cattle grid & up hill, leaving mill on left. Keep left into courtyard at top.

A turreted entrance makes quite an impression as you arrive at this traditional Peeblesshire farmhouse - the old factor's house on the Stobo estate. Built around a courtyard, Hugh and Georgina's home is a place of oak floors, mahogany furniture, attractive pictures and log fires. From the windows you glimpse their large collection of roses. Bedrooms on the first floor are light and airy and have bathrooms en suite; there is also an attic twin-bedded spare room with adjoining bathroom. For those who prefer their own space, there's a cosy self-contained cottage in the outer courtyard.

NETHER SWANSHIEL

Dr Sylvia Auld
Nether Swanshiel,
Hobkirk, Bonchester Bridge, Roxburghshire, Roxburghshire TD9 8JU

tel   01450 860636
fax   01450 860636
e-mail auldsj@globalnet.co.uk
web   www.netherswanshiel.fsnet.co.uk

Shiel (or shieling) means 'summer grazing', a name still apt in this fertile and deeply rural area. Originally built around 1770 as a manse (a Scottish vicarage), Nether Swanshiel is one of four houses in the tiny hamlet of Hobkirk. When the Aulds arrived in 1996 their one acre was a wilderness, but they soon set to, cutting back undergrowth and thinning trees, and opening up the views towards Bonchester Hill and down the river to the church. Gradually the original structure re-emerged; this now forms the basis for their own creation. The garden and house talk to each other through the new terrace, and a herbaceous border around the retaining wall supplies the house with the fresh flowers that Sylvia loves to have in the rooms. The Aulds are keen members of the Henry Doubleday Research Association, and their organic methods are beginning to reap rewards: the garden is alive with birds and an ever-increasing population of bees and butterflies. Old-fashioned yellow azaleas scent the spring, wild orchids flourish under the fruit trees in the wild corner, and martagon lilies pop up in unexpected places. This is a tranquil haven for both wildlife and visitors. *HDRA, Friend of Royal Botanic Garden, Edinburgh.*

rooms	3: 2 twins both with private bathrooms; 1 extra single for members of same party.
price	£50. Single £25.
meals	Dinner £15.
closed	November–February.
directions	B6357 or B6088 to Bonchester Bridge. Turn opp. pub (Horse & Hound). Beyond church 1st lane to right. Set back off road.

Bedouin and Persian rugs and other treasures reveal the Aulds' travelled background: Sylvia, an Islamic art historian, met Graeme (another academic) working in Jerusalem. She is a thoughtful hostess and excellent cook: Aga-baked scones or gingerbread for tea, organic produce (whenever possible) for dinner, and a choice of goodies such as kippers, proper porridge, corn-fritters, compotes and home-made bread for breakfast. You eat by the big Victorian bay window overlooking the terrace in the cosy guest sitting room with a log fire. Sleep deeply in your very private rooms, simply and softly furnished, with good beds and spotless bedspreads.

KILDROCHET HOUSE

Peter & Liz Whitworth
Kildrochet House,
By Stranraer, Wigtownshire DG9 9BB

tel   01776 820216
fax   01776 820216
e-mail   kildrochet@compuserve.com

A gorgeous home, run with great charm by Liz and Peter. Chief among its many architectural virtues is the garden room, a spectacular orgy of glass: books and maps, rugs and wall hangings, all the colours of the rainbow. In the dining room ancestors peer down from the walls; in the hall, the art is modern. Georgian windows give country views, there's an open fire in the drawing room, and the odd sloping floor. Bedrooms are just as good, very private in different wings. One is huge, with room for a sofa, and an armchair in the bathroom. Those who come vow to return.

rooms	2: 1 twin/double with bath/shower; 1 twin/double with bath.
price	£56. Single occ. £34.
meals	Good places to eat nearby.
closed	Occasionally.
directions	From Stranraer, A77 for Portpatrick for 1.5 miles. Straight on at A716 for Drummore. Drive on left after approx. 1 mile, at junc. with B7077 signed Newton Stewart.

Glorious Scottish policies in the rolling Rhins of Galloway – a secret and quiet gem. Kildrochet and its six acres stand at the gateway to the wonderful array of west coast Scottish gardens which owe their existence to the warm Gulf Stream currents. Logan Botanic Garden, Castle Kennedy, Glenwhan and the ferry to Ireland are all on the doorstep. Kildrochet itself is an early 18th-century dower house, its elegant white proportions standing out against the dark foliage of a protective backdrop of mature trees. Like other gardens in the area, this one is particularly spectacular in spring and early summer, with its blaze of azaleas and rhododendrons, carpet of bluebells in the beech wood shelter belt, and camellias in the courtyard. The woodland part is Liz's favourite and reflects her relaxed approach to gardening – she calls herself an amateur but she is just being modest. This is a comfortable and stylish family home, whose handsome façade is covered in clematis, actinidia and wisteria – itself a glory. Step out of the wide windows of the garden room onto the terrace; the scent of the wisteria in spring is a wonderful accompaniment to a quiet cup of tea or an evening drink, and the broad sweep of croquet lawn before you is a delight.

FRANCE

"La terre brilliante de fleurs
Fait éclater mille couleurs …"

VINCENT VOITURE

FRANCE

©Bartholomew Ltd, 2002

A guide to our B&Bs in France

It is entirely fitting that Britain's most celebrated gardener is Lancelot 'Capability' Brown, and France's, André Le Nôtre. For the English garden, no matter how grand, is an outgrowth of nature: Levens Hall, Stourhead, Hatfield House – all have an irregularity of design and an essentially natural, even intimate, feel. The traditional French garden, in contrast, is a place of formality and grandeur, where nature is a force to be tamed. French gardening has undergone some profound changes in recent years, but the great classical heritage lives on, renovated and revived in the châteaux gardens as well as in new, and sometimes stunning, contemporary forms.

All that hedge-clipping was dauntingly impressive and cost a fortune – which was precisely the point! Geometric design and symmetry; alleys of pleached lime and parterres of box; canals, cascades, fountains and statuary; viewpoints, vistas and paths cut with mathematical accuracy through woods; no inclines and few flowers: the French 17th-century nobility sought to express power through the grandeur of their gardens as much as their châteaux. Extravagant topiary did exist before – in 15th-century Italy in particular – but never on this scale. It all culminated in the gardens of the palace of Versailles, designed by Le Nôtre, employed by the Sun King. The orangery alone housed 1,200 orange trees; the fountains were the most extraordinary anyone had ever seen.

The Château de Brécy in Normandy is an early example of the architectural garden; its charming walled topiary sits the other side of meadows grazed by cows. The Château de Courances is a more grandiose garden of the period, and includes *parterres de broderie*: hedges clipped into arabesque shapes. Le Nôtre's first great work was the garden of the Château de Vaux le Vicomte – complex, spectacular and employing, at one time, 18,000 men. Louis XIV was impressed, and immediately appointed Le Nôtre Director of the gardens at Versailles. But the garden of which Le Nôtre himself was most proud was the Château de Chantilly, austerely elegant with its lawn parterres, pools with water jets, canals and even a picturesque 'hamlet'.

The Château de Villandry, west of Tours, has one of the world's greatest gardens, restored to its Renaissance glory in the early 1900s. Its vast potager, divided into nine equal squares, is stuffed with ornamental cabbages, radishes, peas, strawberries, sorrel, leeks, forget-me-nots and daisies – to name but a few – replanted twice a year. It has a dazzling beauty.

In the 18th century the English landscape garden – the clumps of trees, the meandering paths, the temples, grottos, lakes and hills (seemingly so random yet so carefully composed) came to the fore. Out with the fence, in with the ha-ha – so-named because the ditch that allows a "through-view… makes one cry 'Ah! Ah!'" The writer Horace Walpole championed the new romantics, William Kent and 'Capability' Brown, who "leaped the fence and saw that all nature was a garden". The new irregularity was seen as the direct result of admirable British liberalism while scorn was poured on the illiberal French. (Versailles' gardens, pronounced Walpole, were "the gardens of a great child".) In spite of this, *le jardin anglais* became a craze that spilled over into the gardens of France.

The Parc Canon in Normandy is one such natural garden, created by a Parisian barrister, a friend of Walpole, in the late 1700s. A broad path cuts through the woods across the main vista, with a temple at one end, a chinoiserie structure overhanging a stream at the other and open excursions into idyllic nature. Another garden from the same era is Le Désert de Retz near Paris, whose fantastic follies – a giant ruined column disguising a fully furnished house, an Egyptian obelisk, a temple to Pan – were to delight the Surrealists two centuries later. Thirty miles from Paris the philosopher Rousseau, inventor of the phrase "the Noble Savage", lies buried in the arborous landscape of the Parc de Jean-Jacques Rousseau. His tomb rests under poplars on an island on a lake, suitably far from the corrupting influences of civilization. Originally this park contained further romantic conceits: a wilderness and a model farm.

The fashion for landscape among the landowning classes reached its peak in the early 19th century. And in the process most of the old elaborate gardens of England – though not of more conservative Italy and France – were swept away.

Little by little the sedate characteristics of the traditional French garden have given way to a modern eclecticism. Worldwide exchanges of knowledge and increased accessibility of unusual plants have led to new takes on old fashions and a new interest in plantsmanship. A flood of rhododendron introductions began in the 19th century when botanists started collecting in the Himalayas; willows followed from Japan, roses from China; and there was a positive mania for camellias, inspired by the popularity of Alexandre Dumas' *La Dame aux Camélias* in 1848. Although there are still many shrubs and perennials raised in Britain that you would be hard pushed to find across the Channel, recent years have seen a mushrooming of plant nurseries in France. Who knows, the days of the bright begonia may be numbered!

20th-century gardens worth a detour… Kerdalo is a glorious garden in Brittany, planted in the Sixties; among its lakes and follies are 2,000 species of plants and trees — many rare — grouped in subtle harmonies of colour. Le Vasterival in Normandy is a connoisseur's delight, with a heavenly collection of woody plants: rhododendron, hydrangea, maple, birch, viburnum and camellia. La Chèvre d'Or, near Antibes, with its canopies of wisteria and bushes of blue ceanothus, was one of the first gardens planted for year round interest rather than for enjoyment in the fashionable winter months only. The Villa Noailles in Provence is a gem, with its series of softly hedged rooms à la Gertrude Jekyll: gardens within a garden. And the Châteaux de la Ballue in Brittany is a late 20th-century garden of surprises whose parterre is endowed with Gallic wit and fantasy.

The French gardens in this book are a fascinating mix of old and new, from the classical symmetry of the Châteaux du Mesnil Geoffroy and du Longsard to the joyful abandon of the Villamaux' little plot in Normandy inspired by Monet's gardens at Giverny. It has been a huge pleasure seeking out these special gardens and their B&B's; we hope that it will be as much of a treat for you to stay there. Let us know how you get on.

Le Clos

3 rue du Chêne Noir, 60240 Fay les Étangs

The sprucest of farmhouses, whitewashed and Normandy-beamed, sits in the lushest, most secret of gardens, reached via a door in the wall. More English cottage garden than pristine French, it is a tended tumble of colour in every season, a delight to every sense. A vine-embraced walkway, heavy with grapes in summer, leads to the white front door; a weigela, dripping with pink and white flowers in spring, and a wisteria with pale mauve, bloom near by. In the beds: old-fashioned roses, red hot pokers, Welsh poppies, jasmine, irises and lavender, wallflowers, daffodils, azalias, cotoneaster. A potager gives apples and pears, walnuts and plums, sage and thyme; there's a lovely secluded lawn and a neat little parasoled terrace for guests. Inside, timbers glow their 300 years against white walls stencilled in blue. Up an outside stair and into your big, split-level room in the hayloft – converted with originality and sporting red cushions on a butter-yellow bedcover. The separate single is snug and pretty. Dine with your hosts by the old farm fireplace on *tarte aux pommes du jardin*; Monsieur quietly acts as cook while Madame keeps you company, charmingly.

rooms	2: 1 double, 1 single, both with shower
price	€ 46.
meals	Dinner € 19, inc. wine & coffee.
closed	Rarely.
directions	From A16 exit 13 for Gisors & Chaumont en Vexin about 20km; after Fleury left to Fay les Etangs; 2nd left; house on left.

Philippe & Chantal Vermeire

tel	(0)3 44 49 92 38
fax	(0)3 44 49 92 38
e-mail	philippe.vermeire@wanadoo.fr

see French map entry: 182

Ferme de Bannay

51270 Bannay

A garden on a farm – perfect for families. Watch the milking, see how cheese is made. Bannay bustles with hens, ducks, guinea fowl, turkeys, donkey, sheep, nanny goats and cows... the farmyard chatter starts at 6am. The super, three-hectare (seven-acre) garden has a lawn bordered by trees and a pretty little church; there are picnic tables for the school parties who occasionally visit, and loungers for you. Beds burst with daffodils and forsythia in spring; dahlias make their splash in autumn; a carpet of conifers lines a gently stepped path. Breakfast jams come from the fruit trees, vegetables from the potager. As for the house, it is white-walled and beamy, with rooms that dance in swags, flowers and antique bits. A lacey lampshade here, a check tablecloth there, a piano covered with candles and photographs... wonderfully French. Our readers have loved the house, the family and the food. Only Madame's daughter and sister-in-law speak English, but the generosity is so genuine that communication is no problem at all.

rooms	4: 3 doubles, all with bath; 1 suite with shower.
price	€44–€53.
meals	Dinner, with wine, €23; with champagne, €26; restaurants 10km.
closed	Rarely.
directions	From Epernay D51 for Sézanne; at Baye, just before church, right D343; at Bannay right; farm before small bridge.

Muguette & Jean-Pierre Curfs

tel	(0)3 26 52 80 49
fax	(0)3 26 59 47 78

Les Champs Grandmère

Thiamont, 88210 La Petite Raon

An English garden in the Vosges mountains, wildly open to pigs, foxes, heron, hares and deer. It's a heavenly spot surrounded by lakes, pine woods and hills: Grandma's Meadows, three acres carpeted with wild flowers in May. Judith designed the lovely rose arbour 12 years ago and learned by trial and error which varieties withstood the icy winters ('Mme Alfred Carrière', 'New Dawn') and how to protect those that did from gourmandizing deer. Beneath the rose garden: three levels of heather-studded rock garden and lawns (where once a jungle of St John's Wort stood) cascade down to a pond rich with trout, carp and perch. Perfect for fishing, or a dip on a hot day. Rhododendrons, marsh marigolds and flags, seven varieties of honeysuckle, wisteria by the bedroom window, a potager of herbs. The 1960s chalet – tiled downstairs, carpeted up, spotless throughout – is a quiet, bookish home (no telly) where you will relax completely and eat a breakfast that could be French, German or English – you choose. Bedrooms have good repro furniture typical of the region and new beds. A supremely peaceful place – and Judith bakes delicious cakes for tea.

rooms	2 doubles sharing bathroom.
price	€ 53.50.
meals	Choice of restaurants, 2km. Barbecue available.
closed	Rarely.
directions	From Strasbourg A352 W then N420 to St Blaise la Roche (45km); right on D424 14km towards Senones to La Petite Raon; right after church for Moussey; left after café; then left, left & left to house

	Judith Lott
tel	(0)3 29 57 68 08
fax	(0)3 29 57 68 83
e-mail	judelott@aol.com

see French map entry: 184

Château du Mesnil Geoffroy

76740 Ermenouville

This gloriously restored and revived 17th-century château is surrounded by formal gardens designed by a pupil of the great Le Nôtre. Here are the original lime tree avenues and statuary, magnificent topiary, a 600-year-old yew… and a rose garden fit for a prince. Which, of course, it is; Prince Kayali knows every one of the 2,500 varieties by name and the Princess makes rose-petal jelly for breakfast (she also loves to prepare authentic 18th-century dishes from old recipes she has unearthed; do eat in). But perhaps the garden's most intriguing feature is the 17th-century maze, an original and complex structure with a surprise at the finish. The 10 hectares (25 acres) have been officially designated a haven for wild birds and there's an aviary of exotic ones too. Your hosts are charming and attentive and will greet you with an aperitif in the dining room. Each gracefully panelled bedroom overlooks the gardens, each delightfully cosy with canopied beds, delicious bed linen and sweet-smelling bathrooms. Breakfast coffee is poured from a silver pot, croissants served on fine porcelain and dinners illuminated by exquisite candelabra. Can you resist?

rooms	5: 2 doubles, 1 twin, 2 suites, all with bath & shower.
price	€78–€133.
meals	Dinner €42, inc. wine & coffee.
closed	Rarely.
directons	From A13 exit 25 Pont de Bretonne/Yvetot. Through Yvetot for St Valéry en Caux. 2km after Ste Colombe, right towards Houdetot. Château 2km on left.

Prince & Princesse Anne-Marie Kayali

tel	(0)2 35 57 12 77
fax	(0)2 35 57 10 24
e-mail	contact@chateau-mesnil-geoffroy.com
web	www.chateau-mesnil-geoffroy.com

Les Poules Vertes

68 rue de la République, 76490 Caudebec en Caux

A "gentle disorder" reigns in Madame's hilly garden: each level overflows with flowers. She was inspired by the romance of Giverny, but while Monet's garden has seven staff dancing in attendance, Les Poules Verts has just one: Monsieur. He is endowed with the greenest of fingers – "if he were to plant a broom it would sprout leaves", says Madame – and will send you off gladly with cuttings and seeds. The free-range garden is a wonder almost all year round: lilac and wisteria, crocuses, tulips and "the whole family" of jonquils in the spring; roses, hydrangeas, hollyhocks, pelargoniums in summer; dahlias and daisies in September. The old house (once a grange) is on a road which can get noisy during the day, but is quiet at night. Carpeted bedrooms are a characterful jumble of brass beds, flowery wallpapers, ornaments and doilies – inimitably French. Up a velours-dressed stair to the triple with lovely garden views; the small double on the ground floor has its own garden entrance. Madame will give you a terrific welcome and three jams at breakfast, home-made, of course. Her home is named after the topiary in the garden: six chickens fashioned from box.

rooms	4: 2 doubles, 1 triple, 1 quadruple, all with shower.
price	€ 47.
meals	Good restaurant 500m.
closed	Rarely.
directions	In Caudebec, in front of Tourist Office, take Rue de la République (D131) for Yvetot; No. 68 500m on right.

	Christiane Villamaux
tel	(0)2 35 96 10 15
fax	(0)2 35 96 75 25
e-mail	christiane.villamaux@libertysurf.fr
web	www.villamaux.ifrance.com

see French map entry: 186

La Haute Gilberdière

50530 Sartilly

The 18th-century *longère* basks in a delicious forest of flowers: roses and clematis climb and tumble; paths wind past banks of foxglove, lupin, arum and delphinium; fat clumps of hydrangea, gunnera, rhododendron and bamboo contain the peace. Generous, artistic and young in spirit, the Champagnacs are a privilege to meet; Madame is passionate about her *jardin anglais*, the harmonies of colour and shape, and her orchard, for which she's sought out ancient species of apple. A special part of the garden has been allocated to each bedroom, but, of course, you are invited to wander and revel. Find a quiet spot in which to dream: a white bench on the lawns maybe, sweet with the song of birds, or a table for two in a spot fragrant with the spicy floribunda 'Westerland'. Inside: bedrooms are perfect with handsome antiques, pretty bed linen and polished floors, or modern with pale wood, bucolic views and fresh flowers. The honey-coloured sitting/dining room is warmly contemporary, all timber and exposed stone – pots of home-made jam roost between the beams. A deeply romantic place to stay, and Mont St Michel just 15 minutes away. *Gîte space for 4.*

rooms	4: 1 apartment with 2 doubles, both with shower; 1 apartment with 1 double & 1 twin sharing bathroom.
price	€78–€120.
meals	Good restaurants 5–25km.
closed	November–March.
directions	From Avranches D973 for Granville & Sartilly; left at end of village D61 for Carolles; after 800m house on left.

Edith Champagnac

tel	(0)2 33 60 17 44
e-mail	champagnac@libertysurf.fr
web	www.champagnac-farmhouse.com

Château de Montriou

49460 Feneu

Sensational: the 15-hectare (40-acre) park with its English and French gardens (waves of crocuses in spring, lush banks of dahlias in autumn, exquisitely trimmed box and yew), its walled 19th-century potager, its hundred-year-old pear trees and its giant sequoia, the biggest tree in Maine et Loire... and the amazing Jardin de la Princesse, where flowers and curcurbits (70 varieties) flourish side by side. Most impressive is the tunnel of *cucurbitaceae* – squashes, melons, marrows, cucumbers, pumpkins and, Nicole's favourite, the *courge mexicaine* – hanging thinly, fatly, comically from wooden boughs, a glorious tangle of yellows, oranges and greens. Almost as magnificent is the 15th-century château, lived in and tended by the same family for 300 years; the charming de Lotures are bringing fresh energy to the house along with their passion for gardening. A very old stone staircase illuminated by a stained-glass chapel window leads to the properly formal bedrooms whose bold blues and oranges were a design flavour of the period; wooden floors, thick rugs and antiques are only slightly younger. Special at any time of year; ravishing at summer's last flush.

rooms	3: 1 double with bath; 1 double with bath & kitchen; 1 suite for 4 with bath & kitchen.
price	€69–€83; suite €121 for four.
meals	Choice of restaurants nearby.
closed	Rarely.
directions	Le Mans A11 exit 14 for Angers; D52 for Châteauneuf sur Sarthe; at Tiercé left D74 for Ecuillé; D768 junc. straight on; signed 1km on left.

	Regis & Nicole de Loture
tel	(0)2 41 93 30 11
fax	(0)2 41 93 15 63
e-mail	chateau-de-montriou@wanadoo.fr
web	www.chateau-de-montriou.com

see French map Entry: 188

Le Logis du Pressoir

Villeneuve, 49250 Brion

The big windows of this old restored farm open onto a wide, well-tended lawn; hard to believe this was a field where cows once grazed! It is an open garden, gently edged with lime, ash and feathery acacia; secluded yet un-hemmed in. Peaches, cherries and plums flourish in the orchard; roses, irises, clematis, rhododendron and wisteria in the flower garden. There are vines too, and, in the potager, herbs that make their way to your plate – deliciously so: Madame is an imaginative cook. Dinner at the long table in the vast converted stable room is a joyous daily event, thanks to these young, enthusiastic hosts. The bright and simple guest rooms, separate from the main house and each with its own entrance, wear lovingly restored 18th-century beams and honeycomb tiles (Monsieur restores houses – very well): perfect foils for old *armoires* and bedheads. Steep stairs lead up to the children's rooms where everything is in understated good taste. Outside is a pool with its own special pool house (once the old *pressoir* for wine), ping-pong for the children and a bird-watching room provided with binoculars. A serenely happy place.

rooms	5: 1 double, 1 twin, 1 triple, 2 suites, all with bath or shower.
price	€ 49–€ 59.
dinner	€ 20, inc. wine & coffee.
closed	2 weeks in January.
directions	From Saumur N147 N/NW 15km past Longué; D938 right towards Baugé for 2.5km; left to Brion. House signed in village opp. church.

Anne & Jean-Marc Le Foulgocq

tel	(0)2 41 57 27 33
fax	(0)2 41 57 27 33
e-mail	lepressoir@wanadoo.fr
web	www.lepressoir.fr.st

Le Chat Courant

37510 Villandry

If gardens reflect the personality of their owners, then the Gaudouins are the most romantic people you could wish to meet. Stylish, generous too, they attend lovingly to every detail and concoct wonders for you with fruits and (rare) vegetables from their Villandry-style potager. The soft Touraine stone house – opposite the great château itself – is a birdsong-filled haven by the River Cher; its big garden, a combination of formality and *exubérance*, has all-round colour from trees, shrubs, fruits and flowers, and last year won a prize for best in the region. Here are laburnum, magnolia, tamarisk, seringa, clematis, jasmine, roses, camellia, walnut, peach and almond trees and a canopy of wisteria, breathtaking in spring. The box parterres are gayly stuffed with cabbages, lettuces, beetroot, carrots, peas, onions, Jerusalem artichokes, *courgettes spaghetti*, gooseberries, blackcurrants and sweet-smelling herbs. Ducks on the pond, cats in the sun, horses in the fields, a strutting chicken, a big pool and, inside, simple, terracotta-tiled rooms exquisite with country antiques and fresh flowers. A magical place.

rooms	1 family with shower.
price	€ 52 for two, € 90 for four.
meals	Dinner € 18, inc. wine & coffee.
closed	Rarely.
directions	From Tours D7 to Savonnières; right across bridge; left for 3.8km; house on right.

	Anne & Éric Gaudouin
tel	(0)2 47 50 06 94
e-mail	lechatcourant@netcourrier.com
web	www.le-chat-courant.com

see French map entry: 190

Château de Tennessus

79350 Amailloux

Moat, keep, drawbridge, dreams – no wonder children follow Philippa wherever she goes! Her passion has inspired the meticulous restoration: old stones are exposed, furniture is sober (no sagging armchairs here), fires are laid, even in summer. Two stone spirals to the biggest bedroom ever – granite cushioned windowsills, giant hearth, canopied bed, shower snug in what was the original wardrobe. High in the keep, the medieval family room: vast timbers, arrow slits and real windows, all as authentic as can be. As are the gardens which glow from loving care. Pass the granite troughs in the courtyard stuffed with climbing shrubs and roses, through to the medieval-inspired herb garden and rolling lawn with its *tapis de mille fleurs*. In the big potager are rectangular beds and trellises, banks of lavender and avenues of fruit trees, source of breakfast jams. There's a pocket-sized English garden of perennials too, a croquet lawn with roses and an outdoor pool. Pippa is eager and attentive – flowers, bubbly, fishing in the moat – and all around are parkland and sheep. The 360° views from the top of the keep are stupendous. *Gîte space for 5 people.*

rooms	2: 1 double, 1 suite for 4, both with shower.
price	€ 110–€ 135.
meals	Restaurant 4km; choice 9km.
closed	Christmas–New Year.
directions	From A10 exit 29 on N147; N149 W to Parthenay; round Parthenay northbound; cont. N149 for Bressuire; 7km north of Parthenay right at sign for château.

Nicholas & Philippa Freeland

tel	(0)5 49 95 50 60
fax	(0)5 49 95 50 62
e-mail	tennessus@csi.com
web	www.tennessus.com

Les Hortensias

16 rue des Sablières, 17380 Archingeay

Behind its charmingly shuttered stone front, this 17th-century former wine-grower's house hides a magnificent garden that flows through orchard and potager into the countryside. Your hosts, retired from jobs in agricultural safety and country tourism, are wonderfully attentive and like nothing better than to give you a tour. They have carefully ensured that the garden blooms most of the year: tulips and narcissi make a splash in early spring, followed by wisteria, puffs of peonies and a pink rose perfect against an ancient wall. Lupins, irises, red hot pokers, lilies and a tumble of geraniums in the courtyard in high summer; mallows and dahlias in September. On the lawn is a vast weeping willow to sit under. The immaculate potager yields fruits, herbs and veg for dinner – five courses, *aperitif charentais* and wine included. Bedrooms are beautifully maintained too: light, airy, as neat as new pins, with gleaming floors, perfect mattresses on sleigh beds and tiled bathrooms just so; the room for disabled guests is one of the best we've seen. Nearby are Cognac, the beaches of Ré and Oléron islands, and Romanesque wonders galore.

rooms	3: 2 doubles, 1 suite for 4, all with bath & shower.
price	€45–€50.
meals	Dinner €15, inc. wine & coffee.
closed	Rarely.
directions	From A10 exit 34 on D739 to Tonnay Boutonne; left D114 to Archingeay; left for Les Nouillers; house just after turning.

	Marie Therese & Jean-Pierre Jacques
tel	(0)5 46 97 85 70
fax	(0)5 46 97 61 89
e-mail	jpmt.jacques@wanadoo.fr

see French map entry: 192

Les Hauts de Font Moure

17150 St Georges des Agoûts

From wasteland Dinah and Claude are forging a delightful garden for their grand-but-not-too-grand Charantais *maison de maître*. Two young palm trees stand sentinel by the front door, roses tumble over the gate. Behind, a lawn sweeps down to the potager; tucked to one side, an exquisite pool, blessed with views of hills, vineyards, sunflowers and maize. Through the wrought-iron *roseraie*, bursting with ten different types of pale rose, and into a second garden of hollyhocks, lavender, cistus, agapanthus, hydrangea… and a proper English herbaceous border complete with euphorbia and irises and variagated buddleja. Box, palms and maples thrive in the limey soil; fruit from the orchard – apple, cherry, apricot, peach, plum – ends up on the table. Indoors all is serenity and space: lofty light rooms, dark wooden floors, oriental rugs, ravishing antiques. Bedrooms are big and have terrific bathrooms. Your likeable hosts – he French, she English – give you elegant, relaxed dinners and three types of home-grown jam for breakfast. And more all around to delight the senses: Romanesque churches, fishing ports on the estuary, regional wines. A wonderful place.

rooms	4: 2 doubles, 1 twin, 1 family suite, all with bath & shower.
price	€63–€70.
meals	Dinner €23, inc. coffee & wine.
closed	Occasionally.
directions	From A10 exit 37 for Mirambeau. At r'bout pass 'Marché U'; D254 1st right to St Georges des Agoûts; right at church D146; 1st junction left & follow Chambres d'Hôtes signs.

Dinah & Claude Teulet

tel	(0)5 46 86 04 41
fax	(0)5 46 49 67 18
e-mail	cteulet@aol.com
web	www.fontmoure.com

Domaine de la Barde

Route de Perigueux, 24260 Le Bugue

Once a mere weekend cottage for the nobility who owned it, the Domaine today is a luxurious, charming, family-run hotel and restaurant. Beamy, stone-walled, terracotta-tiled rooms are furnished with warm sofas and fine antiques, and bedrooms are divided between mill, forge and manor – even the smallest feel light and inviting. The Darnauds' priority is your comfort; they also have a flair for the dramatic visual touch – like the glass floor under which flows the millstream in the old oil mill. Outdoors, the clipped box *jardin à la francaise* complements to perfection the 17th-century elegance of the manor. There are some fine trees: five planes and an oak, centuries old; maples, elms, bamboo, sequoia, walnuts, hazelnuts, alder and willow; canals and a river of trout. Beyond are orchard and herb garden; beyond that, meadows where wild orchids grow. Roses and clematis – 300 varieties – burgeon in beds alongside neatly gravelled paths. Sit quietly under the trees… or luxuriate in the outdoor pool with jet-stream massage. There's table tennis too and, in the *orangerie*, a sauna. Perfect hosts, rooms, *jardin* and park in one of France's most exquisite areas.

rooms	18 twins/doubles with baths & showers.
price	€72–€196.
meals	Breakfast €11; lunch & dinner €25–€54.
closed	Mid-October–mid-April.
directions	From Périgueux N89; D710 to Le Bugue. 1km before Le Bugue, Domaine signposted on right.

	Andre Darnaud
tel	(0)5 53 07 16 54
fax	(0)5 53 54 76 19

see French map entry: 194

La Missare

9 route de Clermont, 34800 Brignac

A vast and lovely stone winery is the guest wing on this old family property in little Brignac. Your host's sensitive conversion uses old tiles, doors and beams: simple, stylish bedrooms each with an excellent shower room, superb bedding and French windows onto the garden courtyard. Privacy too: big flowering pots separate each entrance. From the sun-caressed courtyard – an attractive jumble of terracotta pots, gravel and grass – wander down soft-pebbled paths to lawned areas and a pool glimmering under a vast umbrella pine. The garden has a Mediterranean theme – olive trees, ancient figs, oleander, palm, old-fashioned roses, herbs and lavender thrive. Fruits too: apples, pears, kiwis, and an orange tree in a stately pot. It is a romantic place, immaculately maintained by Jean-François and his mother; he is a lawyer who swapped advocacy for *chambres d'hôtes*; they happily share their home. Go through the big hall, hung with some fine prints, to breakfast in the living room where a cabinet of treasures will intrigue. You are near the Lac du Salogon – sailing, swimming, walks – and Montpellier, capital of the region. A delightful place.

rooms	4 doubles, all with shower.
price	€ 60–€ 66.
meals	Restaurants 3–12km.
closed	Rarely.
directions	From Clermont L'Hérault N9 r'bout D4 for Brignac 3.5km; house on right entering village.

	Jean-François Martin
tel	(0)4 67 96 07 67
fax	(0)4 67 50 14 11
e-mail	la.missare@free.fr
web	la.missare.free.fr

Les Jardins de Longsard

Château de Longsard, 69400 Arnas

It is grand: an obelisk amid the topiary, Beaujolais from the vines and a seductive 18th-century château. Your Franco-American hosts, sophisticated, multi-lingual and genuinely keen to share their enthusiasm for their estate and its history, have achieved miracles. Yet the actual structure of the garden and park has changed little since 1792: a stone terrace leads to alleys of lime and other ancient trees (the Lebanese cedar is particularly fine), the amazing yew topiary – reminiscent of a chess board – is trimmed every July, and the all-encompassing hedge of neat box remains open at the far end, fronted by a ha-ha, to expand the view: the romantic landscape of the English school was all the rage in the 18th century. There's a winter greenhouse for the oranges, a winery for tastings, and a still-young potager and rose garden, whose fruits and flowers make their way to the dinner table. (Delicious jams for breakfast.) Inside, vast beamed and parquet-floored rooms, some with finely carved doorframes, are eclectically and elegantly furnished in Art Deco mode. If you want to sample *le grand style*, this is for you.

rooms	5: 3 doubles, 2 suites, all with bath.
price	€96.
meals	Dinner €32, inc. wine & coffee.
closed	Rarely.
directions	From A6 exit 'Belleville'; N6 for Lyon 10km; right D43 to Arnas. Through village; château on right after 1.5km.

Alexandra & Olivier du Mesnil

tel	(0)4 74 65 55 12
fax	(0)4 74 65 03 17
e-mail	longsard@wanadoo.fr
web	www.longsard.com

see French map entry: 196

WHAT'S IN THE BACK OF THE BOOK?

Find out more about Alastair Sawday Publishing

GARDEN ORGANISATIONS

You should find your hosts well-informed about gardens and
nurseries in their areas. However, the details of the following
organisations and publications may be of help when planning
a trip. Publications are in italics.

The National Trust (NT)

Britain's premier conservation organisation looks after the
largest and most important collection of historic gardens and
cultivated plants in the world. Over 200 gardens and landscape
parks encompassing over 400 years of history are open to the
public throughout England, Wales and Northern Ireland. They
employ more than 450 skilled gardeners and hundreds more
volunteers.

The National Trust Gardens Handbook and *The National Trust
Handbook 2003* which lists all Trust properties open to the
public, are available at £7.99 each from the Trust's own shops,
good bookshops and from the National Trust.

P.O. Box 39, Bromley, Kent BR1 3XL Tel: 0870 458 4000
www.nationaltrust.org.uk enquiries@thenationaltrust.org.uk

The National Trust for Scotland (NTS)

The conservation charity that protects and promotes Scotland's
natural and cultural heritage for present and future generations
to enjoy. The National Trust for Scotland Guide 2003 features
more than 120 properties in its care, and costs around £2.

Wemyss House, 28 Charlotte Square, Edinburgh EH2 4ET
Tel: 0131 243 9300 Fax: 0131 243 9301
www.nts.org.uk information@nts.org.uk

National Garden Scheme (NGS)

The famous 'yellow book'. A guide to over 3,500 gardens in
England and Wales, the majority of which are not normally
open to the public. Divided by county, this invaluable book
briefly describes the gardens and lists the days on which they
open for charity.

The National Gardens Scheme Charitable Trust,
Hatchlands Park, East Clandon, Surrey GU4 7RT
Tel: 01483 211535 Fax: 01483 211537
www.ngs.org.uk

GARDEN ORGANISATIONS

Scotland's Garden Scheme (SGS)

Scotland's own 'yellow book' features around 350 private gardens north of the border that are not normally open to the public but which open their gates for charity on certain dates. *Gardens of Scotland 2003* will be available from mid-February, and full details of the gardens will also appear on the National Gardens Scheme web site: www.ngs.org.uk.

22 Rutland Square, Edinburgh EH1 2BB
Tel: 0131 229 1870 Fax: 0131 229 0443 sgsoffice@aol.com

The Royal Horticultural Society (RHS)

Since its foundation in 1804, the Royal Horticultural Society has grown to be the world's leading horticultural organisation. It promotes gardens and good gardening practices through its inspirational flower shows, and over 1,000 lectures and demonstrations. Its four flagship gardens are Wisley in Surrey, Rosemoor in Devon, Hyde Hall in Essex, and Harlow Carr in North Yorkshire. The Society has also joined forces with over 80 gardens in the UK and 20 in Europe that offer free access to its members. Among the RHS's many publications, the following are very useful:

The RHS Garden Finder by Charles Quest-Ritson, published by Dorling Kindersley at £9.99. *The RHS Plant Finder* published by Dorling Kindersley at £12.99.

80 Vincent Square, London SW1P 2PE
Tel: 020 7834 4333 Fax: 020 7630 6060
www.rhs.org.uk info@rhs.org.uk

National Council for the Conservation of Plants & Gardens (NCCPG)

The NCCPG seeks to conserve, document, promote and make available Britain and Ireland's great biodiversity of garden plants for the benefit of horticulture, education and science. An independent charity, it has 41 country-wide groups supporting its aims through their membership and their propagation and plant sales efforts. These efforts, together with the dedication and enthusiasm of National Plant Collection[®] Holders enable the NCCPG to fulfil its mission to conserve the vast gene pool of plants cultivated within the British Isles. The *National Plant Collections Directory 2003* listing over 600 National Plant

GARDEN ORGANISATIONS

Collections will be available from February (£6.20 inc. p&p).
The Pink Sheet listing rare and endangered garden plants is
available free on request.

The Stable Courtyard, Wisley Garden, Woking, Surrey
GU23 6QP Tel: 01483 211465 Fax: 01483 212404
www.nccpg.org.uk chrisc@nccpg.org.uk

Henry Doubleday Research Association (HDRA)

The HDRA is Europe's largest organic membership organisation
dedicated to researching and promoting organic gardening,
farming and food. The Association has three organic display
gardens open to the public, at Ryton near Coventry, Yalding
near Maidstone in Kent, and Audley End near Saffron Walden
in Suffolk.

Their guide entitled *Organic Gardening Weekends Directory 2003*
lists organic gardens open to the public during their special
gardening weekends in June and August.

Ryton Organic Gardens, Coventry CV8 3LG
Tel: 024 7630 3517 Fax: 024 7663 9229
www.hdra.org.uk enquiry@hdra.org.uk

Hardy Plant Society (HPS)

The Hardy Plant Society was formed to foster interest in hardy
herbaceous plants. With 12,000 members and over 40 groups
in England, Scotland and Wales, the society aims to provide
information about the wealth of both well and little-known
plants, and to ensure that all worthy plants remain in cultivation
and have the widest possible distribution. The Society's
show garden at Pershore College in the Cotswolds is open
10.00am-4.30pm daily (entrance free). The HPS organises
study days and residential weekends, and publishes an annual
seed list offering over 2,500 varieties, many unobtainable
commercially.

Pam Adams, The Administrator, Little Orchard, Great
Comberton, Pershore, Worcestershire WR10 3DP
Tel: 01386 710317 Fax: 01386 710117
www.hardy-plant.org.uk admin@hardy-plant.org.uk

GARDEN ORGANISATIONS

Cottage Garden Society (CGS)

The CGS was founded in 1982 when many 'old-fashioned' plants were becoming unavailable commercially. Now there are 35 groups, and 9,000 members worldwide, and cottage garden flowers have become more readily available. The CGS continues to help its members find plants that are only produced in a few specialist nurseries, and gives them the opportunity to find 'treasures' through its annual Seed Exchange.

Clive Lane, Administrator, 'Brandon', Ravenshall, Betley, Cheshire CW3 9BH Tel: 01270 820940
clive_lane_cgs@hotmail.com www.thecgs.org.uk

Alpine Garden Society (AGS)

With 14,000 members, the AGS is one of the largest specialist garden societies in the world. Founded in 1929, it promotes interest in alpine and rock garden plants, including small plants and hardy perennials, many bulbs and ferns, hardy orchids, and dwarf trees and shrubs, encouraging their cultivation in rock gardens and conservation in the wild. The AGS has a show garden at Pershore, and organises worldwide tours to see plants in their natural habitats.

AGS Centre, Avon Bank, Pershore, Worcestershire WR10 3JP
Tel: 01386 554790 Fax: 01386 554801
www.alpinegardensociety.org ags@alpinegardensociety.org

Herb Society

The UK's leading society for increasing the understanding, use and appreciation of herbs and their benefits to health. It has its headquarters at the delightful and historic Sulgrave Manor, which dates from 1539, and was once the home of George Washington's ancestors. The Society has been allocated space in the gardens where a herb garden is being created.

Sulgrave Manor, Sulgrave, Nr Banbury, Oxfordshire OX17 2SD
Tel: 01295 768899 Fax: 01295 768069
www.herbsociety.co.uk info@herbsociety.co.uk

Plantlife

Britain's only national membership charity dedicated exclusively to conserving all forms of plant life in its natural habitat – the nation's champion of wild plants!

21 Elizabeth Street, London SW1W 9RP
Tel: 020 7808 0100 Fax: 020 7730 8377
www.plantlife.org.uk

GARDEN ORGANISATIONS

Garden History Society

The Society was founded over 35 years ago, and garden history is now firmly established as a valid academic subject. Through its programme of lectures, visits and conferences the Society carries out its three aims. These are to promote the study of the history of gardening, landscape gardening and horticulture, to promote the protection and conservation of historic parks, gardens and designed landscapes, advising on their restoration, and to encourage the recording of contemporary parks, gardens and landscapes. Although its efforts are concentrated on England, Wales and Scotland, the Society maintains an international interest through its contacts in other countries.

70 Cowcross Street, London EC1M 6EJ
Tel: 020 7608 2409 Fax: 020 7490 2974
www.gardenhistorysociety.org
enquiries@gardenhistorysociety.org

The Association of Gardens Trusts

This national organisation represents the growing number (32) of County Gardens Trusts whose main aim is to assist in the protection, conservation, restoration or creation of garden land in the UK for the education and enjoyment of the public.

70 Cowcross Street, London EC1M 6EJ
Tel/Fax: 020 7251 2610
www.gardenstrusts.org.uk agt@gardenstrusts.org.uk

The Historic Gardens Foundation

A non-profit-making organisation set up in 1995 to create links between everyone concerned with the preservation, restoration and management of historic parks and gardens. Its Historic Gardens Review is published three times a year and offers lively and authoritative coverage of historic gardens worldwide.

34 River Court, Upper Ground, London SE1 9PE
Tel: 020 7633 9165 Fax: 020 7401 7072
www.historicgardens.freeserve.co.uk
office@historicgardens.freeserve.co.uk

GARDEN ORGANISATIONS

Further visiting:

Museum of Garden History

The world's first Museum of Garden History was founded in 1977 at the restored church of St Mary-at-Lambeth next to Lambeth Palace, the London residence of the Archbishop of Canterbury, just across the Thames from the Houses of Parliament. The Museum's unique collection tells the story of the history of gardening and the work of celebrated gardeners. Special focus is given to the Tradescant family who were gardeners to Charles I and Charles II. Plants first introduced to Britain by the Tradescants in the 17th century feature in the Museum's garden, as does the Tradescant family tomb.

Lambeth Palace Road, London SE1 7LB Open daily Feb-Dec, 10.30am-5pm Tel: 020 7401 8865 Fax: 020 7401 8869
www.museumgardenhistory.org
info@museumgardenhistory.org

Border Lines

Day courses, and tours of outstanding private gardens not normally open to the public. Each garden tour is led by the owner or head gardener who shares ideas and expertise. Visitors are offered a two-course lunch with wine at the host's home, and there is also an opportunity to buy plants. Courses consist of illustrated lectures, demonstrations in the garden and informal discussions. For a brochure, contact Ruth Arnold.

Quadrille Court, St Thomas' Street, Lymington, Hampshire SO41 9NA Tel: 01590 677994 Fax: 01590 678592
www.border-lines@quadrille.uk.com
border-lines@quadrille.uk.com

Rare plant Fairs

A unique opportunity for plant hunters and gardeners to source rare and unusual plants at reasonable prices. The fairs (listed overleaf) are attended by specialist nursery experts who, as well as growing the plants, give top advice on their care and planting. All the fairs take place in great locations... worth a day out in themselves! For further information telephone Maureen Willson on 0117 956 2566 or visit www.rareplantsfair.com

GARDEN ORGANISATIONS

Other charities:

The Quiet Garden Trust
A charity that oversees a network of gardens attached to private houses and churches, which provide occasional days of stillness and reflection for those in search of spiritual refreshment.

Stoke Park Farm, Park Road, Stoke Poges, Buckinghamshire SL2 4PG Tel: 01753 643050 Fax: 01753 643081. www.quietgarden.co.uk quiet.garden@ukonline.co.uk

Gardening for Disabled Trust
This charity gives small grants to people all over the UK in order that they may continue to garden despite advancing age, illness, or disability. Information from and donations to:

Julia Sebline, Hayes Farmhouse, Hayes Lane, Peasmarsh, Rye, East Sussex TN31 6XR Fax: 01424 882876 julia.sebline@virgin.net.

Main Garden and Flower Show dates 2003

Harrogate Spring Show	24-27 April
Spring Gardening Show at Malvern	9-11 May
Chelsea Flower Show	20-23 May
BBC Gardeners World Live	11-15 June
Hampton Court Palace Flower Show	8-13 July
RHS Flower Show at Tatton Park	23-27 July
Harrogate Autumn Show	12-14 September
Malvern Autumn Garden & Country Show	27-28 September
RHS London Flower Shows	monthly

RARE PLANT FAIRS 2003

12 April Queen Charlotte Hall, Parkshott, Richmond, London
11am-3pm; admission £3.50

19 April Pittville Pump Room, Pittville Park, Cheltenham
11am-3pm; admission £3.50

4 May Caldicot Castle, Caldicot, Nr Chepstow, Monmouthshire
11am-5pm; admission £3

11 May University of Oxford Botanic Garden. Rose Lane, Oxford
11am-5pm; admission £3.50

25 May Castle Bromwich Hall Gardens, Castle Bromwich,
Nr Birmingham; 11am-4pm; admission £3.50

1 June Lackham Country Park, Nr Chippenham, Wiltshire
11am-4pm; admission £4

8 June The Manor House. Birlingham, Nr Pershore, Worcestershire
11am-4pm; admission £3.50

22 June Fonmon Castle, Nr Barry, Glamorgan
11am-4pm; admission £3.50

29 June The Old Rectory, Burghfield, Nr Reading
11am-4pm; admission £3.50

13 July Caldicot Castle, Nr Chepstow, Monmouthshire
11am-5pm; admission £3

31 August Abergavenny Castle, Abergavenny, Monmouthshire
11am–5pm; admission £3

7 September Wombourne Wodehouse, Wombourne, Nr Wolverhampton
11am-5pm; admission £3.50

GOOD GARDENS

We would like to have included all the gardens we know of in this section, and nurseries too, but sadly we don't have the space, so here is a selection of gardens from *The Good Gardens Guide*: its 2* gardens and those with 1* most regularly open to the public. For planning garden visits this is an invaluable guide, as is the NGS yellow book (www.ngs.org).

Bedfordshire

The Manor House *
Church Road, Stevington, Bedford 01234 822064
www.kathybrownsgarden.homestead.com Kathy Brown

Seal Point *
7 Wendover Way, Luton 01582 611567 Mrs Danae Johnston

Toddington Manor *
Toddington 01525 872576 Sir Neville & Lady Bowman-Shaw

Berkshire

Cliveden **
Taplow, Maidenhead 01628 605069 The National Trust

The Old Rectory *
Burghfield, Reading 0118 983 3200 Mr A R Merton

Scotlands *
Cockpole Green, Wargrave, Reading 01628 822648
Mr Michael & The Hon. Mrs Payne

Waltham Place *
White Waltham, Maidenhead 01628 825517
www.waltham-place.org.uk Mr & Mrs N F Oppenheimer

Birmingham area

The Birmingham Botanical Gardens & Glasshouses *
Westbourne Road, Edgbaston 0121 454 1860
www.bham-bot-gdns.demon.co.uk

Castle Bromwich Hall Gardens *
Chester Road, Castle Bromwich 0121 749 4100
Castle Bromwich Hall Gardens Trust

Bristol area

Blaise Castle House *
Henbury, Bristol 0117 950 6789 Bristol City Museum

Buckinghamshire

Ascott **
Wing, Leighton Buzzard 01296 688242
www.ascottestate.co.uk The National Trust

Stowe Landscape Gardens **
Buckingham 01280 822850 The National Trust

Waddesdon Manor **
Waddesdon, Aylesbury 01296 653211
www.waddesdon.org.uk The National Trust

West Wycombe Park **
West Wycombe 01628 488675 The National Trust

GOOD GARDENS

Cambridgeshire

Abbots Ripton Hall *****
Abbots Ripton, Huntingdon 01487 773555
Lord & Lady De Ramsey

Anglesey Abbey Gardens & Lode Mill ******
Lode, Cambridge 01223 811200
www.nationaltrust.org.uk/angleseyabbey The National Trust

Christ's College ******
St Andrew's Street, Cambridge 01223 334900

University Botanic Garden ******
Cambridge 01223 336265 University of Cambridge

Cheshire

Arley Hall & Gardens *****
Arley, Great Budworth, Northwich 01565 777353
www.arleyestate.zuunet.co.uk Viscount Ashbrook

Capesthorne Hall & Gardens *****
Macclesfield 01625 861221 www.capesthorne.com
Mr W A Bromley Davenport

Cholmondeley Castle Gardens *****
Cholmondeley Castle, Malpas 01829 720383
The Marquess of Cholmondeley

Ness Botanic Gardens ******
Neston Road, Ness, Wirral 0151 353 0123
www.merseyworld.com/nessgardens/
University of Liverpool

Norton Priory Museum & Gardens *****
Manor Park, Runcorn 01928 569895 www.nortonpriory.org
The Norton Priory Museum Trust

Tatton Park ******
Knutsford 01625 534400
Cheshire County Council/The National Trust

Cornwall

Antony *****
Torpoint 01752 812364
The National Trust & Trustees of Carew Pole Garden Trust

Bosahan *****
Manaccan, Helston 01326 231351
Mr & Mrs R J Graham-Vivian

Bosvigo *****
Bosvigo Lane, Truro 01872 275774 www.bosvigo.com
Mr Michael & Mrs Wendy Perry

Caerhays Castle Garden ******
Caerhays, Gorran, St Austell 01872 501310
www.caerhays.co.uk Mr F J Williams

GOOD GARDENS

Chyverton **
Zelah, Truro 01872 540324 Mr N Holman

Cotehele *
St Dominick, Saltash 01579 351346 The National Trust

Glendurgan Garden *
Mawnan Smith, Falmouth 01326 250906 The National Trust

Heligan **
Pentewan, St Austell 01726 845100 www.heligan.com
The Lost Gardens of Heligan

Lamorran House *
St Mawes 01326 270800 Mr & Mrs R Dudley-Cooke

Lanhydrock *
Bodmin 01208 73320 The National Trust

Mount Edgcumbe House & Country Park *
Cremyll, Torpoint 01752 822236
Cornwall County Council & Plymouth City Council

Pencarrow *
Washaway, Bodmin 01208 841369 www.pencarrow.co.uk
The Molesworth-St Aubyn family

Pine Lodge Garden & Nursery *
Cuddra, Holmbush, St Austell 01726 73500
www.pine-lodge.co.uk Mr & Mrs R Clemo

St Michael's Mount *
Marazion, Penzance 01736 710507 The National Trust

Trebah **
Mawnan Smith 01326 250448 www.trebah-garden.co.uk
Mr & Mrs J A Hibbert (Trebah Garden Trust)

Tregrehan *
Par 01726 814389 The Carlyon Estate/Mr T Hudson

Trelissick *
Feock, Truro 01872 862090 The National Trust

Trengwainton Garden *
Penzance 01765 362297 The National Trust

Tresco Abbey **
Tresco, Isles of Scilly 01720 424105 Mr R A Dorrien-Smith

Trewithen **
Truro 01726 883647 Mr & Mrs A M J Galsworthy

Cumbria   Brockhole *
Lake District Visitor Centre, Windermere
015394 46601 Lake District National Park Authority

GOOD GARDENS

Holehird **
Patterdale Road, Windermere 015394 46008
Lakeland Horticultural Society

Holker Hall **
Cark-in-Cartmel, Grange-over-Sands 015395 58328
www.holker-hall.co.uk Lord & Lady Cavendish

Levens Hall **
Kendal 015395 60321 www.levenshall.co.uk Mr C H Bagot

Muncaster Castle *
Ravenglass 01229 717614 www.muncastercastle.co.uk
Mr & Mrs Gordon-Duff-Pennington

Derbyshire

Chatsworth **
Bakewell 01246 582204 www.chatsworth.org
The Duke & Duchess of Devonshire

Devon

Castle Drogo **
Drewsteignton 01647 433306 The National Trust

Coleton Fishacre Garden **
Brownstone Road, Kingswear, Dartmouth 01803 752466
www.nationaltrust.org.uk The National Trust

Dartington Hall *
Dartington, Totnes 01803 862367 www.dartington.u-net.com
Dartington Hall Trust

Killerton *
Broadclyst, Exeter 01392 881345 The National Trust

Knightshayes **
Bolham, Tiverton 01884 254665 The National Trust

Marwood Hill **
Marwood, Barnstaple 01271 342528 Dr J A Smart

Overbecks Museum & Garden *
Sharpitor, Salcombe 01548 842893 The National Trust

RHS Garden Rosemoor **
Great Torrington 01805 624067
The Royal Horticultural Society

Dorset

Abbotsbury Sub-Tropical Gardens *
Abbotsbury, Weymouth 01305 871387
www.abbotsbury-tourism.co.uk Ilchester Estates

Cranborne Manor Garden **
Cranborne, Wimborne Minster 01725 517248
www.cranborne.co.uk Viscount & Viscountess Cranborne

GOOD GARDENS

Mapperton **
Beaminster 01308 862645 www.mapperton.com
The Earl & Countess of Sandwich

Essex

The Beth Chatto Gardens **
Elmstead Market, Colchester 01206 822007
www.bethchatto.co.uk Mrs Beth Chatto

R & R Saggers *
Waterloo House, High Street, Newport, Saffron Walden
01799 540858 R & R Saggers

Gloucestershire

Barnsley House **
Barnsley, Nr Cirencester 01285 740561
www.opengarden.co.uk Mr & Mrs Charles Verey

Hidcote Manor Garden **
Hidcote Bartrim, Chipping Campden 01386 438333
The National Trust

Kiftsgate Court **
Chipping Campden 01386 438777 www.kiftsgate.co.uk
Mr & Mrs J G Chambers

The National Arboretum, Westonbirt **
Westonbirt, Tetbury 01666 880220 The Forestry Commission

Sezincote **
Moreton-in-Marsh Mr & Mrs D Peake

Hampshire & Isle of Wight

Exbury Gardens **
Exbury, Southampton 023 8089 1203
www.exbury.co.uk Mr E L de Rothschild

Furzey Gardens *
Minstead, Lyndhurst 023 8081 2464 Mrs M M Cole

Longstock Park Water Gardens **
Longstock, Stockbridge 01264 810894 John Lewis Partnership

Mottisfont Abbey Garden **
Mottisfont, Romsey 01794 340757 The National Trust

The Sir Harold Hillier Gardens & Arboretum **
Jermyns Lane, Ampfield, Romsey 01794 368787
www.hillier.hants.gov.uk Hampshire County Council

Spinners *
School Lane, Boldre, Lymington 01590 673347
Mr & Mrs P G G Chapel

West Green House Garden **
West Green, Hartley Wintney, Hook 01252 844611
Miss Marylyn Abbott

GOOD GARDENS

Ventnor Botanic Garden **
The Undercliffe Drive, Ventnor 01983 855397
www.botanic.co.uk Isle of Wight Council

Herefordshire Hergest Croft Gardens *
Kington 01544 230160 www.hergest.co.uk W L Banks

Hertfordshire Benington Lordship **
Benington, Stevenage 01438 869668
www.beningtonlordship.co.uk Mr & Mrs C H A Bott

Chenies Manor House *
Chenies, Rickmansworth 01494 762888
Lt. Col. & Mrs Macleod Matthews

Crossing House Garden *
Shepreth, Royston 01763 261071
Mr & Mrs Douglas Fuller

Hatfield House, Park & Gardens **
Hatfield 01707 287010 www.hatfield-house.co.uk
The Marquess of Salisbury

Hopleys *
Much Hadham 01279 842509 Mr A Barker

Kent Emmetts Garden *
Ide Hill, Sevenoaks 01732 868381 The National Trust

Goodnestone Park **
Goodnestone, Nr Wingham, Canterbury 01304 840107
Lady FitzWalter

Great Comp *
Platt, Borough Green, Sevenoaks 01732 882669
www.greatcomp.co.uk Great Comp Charitable Trust

Hever Castle & Gardens **
Hever, Edenbridge 01732 865224 www.hevercastle.co.uk
Broadlands Properties Ltd

Leeds Castle Park & Gardens *
Maidstone 01622 765400 www.leeds-castle.co.uk
Leeds Castle Foundation

Scotney Castle Garden *
Lamberhurst, Tunbridge Wells 01892 891081
The National Trust

Sissinghurst Castle Garden **
Sissinghurst, Cranbrook 01580 710701 The National Trust

Lancashire Catforth Gardens *
Roots Lane, Catforth, Preston 01772 690561
Mr & Mrs T A Bradshaw

GOOD GARDENS

Gresgarth Hall **
Caton 01524 770313 www.arabellalennoxboyd.com
Sir Mark & Lady Lennox-Boyd

Leicestershire   **Long Close** *
Main Street, Woodhouse Eaves, Loughborough 01509 890616
Mr J T Oakland & Miss P Johnson

Lincolnshire   **Aubourn Hall** *
Aubourn, Lincoln 01522 788270 Lady Nevile

Belton House *
Belton, Grantham 01476 566116 The National Trust

London area   **Chiswick House** **
Burlington Lane, Chiswick, London 020 8995 0508
London Borough of Hounslow & English Heritage

Ham House *
Ham Street, Richmond, Surrey 020 8940 1950
The National Trust

Hampton Court Palace **
East Molesey, Surrey 020 8781 9500 www.hrp.org.uk
Historic Royal Palaces Trust

Isabella Plantation *
Richmond Park, Richmond, Surrey 020 8948 3209 Royal Parks

Royal Botanic Gardens **
Kew, Richmond, Surrey 020 8940 1171 www.kew.org Trustees

Syon Park *
Brentford, Middlesex 020 8560 0881 www.syonpark.co.uk
The Duke of Northumberland

Manchester area   **Lyme Park** *
Disley, Stockport, Cheshire 01663 762023
The National Trust

Norfolk   **Blickling Hall** *
Aylsham, Norwich 01263 738030 www.nationaltrust.org,uk
The National Trust

The Dell Garden *
Bressingham, Diss 01379 688585 www.blooms-online.com
Mr Alan Bloom

East Ruston Old Vicarage **
East Ruston, Norwich 01692 650432
www.e-ruston-oldvicaragegardens.co.uk
Graham Robeson & Alan Gray

Fairhaven Woodland & Water Garden *
School Road, South Walsham, Norwich 01603 270449
www.norfolkbroads.com/fairhaven The Fairhaven Garden Trust

GOOD GARDENS

Foggy Bottom *
Bressingham, Diss 01379 688585 www.blooms-online.com
Mr & Mrs Adrian Bloom

Holkham Hall *
Wells-next-the-Sea 01328 710227 www.holkham.co.uk
The Earl of Leicester

Sheringham Park *
Upper Sheringham 01263 823778 The National Trust

Northamptonshire Coton Manor Gardens *
Guilsborough, Northampton 01604 740219
www.cotonmanor.co.uk Mr & Mrs Ian Pasley-Tyler

Cottesbrooke Hall **
Cottesbrooke, Northampton 01604 505808
www.cottesbrookehall.co.uk
Capt. & Mrs J Macdonald-Buchanan

Kelmarsh Hall *
Kelmarsh, Northampton 01604 686543 The Kelmarsh Trust

Northumberland Belsay Hall, Castle & Gardens **
Belsay, Newcastle-upon-Tyne 01661 881636 English Heritage

Howick Hall *
Howick, Alnwick 01665 577285 Lord Howick of Glendale

Wallington *
Cambo, Morpeth 01670 774283 www.ntnorth.demon.co.uk
The National Trust

Nottinghamshire Felley Priory *
Underwood 01773 810230 The Hon. Mrs Chaworth Musters

Newstead Abbey *
Newstead Abbey Park, Nottingham 01623 455900
Nottingham City Council

Oxfordshire Blenheim Palace **
Woodstock, Oxford 01993 811091 The Duke of Marlborough

Broughton Castle *
Broughton, Banbury 01295 276070
www.broughtoncastle.demon.co.uk Lord Saye & Sele

Greys Court *
Rotherfield Greys, Henley-on-Thames 01491 628529
The National Trust

Oxford Botanic Garden **
Rose Lane, Oxford 01865 286690 University of Oxford

GOOD GARDENS

Rousham House **
Nr Steeple Aston, Bicester 01869 347110 www.rousham.org
Charles Cottrell-Dormer

Upton House *
Banbury 01295 670266 www.ntrustsevern.org.uk The
National Trust

Waterperry Gardens *
Wheatley, Oxford 01844 339226
www.waterperrygardens.co.uk

Shropshire

The Dorothy Clive Garden *
Willoughbridge, Market Drayton 01630 647237
Willoughbridge Garden Trust

Hodnet Hall **
Hodnet, Market Drayton 01630 685202
Mr A E H & The Hon Mrs Heber-Percy

Weston Park *
Weston-under-Lizard, Shifnal 01952 852100
www.weston-park.com Weston Park Enterprises

Wollerton Old Hall **
Wollerton, Hodnet, Market Drayton 01630 685760
John & Lesley Jenkins

Somerset

Barrington Court Garden *
Barrington, Ilminster 01460 241938 The National Trust

Cothay Manor **
Greenham, Wellington 01823 672283 Mr & Mrs Alastair Robb

Dunster Castle *
Dunster, Minehead 01643 821314 The National Trust

East Lambrook Manor Gardens *
South Petherton 01460 240328 www.eastlambrook.com
Robert & Marianne Williams

Forde Abbey **
Chard 01460 221290 www.fordeabbey.co.uk
Mr M Roper

Greencombe **
Porlock 01643 862363 Greencombe Garden Trust

Hadspen Garden & Nursery **
Castle Cary 01749 813707 Mr N A Hobhouse & N & S Pope

Hestercombe Gardens *
Cheddon Fitzpaine, Taunton 01823 413923
www.hestercombegardens.com
HGP Ltd/Somerset County Council

GOOD GARDENS

Montacute House *
Montacute 01935 823289 The National Trust

Tintinhull House Garden *
Farm Street, Tintinhull, Yeovil 01935 822545
The National Trust

Staffordshire

Biddulph Grange Garden **
Grange Road, Biddulph, Stoke-on-Trent 01782 517999
The National Trust

Shugborough *
Milford, Stafford 01889 881388 www.staffordshire.gov.uk
Staffordshire County Council / The National Trust

Suffolk

Helmingham Hall Gardens **
Stowmarket 01473 890363 www.helmingham.com
Lord Tollemache

Somerleyton Hall & Gardens **
Somerleyton, Lowestoft 01502 730224
www.somerleyton.co.uk Lord & Lady Somerleyton

Wyken Hall *
Stanton, Bury St Edmunds 01359 250287
Sir Kenneth & Lady Carlisle

Surrey

Claremont Landscape Garden *
Portsmouth Road, Esher 01372 467806 The National Trust

Painshill Landscape Garden **
Portsmouth Road, Cobham 01932 868113
www.painshill.co.uk Painshill Park Trust

Polesden Lacey *
Great Bookham, Dorking 01372 452048
The National Trust

RHS Garden Wisley **
Wisley, Woking 01483 224234 www.rhs.org.uk
Royal Horticultural Society

The Savill Garden (Windsor Great Park) **
Wick Lane, Englefield Green 01753 847518
Crown Estate Commissioners

Sutton Place **
Guildford 01483 504455 Sutton Place Foundation

The Valley Gardens (Windsor Great Park) **
Wick Road, Englefield Green 01753 860222
Crown Estate Commissioners

Sussex

Borde Hill Garden *
Balcombe Road, Haywards Heath 01444 450326
Borde Hill Gardens Ltd

GOOD GARDENS

Cabbages & Kings *
Wilderness Farm, Hadlow Down, Uckfield 01825 830552
www.ckings.co.uk Ryl & Andrew Nowell

Denmans *
Fontwell, Arundel 01243 542808 www.denmans-garden.co.uk
John Brookes

Great Dixter **
Dixter Road, Northiam, Rye 01797 252878
www.greatdixter.co.uk Christopher Lloyd & Olivia Eller

Leonardslee Gardens **
Lower Beeding, Horsham 01403 891212
www.leonardslee.com The Loder family

Nymans **
Handcross, Haywards Heath 01444 400321
The National Trust

Pashley Manor *
Ticehurst 01580 200888 Mr & Mrs James A Sellick

Petworth House *
Petworth 01798 342207 www.nationaltrust.org.uk
The National Trust

Sheffield Park Garden **
Sheffield Park 01825 790231 The National Trust

Wakehurst Place Garden & Millennium Seed Bank **
Ardingly, Haywards Heath 01444 894066 www.kew.org
The Royal Botanic Gardens, Kew

West Dean Gardens *
West Dean, Chichester 01243 818210 www.westdean.org.uk
Edward James Foundation

Warwickshire Coughton Court *
Alcester 01789 400777 Mrs C Throckmorton

Warwick Castle *
Warwick 0870 442 2000 www.warwick-castle.co.uk
The Tussauds Group

Wiltshire Heale Gardens *
Middle Woodford, Salisbury 01722 782504
Mr & Mrs Guy Rasch

Iford Manor **
Bradford-on-Avon 01225 863146 Mrs Cartwright-Hignett

Stourhead **
Stourton, Warminster 01747 841152
www.nationaltrust.org.uk The National Trust

GOOD GARDENS

Wilton House *
Wilton, Salisbury 01722 746720 www.wiltonhouse.com
The Earl of Pembroke

Worcestershire

Eastgrove Cottage Garden Nursery *
Sankyns Green, Shrawley, Little Witley 01299 896389
www.eastgrove.co.uk Malcolm & Carol Skinner

Stone House Cottage Gardens *
Stone, Kidderminster 01562 69902
Mr & Mrs James Arbuthnott

Yorkshire

Castle Howard **
York 01653 648444 ext. 220 www.castlehoward.co.uk
Castle Howard Estates Ltd

Golden Acre Park *
Otley Road, Leeds 0113 246 3504 Leeds City Council

Harewood House *
Harewood, Leeds 0113 218 1010 www.harewood.org
The Earl & Countess of Harewood

Harlow Carr Botanical Gardens *
Crag Lane, Harrogate 01423 565418
www.harlowcarr.fsnet.co.uk Royal Horticultural Society

The Hollies Park *
Weetwood Lane, Leeds 0113 247 8361 Leeds City Council

Millgate House *
Richmond 01748 823571
www.millgatehouse.com Austin Lynch & Tim Culkin

Newby Hall & Gardens **
Ripon 01423 322583 R Compton

Rievaulx Terrace & Temples *
Rievaulx, Helmsley 01439 798340 The National Trust

Studley Royal & Fountains Abbey **
Ripon 01765 608888 www.fountainsabbey.org,uk
The National Trust

GOOD GARDENS

Wales

Dyffryn Gardens *
St Nicholas, Cardiff 029 2059 3328
www.dyffryngardens.org.uk Vale of Glamorgan Council

Cae Hir *
Cribyn, Lampeter, Ceredigion 01570 470839
Mr W Akkermans

Chirk Castle *
Chirk, Wrexham, Clwyd 01691 777701 The National Trust

Bodnant Garden **
Tal-y-Cafn, Colwyn Bay, Conwy 01492 650460
www.oxalis.co.uk/bodnant The National Trust

Clyne Gardens **
Blackpill, Swansea, West Glamorgan 01792 401737
Swansea City Council

Singleton Botanic Gardens *
Singleton Park, Swansea, West Glamorgan 01792 302420
Swansea City Council

Bodysgallen Hall *
Llandudno, Gwynedd 01492 584466 www.bodysgallen.com
Historic House Hotels

Plas Brondanw Gardens *
Llanfrothen, Penrhyndeudraeth, Gwynedd 07880 766741

Hilton Court *
Roch, Haverfordwest, Pembrokeshire 01437 710262
www.hiltongardensandcrafts.co.uk Mr & Mrs Peter Lynch

The Dingle *
Welshpool, Powys 01938 555145 Mr & Mrs Roy Joseph

Powis Castle & Garden **
Welshpool, Powys 01938 554338 The National Trust

GOOD GARDENS

Scotland

Crathes Castle Garden **
Crathes Castle, Banchory, Aberdeenshire 01330 844525
The National Trust for Scotland

Leith Hall & Gardens *
Huntly, Aberdeenshire 01464 831216 www.nts.org.uk
The National Trust for Scotland

Pitmedden Garden *
Pitmedden Village, Ellon, Aberdeenshire 01651 842352
The National Trust for Scotland

Edzell Castle *
Edzell, Brechin, Angus 01356 648631 Historic Scotland

House of Pitmuies **
Guthrie, By Forfar, Angus 01241 828245 Mrs Farquhar Ogilvie

Achamore Gardens *
Isle of Gigha, Argyll & Bute 01583 505267
www.isle-of-gigha.co.uk Mr & Mrs Derek Holt

Arduaine Garden **
Oban, Argyll & Bute 01852 200366
The National Trust for Scotland

Benmore Botanic Garden **
Dunoon, Argyll, Argyll & Bute 01369 706261
Royal Botanic Garden Edinburgh

Crarae Garden **
Minard, Inveraray, Argyll & Bute 01546 886614
Crarae Gardens Charitable Trust

Mount Stuart **
Rothesay, Isle of Bute, Argyll & Bute 01700 503877
Mount Stuart Trust

Culzean Castle & Country Park **
Maybole, South Ayrshire 01655 884400
The National Trust for Scotland

Castle Kennedy & Lochinch Gardens **
Stranraer, Wigtownshire, Dumfries & Galloway 01776 702024
The Earl & Countess of Stair

Logan Botanic Garden **
Port Logan, Stranraer, Wigtownshire, Dumfries & Galloway
www.nbge.org.uk Royal Botanic Garden Edinburgh

Threave Garden & Estate *
Stewartry, Castle Douglas, Dumfries & Galloway
01556 502575 The National Trust for Scotland

GOOD GARDENS

Glenarn *
Rhu, Helensburgh, Dunbartonshire 01436 820493
Michael & Sue Thornley

Royal Botanic Garden Edinburgh **
Inverleith Row, Edinburgh 0131 552 7171

Greenbank Garden *
Flenders Road, Clarkston, Glasgow 0141 639 3281
The National Trust for Scotland

Castle of Mey **
Thurso, Caithness, Highland
The Queen Elizabeth Castle of Mey Trust

Dunrobin Castle Gardens *
Golspie, Sutherland, Highland 01408 633177
The Sutherland Trust

Inverewe Garden **
Poolewe, Ross & Cromarty, Highland 01445 781200
The National Trust for Scotland

Little Sparta **
Dunsyre, Lanark, South Lanarkshire Dr Ian Hamilton Finlay

Blair Castle *
Blair Athol, Pitlochry, Perth & Kinross 01796 481207
The Blair Charitable Trust

Drummond Castle Gardens **
Muthill, Crieff, Perth & Kinross 01764 681257
Grimsthorpe & Drummond Castle Trust Ltd

Manderston **
Duns, Scottish Borders 01361 883450
www.manderston.co.uk Lord Palmer

WHAT IS ALASTAIR SAWDAY PUBLISHING?

A dozen or more of us work in converted barns on a farm near Bristol, close enough to the city for a bicycle ride and far enough for a silence broken only by horses and the occasional passage of a tractor. Some editors work in the countries they write about, e.g. France; others work from the UK but are based outside the office. We enjoy each other's company, celebrate every event possible, and work in an easy-going but committed environment.

These books owe their style and mood to Alastair's miscellaneous career and his interest in the community and the environment. He has taught overseas, worked with refugees, run development projects abroad, founded a travel company and several environmental organisations. There has been a slightly mad streak evident throughout, not least in his driving of a waste-paper-collection lorry for a year, the manning of stalls at jumble sales and the pursuit of causes long before they were considered sane.

These books owe their style and mood to Alastair's miscellaneous career and his interest in the community and the environment

Back to the travel company: trying to take his clients to eat and sleep in places that were not owned by corporations and assorted bandits he found dozens of very special places in France – farms, châteaux etc – a list that grew into the first book, French Bed and Breakfast. It was a celebration of 'real' places to stay and the remarkable people who run them.

The publishing company grew from that first and rather whimsical French book. It started as a mild crusade, and there it stays – full of 'attitude', and the more appealing for it. For we still celebrate the unusual, the beautiful, the individual. We are passionate about rejecting the banal, the ugly, the pompous and the indifferent and we are passionate too about 'real' food. Alastair is a trustee of the Soil Association and keen to promote organic growing and consuming by owners and visitors.

It is a source of deep pleasure to us to know that there are many thousands of people who share our views. We are by no means alone in trumpeting the virtues of resisting the destruction and uniformity of so much of our culture – and the cultures of other nations, too.

We run a company in which people and values matter. We love to hear of new friendships between those in the book and those using it, and to know that there are many people – among them farmers – who have been enabled to pursue their decent lives thanks to the extra income our books brings them.

Britain

France

Ireland

Italy

Portugal

Spain...

all in one place!

On the unfathomable and often unnavigable sea of internet accommodation pages, those who have discovered **www.specialplacestostay.com** have found it to be an island of reliability. Not only will you find a database full of honest, trustworthy, up-to-date information about Special Places to Stay across Europe, but also:

- Links to the web sites of well over a thousand places from the series
- Colourful, clickable, interactive maps to help you find the right place
- The facility to make most bookings by e-mail – even if you don't have e-mail yourself
- Online purchasing of our books, securely and cheaply
- Regular, exclusive special offers on titles from the series
- The latest news about future editions, new titles and new places
- The chance to participate in the evolution of the site and the books

The site is constantly evolving and is frequently updated. We've revised our maps, adding more useful and interesting links, providing news, updates and special features that won't appear anywhere else but in our window on the world wide web.

Just as with our printed guides, your feedback counts, so when you've surfed all this and you still want more, let us know – this site has been planted with room to grow.

Russell Wilkinson, Web Producer
website@specialplacestostay.com

If you'd like to receive news and updates about our books by e-mail, send a message to newsletter@specialplacestostay.com

ALASTAIR SAWDAY'S

**British Hotels, Inns
& Other Places**
Edition 4   £12.99

**British Bed &
Breakfast**
Edition 7   £14.99

**British Holiday
Homes**
Edition 1   £9.99

**Bed & Breakfast
For Garden Lovers**
Edition 2   £14.99

**French Bed &
Breakfast**
Edition 8   £15.99

**French Hotels, Inns &
Other Places**
Edition 2   £11.95

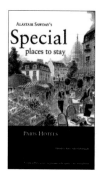

Paris Hotels
Edition 3   £8.95

**French Holiday
Homes**
Edition 1   £11.99

SPECIAL PLACES TO STAY SERIES

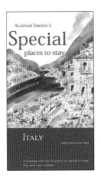

Italy
Edition 2   £11.95

Portugal
Edition 1   £8.95

Spain
Edition 4   £11.95

London
Edition 1   £9.99

Ireland
Edition 3   £10.95

THE LITTLE EARTH BOOK

Over 30,000 copies sold.

A fascinating read. The earth is now desperately vulnerable; so are we. Original, stimulating short essays about what is going wrong with our planet, and about the greatest challenge of our century: how to save the Earth for us all. It is succinct, yet intellectually credible, well-referenced, wry yet deadly serious.

Researched and written by a Bristol architect, James Bruges, The Little Earth Book is a clarion call to action, a stimulating collection of short essays on today's most important environmental concerns, from global warming and poisoned food to unfettered economic growth, Third World debt, genes and 'superbugs'. Undogmatic but sure-footed, the style is light, explaining complex issues with easy language, illustrations and cartoons. Ideas are developed chapter by chapter, yet each one stands alone. It is an easy browse.

The Little Earth Book provides hope, with new ideas and examples of people swimming against the current, for bold ideas that work in practice. It is a book as important as it is original. Learn about the issues and join the most important debate of this century.

Did you know?

- If everyone adopted the Western lifestyle we would need five earths to support us.
- In 50 years the US has — with intensive pesticide use — doubled the amount of crops lost to pests.
- Environmental disasters have already created more than 80 MILLION refugees.

www.littleearth.co.uk

And now The Little Food Book! Same style, same purpose: it blows the lid off the food 'industry' — in a concise, entertaining way. Written by Craig Sams, Chairman of the Soil Association, it is pithy, deeply informative and an important contribution to the great food debate.

ORDER FORM UK

All these Special Places to Stay books are available in major bookshops or you may order them direct.
Post and packaging are FREE.

		Price	No. copies
French Bed & Breakfast	Edition 8	£15.99	
French Hotels, Inns and other places	Edition 2	£11.99	
French Holiday Homes	Edition 1	£11.99	
Paris Hotels	Edition 4	£ 9.99	
British Bed & Breakfast	Edition 7	£14.99	
British Hotels, Inns and other places	Edition 4	£12.99	
British Holiday Homes	Edition 1	£ 9.99	
Garden Bed & Breakfast	Edition 2	£14.99	
London	Edition 1	£ 9.99	
Ireland	Edition 4	£12.99	
Spain (available February 2003)	Edition 5	£11.99	
Portugal	Edition 1	£ 8.95	
Italy	Edition 2	£11.95	
The Little Earth Book	Edition 3	£ 6.99	
The Little Food Book	Edition 2	£ 6.99	
Please make cheques payable to	Total £		

**Please make cheques payable to
Alastair Sawday Publishing**

Please send cheques to: Alastair Sawday Publishing,
The Home Farm Stables, Barrow Gurney, Bristol BS48 3RW.
For credit card orders call 01275 464891 or order directly
from our web site www.specialplacestostay.com

Title   First name

Surname

Address

Postcode

Tel

If you do not wish to receive mail from other
like-minded companies, please tick here ☐

If you would prefer not to receive information about
special offers on our books, please tick here ☐

GBB2

REPORT FORM

If you have any comments on entries in this guide, please let us
have them. If you have a favourite house, hotel, inn or other
new discovery, not just in Britain, please let us know about it.

Book title: _____

Entry no: _____

New
recommendation: _____

Country: _____

Name of property: _____

Address: _____

_____

_____

Postcode: _____

Tel: _____

Date of stay: _____

Comments: _____

_____

_____

From: _____

Address: _____

_____

_____

Postcode: _____

Tel: _____

Please send the completed form to:

Alastair Sawday Publishing,
The Home Farm Stables, Barrow Gurney, Bristol BS48 3RW,
or go to www.specialplacestostay.com and click on 'contact'.

Thank you.

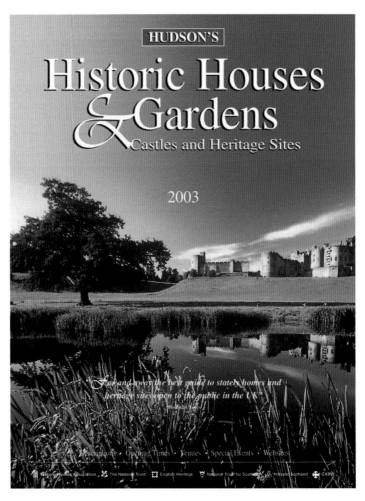

Discover the best-selling, definitive annual heritage guide to Britain's castles, stately homes and gardens open to the public.

600 pages featuring 2000 properties with
more than 1500 colour photographs.
An invaluable reference source <u>and</u> a good read.

THE GOOD GARDENS GUIDE 2003

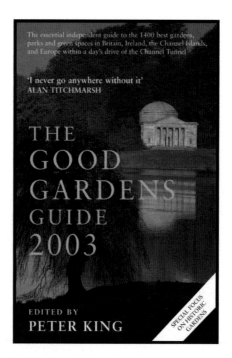

After a comfortable bed and excellent breakfast, garden lovers can do no better than set out for the day armed with a copy of *The Good Gardens Guide*. Now in its fourteenth year, this is the only independent guide to the best of British gardens open to the public in all their extraordinary variety. Baroque extravaganzas set within parkland jostle with traditional cottage-garden plots, clean-cut modern designs of glass and water, even a London roof garden colonised by flamingos. The descriptions are written by a team of dedicated enthusiasts, and the entries include all the up-to-date information necessary for a successful visit. The 2003 edition of the *Guide* focuses on Britain's historic parks and gardens – over 500 are listed and described, and in a special introductory section a thought-provoking series of articles celebrates them as brave survivors, visited and enjoyed by millions each year.

'By far the best of the available garden guides' Anna Pavord

'You can never go wrong by buying the latest edition' Stephen Anderton

'Indispensable' Sir Roy Strong

Published by Bloomsbury
672 pages   ISBN 0 7475 5655 5   £14.99

QUICK REFERENCE INDICES

BBGL

These houses were in the 2002 BBGL brochure.

England

Bath & N.E. Somerset • 1 • 2 • Bristol • 6 • Cheshire • 8 • Cornwall • 9 • 11 • 12 • 13 • 15 • 16 • Cumbria • 18 • Derbyshire • 19 • Devon • 22 • 23 • 28 • 30 • 32 • 33 • 34 • Dorset • 35 • 36 • Essex • 39 • Gloucestershire • 42 • 43 • 44 • 46 • Hampshire • 50 • Herefordshire • 51 • 57 • Isle of Wight • 60 • Kent • 62 • 63 • 67 • 68 • Lancashire • 71 • London • 76 • Norfolk • 79 • 80 • 82 • Northamptonshire • 83 • 84 • Nottinghamshire • 85 • Oxfordshire • 88 • 89 • 92 • 93 • Shropshire • 95 • 96 • 99 • 101 • Somerset • 105 • 106 • 108 • 109 • 110 • Suffolk • 117 • 118 • 119 • 120 • Surrey • 121 • Sussex • 125 • 127 • 127 • 128 • 129 • 130 • 131 • Warwickshire • 134 • 135 • 137 • Wiltshire • 138 • 141 • 143 • 146 • 147 • 148 • Worcestershire • 149 • Yorkshire • 152 • 153 • 157 • 158 • 159 •

Wales

Ceredigion • 162 • Gwent • 163 •

Scotland

Argyll & Bute • 166 • Ayrshire • 168 • Edinburgh • 169 • Fife • 170 • Highland • 172 • Isle of Bute • 173 • Midlothian • 174 • Perthshire • 176 • 177 • Renfrewshire • 178 • Roxburghshire • 180 • Wigtownshire • 181 •

Limited mobility

Need a ground-floor bedroom and bathroom? Ask these owners.

England

Cornwall • 10 • 17 • Devon • 22 • Gloucestershire • 44 • 45 • Hampshire • 49 • Herefordshire • 59 • Oxfordshire • 92 • Shropshire • 98 • Somerset • 102 • 114 • Suffolk • 117 • Surrey • 122 •

Scotland

Highland • 172 • 178 •

France

Maine-et-Loire • 189 • Hérault • 196 •

Wheelchair friendly

If you need houses which are wheelchair-friendly, contact these owners.

England

Derbyshire • 20 • Essex • 40 • Herefordshire • 53 • Kent • 69 • Leicestershire • 72 • Oxfordshire • 92 • Shropshire • 95 • Somerset • 114 • Warwickshire • 133 •

Scotland

Highland • 172 • Renfrewshire • 178 •

France

Charente-Maritime • 192 • Dordogne • 194 •

QUICK REFERENCE INDICES

Child friendly

The owners of these houses welcome children of any age but may not have all the equipment you need, so discuss beforehand.

England

Bath & N.E. Somerset • 1 • 2 • 4 • Cornwall • 10 • 16 • Cumbria • 18 • Derbyshire • 20 • Devon • 25 • 26 • 27 • 28 • 32 • 34 • Dorset • 35 • 36 • Essex • 40 • Gloucestershire • 42 • 43 • 45 • 47 • Herefordshire • 51 • 55 • Kent • 65 • 69 • Lancashire • 71 • Leicestershire • 72 • Lincolnshire • 73 • 74 • Norfolk • 80 • 82 • Nottinghamshire • 85 • 86 • Oxfordshire • 90 • Shropshire • 100 • Somerset • 104 • 106 • 107 • 112 • 114 • Suffolk • 115 • Surrey • 123 • Sussex • 124 • 126 • 130 • Warwickshire • 133 • 134 • 136 • 137 • Wiltshire • 141 • 148 • Yorkshire • 154• 155 • 157 • 159 •

Wales

Carmarthenshire • 160 • Ceredigion • 162 • Gwent •163 • Powys • 165 •

Scotland

Argyll & Bute • 166 • Ayrshire • 168 • Edinburgh • 169 • Fife • 170 • 171 • Highland • 172 • Midlothian • 174 • Perthshire • 175 • 176 • Renfrewshire • 178 • Peeblesshire • 179 • Roxburghshire • 180 • Wigtownshire • 181 •

France

Oise • 182 • Marne • 183 • Seine-Maritime • 185 • 186 • Maine-et-Loire • 188 • 189• Indre-et-Loire • 190 • Deux Sèvres • 191 • Charente-Maritime • 192 • Rhône • 195 •

Organic & home-grown produce

These owners use mostly home-grown, locally-grown or organically-grown produce.

England

Bath & N.E. Somerset • 1 • 2 • 4 • Buckinghamshire • 7 • Cornwall • 9 • 10 • Derbyshire • 19 • Devon • 21 • 22 • 24 • 25 • 26 • 27 • 28 • 29 • 30 • 32 • 33 • 34 • Dorset • 35 • 36 • 37 • Essex • 38 • 39 • Gloucestershire • 42 • Herefordshire • 51 • 52 • 53 • 54 • 55 • 58 • Isle of Wight • 60 • Kent • 61 • 67 • 69 • Leicestershire • 72 • London • 75 • 77 • Norfolk • 79 • Oxfordshire • 89 • 91 • 92 • 93 • Rutland • 94 • Shropshire • 96 • 97 • 98 • 99 • 100 • 101 • Somerset • 102 • 103 • 106 • 107 • 111 • 112 • Suffolk • 115 • 117 • 119 • Sussex • 129 • 132 • Warwickshire • 133 • 137 • Wiltshire • 138 • 140 • 141 • 142 • 148 • Worcestershire • 150 • Yorkshire • 153 • 158 • 159 •

Wales

Carmarthenshire • 160 • Ceredigion • 161 • 162 • Gwent • 163 • Powys • 165 •

QUICK REFERENCE INDICES

Scotland

Ayrshire • 167 • Fife • 170 • 171 • Highland • 172 • Midlothian • 174 •
Perthshire • 176 • 177 • Renfrewshire • 178 • Roxburghshire • 180 •

France

Seine-Maritime • 185 • Indre-et-Loire • 190 • Charente-Maritime •
192 • 193 • Rhône • 195 •

Pets welcome Your pets are generally welcome at these houses. Always check.

England

Bath & N.E. Somerset • 4 • Cornwall • 10 • Derbyshire • 20 • Devon •
25 • 28 • 31 • Dorset • 36 • 37 • Essex • 40 • Gloucestershire • 45 •
Herefordshire • 52 • 55 • 56 • 59 • Lancashire • 71 • Leicestershire •
72 • Norfolk • 80 • 81 • Nottinghamshire • 85 • 86 • Shropshire • 98 •
Somerset • 106 • 114 • Suffolk • 115 • 117 • Sussex • 126 •
Warwickshire • 134 • 136 • Wiltshire • 139 • 147 • 148 • Yorkshire •
152 • 154 • 155 • 158 • 159 •

Wales

Ceredigion • 161 •

Scotland

Argyll & Bute • 166 • Highland • 172 • Midlothian • 174 • Perthshire •
177 • Renfrewshire • 178 •

France

Oise • 182 • Seine-Maritime • 186 • Maine-et-Loire • 188 • 189 •
Indre-et-Loire • 190 • Dordogne • 194 •

All day You are welcome to stay all day at these houses.

England

Bath & N.E. Somerset • 2 • 4 • Buckinghamshire • 7 • Cheshire • 8 •
Cornwall • 9 • 14 • 15 • Derbyshire • 19 • 20 • Devon • 21 • 22 • 23 •
24 • 25 • 26 • 29 • 30 • 31 • Dorset • 36 • 37 • Herefordshire • 54 • 56
• Kent • 61 • 65 • 68 • Lancashire • 71 • London • 78 • Norfolk • 81 •
Oxfordshire • 87 • Shropshire • 95 • 96 • 98 • Somerset • 102 • 104 •
107 • 111 • 112 • 113 • 114 • Suffolk • 117 • Surrey • 123 • Sussex •
126 • 129 • 131 • 132 • Warwickshire • 133 • 136 • Wiltshire • 142 •
Yorkshire • 151 • 155 • 156 •

Wales

Ceredigion • 161 • Monmouthshire • 164 • Powys • 165 •

Scotland

Argyll & Bute • 166 • Midlothian • 174 • Renfrewshire • 178 •
Peeblesshire • 179 • Wigtownshire • 181 •

QUICK REFERENCE INDICES

Dinner

These owners can provide dinner, by arrangement.

England

Bath & N.E. Somerset • 3 • 4 • Berkshire • 5 • Buckinghamshire • 7 • Cornwall • 9 • 10 • 13 • 15 • 16 • Cumbria • 18 Devon • 21 • 24 • 25 • 27 • 31• 32 • 33 • 34 • Dorset • 36 • 37 • Essex • 38 • 39 • Gloucestershire • 41 • 45 • 46 • 47 • Herefordshire • 51 • 52 • 53 • 54 • 55 • 58 • 59 • Isle of Wight • 60 • Kent • 67 • Lincolnshire • 73 • London • 75 • 76 • 78 • Norfolk • 79 • 80 • 81 • Nottinghamshire • 85 • Oxfordshire • 87 • 88 • 89 • Rutland • 94 • Shropshire • 96 • 97 • 100 • 101 • Somerset • 103 • 104 • 105 • 106 • 107 • 108 • 110 • 111 • 114 • Suffolk • 115 • 120 • Sussex • 130 • Warwickshire • 133 • 136 • 137 • Wiltshire • 138 • 139 • 140 • 141 • 142 • 143 • 144 • Worcestershire •150 • Yorkshire • 153 • 154 • 155 • 156 • 158 • 159 •

Wales

Carmarthenshire • 160 • Ceredigion • 161 • 162 • Gwent • 163 • Powys • 165 •

Scotland

Ayrshire • 167 • 168 • Fife • 170 • 171 • Highland • 172 • Isle of Bute • 173 • Midlothian • 174 • Perthshire • 177 • Renfrewshire • 178 • Peeblesshire • 179 • Roxburghshire • 180 •

France

Oise • 182 • Marne • 183 • Seine-Maritime • 185 • Maine-et-Loire • 189 • Indre-et-Loire • 190 • Charente-Maritime • 192 • 193 • Dordogne • 194 • Rhône •195 •

Licensed

These places are licensed.

Cornwall • 9 • 15 • Derbyshire • 20 • Devon • 24 • 34 • Gloucestershire • 45 • Herefordshire • 51 • 53 • Nottinghamshire • 85 • Rutland • 94 • Shropshire • 97 • 101 • Somerset • 111 • 114 • Suffolk • 119 • Suffolk • 120 • Wiltshire • 139 • 140 • Yorkshire • 155 • 156 • 159 •

Wales

Carmarthenshire • 160 • Powys • 165 •

Scotland

Argyll & Bute • 166 •

INDEX – SURNAME

INDEX – SURNAME

INDEX – SURNAME

INDEX – PLACE NAME

INDEX – PLACE NAME

INDEX – PLACE NAME

EXCHANGE RATE TABLE

£ Sterling	US$	Euro€
1	1.59	1.57
5	7.85	7.83
7	11.13	10.96
10	15.90	15.66
15	23.85	23.48
17	27.03	26.61
20	31.80	31.31
25	39.75	39.14
30	47.70	46.97
35	55.65	54.79
40	63.60	62.62
45	71.55	70.45
50	79.50	78.28
70	111.30	109.58
90	143.10	140.90

November 2002

EXPLANATION OF SYMBOLS

Treat each one as a guide rather than a statement of fact and check important points when booking.

Children are positively welcomed, with no age restrictions, but cots, high chairs etc are not necessarily available.

Full and approved wheelchair facilities for at least one bedroom and bathroom and access to all ground-floor common areas.

Ground-floor bedrooms for people of limited mobility.

No smoking anywhere in the house.

Pets are welcome but may have to sleep in an outbuilding or your car. Check when booking.

Credit cards accepted; most commonly Visa and MasterCard.

Vegetarians catered for with advance warning. All hosts can cater for vegetarians at breakfast.

Most, but not necessarily all, ingredients are organically grown, home-grown or locally grown.

The premises are licensed.

Working farm.